VULCAN TEST PILOT

Books by same author

Autobiography:
Flight Testing to Win
ISBN 1-4116-4825-0

Mystery Fiction – a Trilogy:
A Flight Too Far
A mysterious disaster at Heathrow
ISBN 0-9553856-3-6

The Final Flight
A Bermuda Triangle mystery
ISBN 0-9553856-0-1

The Right Choice
An aviation story of deceit and disaster
ISBN 0-9553856-2-8

VULCAN

TEST PILOT

MY EXPERIENCES IN THE COCKPIT OF A COLD WAR ICON

TONY BLACKMAN

GRUB STREET · LONDON

Published by
Grub Street
4 Rainham Close
London
SW11 6SS

First published in hardback 2007
This edition first published 2009

Reprinted 2009, 2011, 2016

British Library Cataloguing in Publication Data
Blackman, Tony
Vulcan test pilot : my experiences in the cockpit of a Cold War icon
1. Blackman, Tony 2. Vulcan (Jet bomber)
I. Title
623.7'463'0941

ISBN-13: 9781906502300

Cover design by Lizzie B design

Typeset by Pearl Graphics, Hemel Hempstead

Printed and bound by Finidr, Czech Republic

CONTENTS

DEDICATION

First of all I want to dedicate this book to Roly Falk and to Jimmy Harrison; their superb test flying helped to make the Vulcan such a wonderful and effective aircraft and they, alas, can no longer relate this incredible story themselves.

The other dedication I want to make is to Margaret my wife. She was my editor, my proof reader and knew almost as much about the Vulcan as I did by the time the book was finished. Together we went to Bruntingthorpe, to the National Archives and to the publisher and she was an everlasting inspiration and ideas person. We were both at Boscombe when the Vulcan arrived and I am sure being the first lady to fly in the co-pilot's seat also helped. I consider myself very fortunate to have had such outstanding support.

ACKNOWLEDGEMENTS

I have had an enormous amount of help and support writing this book so it is difficult to know where to begin. However, perhaps I should start with Peter Clegg who has given me so much material, unstinted support and saved me years of work.

One of the splendid pleasures I have had researching the book was making contact again with so many old friends and colleagues and if I have left someone out I hope they will forgive me. Wason Turner was in charge of the technical office in B Squadron at Boscombe Down when I was there and it was a real pleasure to work with him again. He has helped me enormously in making sure that this book is not a work of fiction and providing me with the graphs of the measurements we made at Boscombe Down.

At Avros, Harry Holmes was in the marketing department and Mike Taylor in the flight test office at Woodford in my time; they found invaluable photos, documents, and flight test reports for me besides advising me and jogging my memory. John MacDaniel's book *Tales of the Cheshire Planes* was another useful technical source that I needed, as was Laurie Trier on Vulcan structures and the frailties thereof. Bob Pogson was my AEO and he reminded me of extra things that I had forgotten. I have almost forgiven him for flying in even more Vulcans than I did.

Researching accidents was a difficult but important task and I would like to thank Mary Hudson of the Historical Branch, and Peter Elliott of the Royal Air Force Museum for pointing me in the right direction. I would also like to express my unbounded admiration for the National Archives.

From the other side of the world in Canberra, I would like to thank John Saxon for helping me with the Blue Steel story and Milt Cottee for setting the speed limit of the Vulcan Mk 1, telling me about it and, of course, flying with me all those years ago.

I was also lucky in getting help from 'old' Royal Air Force Vulcan aircrew, Peter Lawrence, Rod Powell and Roy Ashton amongst others.

Some of the basic Vulcan information I garnered from web sites and in particular I used Guy Bartlett's which was a mine of information. With regard to photos, I have tried to acknowledge all as appropriate but if I have missed any out or got some wrong please let me know and I can only apologise.

Finally, any mistakes which have crept in are, of course, entirely my responsibility.

FOREWORD

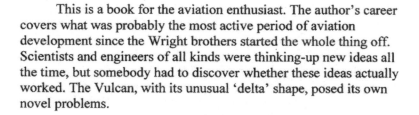

This is a book for the aviation enthusiast. The author's career covers what was probably the most active period of aviation development since the Wright brothers started the whole thing off. Scientists and engineers of all kinds were thinking-up new ideas all the time, but somebody had to discover whether these ideas actually worked. The Vulcan, with its unusual 'delta' shape, posed its own novel problems.

Most people, who can drive a car safely, can probably fly an aeroplane, but taking up a newly designed and built aircraft for the first time requires quite exceptional skills - and nerve. In these days, the whole aircraft industry has more experience, and much preparatory work can be done by simulation, even so the first time into the air for a new design is always going to be a tense experience.

In this book, the author tells the story of flight-testing the Vulcan from the first scale model 707, to the flight of the two prototypes. He then traces the development of the aircraft and its entry into service with the Royal Air Force.

I found this book particularly interesting, as I had the pleasure of flying in a Vulcan in 1958 with Wing Commander Frank Dodd from Wyton to Farnborough. I will not forget the experience.

HRH The Duke of Edinburgh

APPRECIATION

I am so glad to have the opportunity to say thank you to Tony for writing this splendid book. Among the many books written about the Vulcan this one is unique in describing so well, in mainly non technical terms, the birth pangs of the aircraft and the work it took to make it such an outstanding success.

Not surprisingly, one of the things I really liked about this book was the fact that Tony realised that Roly not only tested the Vulcan but also sold it to the Royal Air Force, the politicians and above all, to the public, including the time he rolled the Vulcan for the first time at the Farnborough Air Display in 1955. Of course Tony has been able to write this account first hand because he was so intimately involved; Roly recruited Tony and he took over the Vulcan testing with Jimmy Harrison.

The Spitfire is the aircraft icon of the Second World War and, thanks to Roly, Jimmy, Tony and RAF crews, the Vulcan is the aircraft icon of the Cold War. There are quite a few Spitfires still flying but to get a Vulcan flying again would be a magnificent achievement and this book will be a fitting backcloth to XH558 display flying again and will remind those who fly it, and those who watch, of the hard work that took place to make it all possible.

Leysa Falk

INTRODUCTION

There have been various books written about the Vulcan, telling in great detail the operation of the aircraft and maybe a little bit about the early years. However, as far as I know there has never been a book written about test flying the Vulcan by someone who was actually there at the time doing a lot of the flight testing. The aerodynamic shape of the Vulcan had some unusual flying characteristics which needed to be dealt with; its relatively benign flying qualities didn't happen by accident! This book explains how the aircraft was made to work and be safe to fly.

It seemed an ideal time to write it to celebrate Vulcan XH558 flying again, forty-six years after I first flew it on its production schedule. I not only tested the aircraft then but, as it was the first Mk 2, I delivered it to Waddington, and flew it again five years later after modifications had been fitted. During my research I found that I had flown 105 of the aircraft out of the 136 built, 850 flights and 1,327 hours. However Bob Pogson, our main Avro AEO who controlled all the vital electrical power in the aircraft, soon put me in my place as he had flown in 123 Vulcans and, recently, I met a 9 Squadron AEO who had achieved 3,500 hours but I don't know how many flights he had done.

The sort of flying 558 is going to do is of course all display flying and so this book fits in very well, since at Woodford where the aircraft were built, we not only tested the Vulcan but we used to do demonstration flying at Farnborough and the history of these demonstrations is discussed.

The book does not aim to be a technical primer or a flight by flight tale of test flying, though I have added one or two flight test records to give the reader a feel of how it was done and also some graphs of the measurements I helped to make before the first Vulcan was delivered to the Royal Air Force. The book is mainly for people not particularly associated with the Vulcan, though it is hoped that the aficionados will enjoy having their memories jogged. I have tried to explain some of the more complicated aeronautical expressions and included a glossary to help readers who are not familiar with the jargon. I have done this because the Vulcan is a UK icon and I want as many people as possible to appreciate the work that went into developing the aircraft. It has captured the imagination of the whole country and represents what this country can achieve when it sets its mind to it.

I make no apologies for the personal stories which I tell because I want people to be able to feel as I did when I flew the aircraft and experience the excitement of handling an incredibly powerful machine, knowing that at any could and did happen.

ALB June 2007

PROLOGUE

Tester 27, you are clear to taxi, Runway 24

It was 29th March 1956, my usual callsign but this time flying a Vulcan. We had left the huge Weighbridge hangar at Boscombe Down and walked across the vast expanse of concrete towards the silver Vulcan which towered above us. For me it was a very special day as it was to be my first flight as captain of the aircraft. It all seemed incredible. Just over twelve months earlier I had been finishing a year's course learning how to be a test pilot at the Royal Air Force's world famous Empire Test Pilots School, ETPS, at Farnborough[1]. I had been an RAF fighter pilot in Germany and now had become an important heavy bomber test pilot, part of a team of three tasked with deciding whether this strangely shaped delta aircraft was safe to fly and whether it had the required performance to spearhead the UK's defence effort. Would it be an effective operational aircraft and nuclear deterrent in the turbulent Iron Curtain years of the second half of the twentieth century?

The heavy electrical cable from the noisy Houchin electrical generator was plugged into the power socket underneath the fuselage near the back of the aircraft, keeping all the aircraft systems alive until the engines were started and their electrical generators could take over from the ground supply. The civilian ground crew were waiting for us and the crew chief, with his headphones plugged into a socket on the nosewheel undercarriage leg, watched us clamber into the aircraft. I climbed first up the removable ladder fixed to the emergency escape door into the rear crew compartment. Graham Moreau, who had been on the test pilot course with me at Farnborough and was to be my co-pilot was next, followed by the other three crew members. The space was almost completely dark apart from a few instrument lights and two very small windows in the roof. There were three seats facing rearwards for the rear crew with the instruments and switches for the systems they controlled in front of them and there was a prone crew position with a window on the floor for visual bombing which was covered over. Above that, there was a space and, on this aircraft, a very large vertical panel was fitted with rows and rows of instruments, recording all the vital information of the flight for analysis afterwards. Two cameras, to be operated by the flight test observer sitting in the seat normally occupied by the radar navigator, were pointed at these instruments.

---

[1] See *Flight Testing to Win* by author.

We had assembled earlier in a briefing room to decide what measurements were required on this the fourth flight of a series to enable the Ministry of Supply's Aircraft and Armament Experimental Establishment, A&AEE, to advise the Government whether the Vulcan, being developed by A V Roe and Co Ltd in Manchester, was satisfactory to be accepted into the Royal Air Force, a procedure which, when completed, would enable a so-called CA release to be given. Wason Turner, head of the B Squadron technical office responsible for writing the CA release, had discussed the required tests with us and Brian Ramsdale, who worked in the tech office, was flying with us as flight test observer to control all the instrumentation so essential to measure and determine what actually happened during the flight. Besides Graham, as flight crew we had a RAF navigator and an air electronics officer, AEO, who had to control the electrical power on the aircraft, vital on the Vulcan with all its flying controls operated by electrically driven hydraulic motors.

The two pilots' ejection seats were above us so I carried on climbing up another ladder to get into my seat. The flight deck was tiny with the seats very close together. This was to be only my fourth flight in the Vulcan and I was just getting used to the contortions required to get from the top of the ladder onto the ejection seat, though I got a lot more adept at it during the weeks that followed. Once in my seat I buckled on the harness of my parachute, which acted as a very uncomfortable seat cushion, and then attached the ejector seat straps over the top of the parachute harness. The safety equipment specialist helped Graham and myself with strapping in and then, when we had finished, he armed the ejection seats by removing the safety pins which prevented the seats from firing on the ground, and put the pins in their correct stowages. Finally, after a careful check around he climbed down to leave the aircraft.

I looked through the front windscreens at the ground crew and the Boscombe tarmac. The view through the three narrow long pieces of glass was much less than on any of the twenty or so other types of aircraft I had flown and, in my opinion, was undesirably small though acceptable. Luckily there was a large circular window on my left which had a very good side view, which I found invaluable in the years ahead.

The instrument panel seemed large but in reality was basically the same as on my first jet, the Vampire twin-boom fighter; airspeed indicator, machmeter, artificial horizon, altimeter, rate of climb and the turn and slip indicator all seemed very familiar. The panel between the two pilots' instruments was filled with engine displays. The chief difference between the Vampire and the Vulcan was the plethora of small black and white indicators, dolls eyes, and a myriad of warning lights. These were the indicators for the systems of the aircraft and it was the correct functioning of these systems that was so vital for the safe operation of the Vulcan. However, like the Vampire, the aircraft

Vulcan flight deck as pictured in pilots' notes.

had a stick and not a control column so I felt very much at home.

Graham read out the pre-starting checks and then, when the rear crew told me they were ready and the entrance door, now serving as an escape chute, was shut, I got permission from the crew chief, who had his headphones on, to start the first engine. There was a faint humming noise which gradually got louder and I lifted the left, number one, throttle lever over a mechanical stop called a gate, and moved it forward slightly thus opening the high pressure cock and allowing fuel into the engine. There was a distinctive rumble as the fuel in the engine ignited and the engine jet pipe temperature needle moved off its stops and stabilised at about 400°C. The AEO called out on the intercom that the engine's generator was on line and I started the other three engines in turn. After carrying out the after-starting checks and pre-taxi checks I instructed the crew chief to unplug the Houchin, remove the chocks and clear the aircraft. After a minute or so he waved to me and I could see him walking towards the left wing tip, where he was joined by a tractor towing the Houchin power rig. We were free and I relished the thought that what happened in the next few hours was now all up to me.

I called air traffic for permission to taxi and only then, as I opened the throttles, as the engine noise increased, as the engines 'spooled up' and as I pressed the nosewheel steering button and the aircraft started to move, did I realise that what was happening was like a dream come true. Now I was in charge of one of the country's newest and most advanced aircraft on which a vast amount of money and effort had been spent. Maybe that was why I was a little more careful than usual as I threaded my way between the parked aircraft, most of them in the process of being evaluated by A&AEE, fighters, bombers, maritime reconnaissance and naval airplanes.

Tester 27, you are cleared on to Runway 24

Boscombe air traffic cleared me to taxi on to the main runway and I lined up Vulcan XA889 in the middle of the 150ft wide runway ready for take-off.

Tester 27, you are cleared for take-off

The concrete stretched thousands of feet into the distance ahead of us. As air traffic gave clearance for take-off I grasped the four small engine throttle levers in my right hand and moved them forward together. The engine noise increased and I took my feet off the rudder pedal brakes to let the aircraft roll. We accelerated, going faster and faster as I pushed the throttles fully forward, and the runway started flying by. The speed increased at what seemed like an unstoppable rate and Graham called out 'rotate' as we reached the pre-calculated speed to raise the nosewheel off the runway, V_R, and I pulled the stick backwards. The nose of the aircraft rose blocking my view of the runway and then, as Graham called out V_2, I pulled the stick back further and we lifted smoothly off the runway. I reached forward with my right hand to press the button to raise the landing gear. I had to increase the pull force on the stick very quickly after 'unstick' and make the aircraft climb steeply to ensure the undercarriage was locked up before its maximum operating speed was exceeded. In what seemed like an incredibly short time we were racing upwards, Boscombe and the Salisbury Plain had disappeared below and we were ready to start work, which was, after all, the object of the exercise, though nothing could diminish the thrill of actually flying the aircraft.

Extract from author's log book. First four flights.

CHAPTER 1

FROM THE BEGINNING

The whole concept of the Vulcan had been triggered in 1946 by the Ministry of Defence, which issued an operational requirement, OR229, specifying a bomber with a top speed of 500 knots, an operating height of 50,000ft and a range of 3,350 nautical miles. The bomb load was to be 10,000lbs and it was intended as part of the nuclear deterrent. The requirement was generated by the US nuclear explosions at Hiroshima and Nagasaki and the perceived need to keep up the UK's position as a world power; it was a response to inter-national events and the fact that the UK, still in the throes of post-war euphoria, believed that it was going to be possible to remain a major world player. Thus this whole concept of the V Bomber force was to act as a carrier for the potential nuclear deterrent.

The desire to have an independent nuclear deterrent was fuelled by the political tensions existing between the US and the UK at the end of the Second World War, which had been further exacerbated by the change of government in the UK in 1945. The US administration was deeply suspicious of a Labour Government which might well have sympathy with the newly emerging power of Communist Russia. This US suspicion of the UK was intensified when it was discovered that some significant people who had a lot of classified information had defected to Russia. The UK Government in turn was wary of relying too heavily on US co-operation for the country's national security. It had become quite clear during the war that though the US had supported the UK with Lend/Lease, they would only actively intervene to promote their own interests, which were not necessarily the same as those of the UK.

Even though a number of British scientists and engineers had been closely involved in the research and development of the atom bomb in the US, the post-war US Government was reluctant to share its nuclear secrets with the UK, preferring the option of a NATO force which would remain under US dominance. However, the UK Government was determined to achieve its own independent nuclear capacity, partly for the perceived prestige it would bestow and partly because of the distrust of US motives and actions, so that now the task of building a British nuclear weapons system had become a high priority.

However, as the Russian threat loomed ever larger, it finally became clear to the US decision makers that a well armed UK would act as her front line of defence in any attack from the Soviet Union and, indeed, there is no question that the reality of the V Force with nuclear weapons patrolling the skies and the avowed policy of instant response safeguarded the United States as well as Europe from attack throughout the height of the cold war.

This ongoing ambition of the UK Government to have its own nuclear deterrent was to cause endless trouble in the ensuing decades, as successive administrations sought to equate these aspirations with the realities of national defence and economic necessity; perhaps it is true to say as an aside that, though the Vulcan as a prime defence project has long since gone, the same political conflicts still exist even today.

Many projects were commissioned, then subsequently cancelled, thus wasting manufacturers' time and large sums of tax payers' money, though I suspect the firms concerned didn't mind too much. These included the Avro 720 supersonic fighter, Avro 730 supersonic bomber proposed as a successor to the Vulcan, the British Aircraft Corporation TSR2 strike fighter and, at the project level, the Douglas Skybolt ICBM, to name but a few. This frenetic activity has been described as 'the usual lunatic manner of the Air Ministry dealings with Industry throughout the 1950s and 1960s' but to be fair I am sure the aspirations of the three services were initially encouraged by the politicians, who then changed their minds when faced with either financial constraints or changes in government policy. Unfortunately, almost every decision taken eventually proved to be both costly and mistaken, so that the technical advantages gained at the end of World War 2 were largely squandered.

Although the new operational requirement for what was to become the V Bombers, conceived in 1947, was clearly going to push the engineering of the day to its limits, the intention was to get the aircraft into service by 1951, which in itself demonstrates how little idea the Air Staff had of the task they had laid before the various manufacturers. Nevertheless, the challenge was welcomed and six companies tendered bids.

The specification was refined and issued in detail and called B35/46. Of the six companies who originally responded, Armstrong Whitworth and English Electric were soon eliminated leaving four companies attempting to respond to the full specification, Shorts at Belfast, Vickers with their airfield at Wisley and their factory at Brooklands, Handley Page at Radlett and A V Roe and Co Ltd based in Manchester with their airfield at Woodford just south of Stockport in Cheshire. The first approved design was that of the Shorts A4, a relatively simple interim solution later called the Sperrin, but by the time it flew in 1951 it was obvious that, as an interim bomber, it would not be required, the first of many wasteful mistakes. Eventually, three separate designs were chosen in order to spread the risk. The Vickers proposal was very conventional and could not hope to meet the full requirement but was regarded by the government as an intermediate solution, whilst waiting for the development of the more adventurous designs.

Innovative aerodynamics and structural design were clearly required to meet the exacting demands of this specification and Roy Chadwick, who had designed the Lancaster, which only three years earlier had been considered a state of the art bomber, was Avro's chief designer at the time and he had the idea of meeting the specification with a delta wing aircraft with an integrated wing and fuselage.

When the decision was taken to go for the delta design there was very little background experience; the delta is generally attributed to Dr Alexander M Lippisch in Germany during the Second World War. At the end of the war, US government agencies and many US aircraft corporations studied captured German reports on delta-winged aircraft; Lippisch himself went to the States in 1946, initially to Naval Air Materiel Center in Philadelphia, Pennsylvania. In addition, the National Advisory Committee for Aeronautics, the forerunner of National Aeronautics and Space Administration, had been studying the delta design in some detail. It is assumed that Avros had some knowledge of this work, probably through the Royal Aircraft Establishment.

The Handley Page design opted for an original crescent wing with a high tailplane. The Avro Delta type 698, emerged as the clear favourite to win the contest but, as an insurance, the runner-up design of the Handley Page HP80 was also selected for further development. Very unfortunately, Chadwick never survived to see his brilliant brain child accepted as he and the chief test pilot, Bill Thorne, died in an aborted take-off from Woodford in an Avro Tudor on 23rd August 1947, when the aileron controls were connected the wrong way round, in the wrong sense as we say, after maintenance had been carried out. Consequently, though the Avro design was endorsed as the best at the conference of 15th January 1948, the instructions to proceed were delayed until the Ministry of Supply was convinced that the Avro team had sufficient technical competence to handle the project following Chadwick's death. Meanwhile, Vickers received an instruction to proceed on 16th April 1948 and in the same month Handley Page was contracted to produce two HP80 prototypes.

Avros finally received an order for the Type 698 in June 1948 but I do wonder whether the Vulcan would have been any different had the development proceeded under Chadwick's innovative eye. The integrated wing fuselage concept was abandoned and the final design had fuselage with the delta wings attached. The attractions of the Vulcan design were:

1.   The ability to have pronounced sweepback in order to delay buffet, the onset of which would cause drag due to high local mach numbers on the top surface of the wing.

2.   The delta had a large wing area without going to an excessive span.

3.   The delta wing could be made very stiff by having two spars, one at the leading edge and the other at the trailing edge of the wing meeting at the wing tip.

4.   Another benefit of the delta was that by the very nature of its wing shape with its very long distance between the leading and trailing edge of the wing next to the fuselage, chord in aeronautical terms, it was possible to have a very thick wing inboard. This thickness at the wing root made it possible to have large buried engine air intakes in the leading edge of the wing and also sufficient depth for retracting the undercarriage. A further advantage of a thick wing was that there was plenty of room for the fuel tanks, though Avros decided not to take full advantage of the thickness by having integral tanks sealed in the wing; instead the fuel tanks were bag tanks which meant that the skinning on the wing was much less critical during construction. I always regretted that decision since I found the Vulcan's range rather disappointing whereas the aircraft's great competitor, the Victor, had external tanks and therefore a greater fuel capacity and range.

5.   There was another aerodynamic plus for the delta which was that by making the wing thinner at the wing tip than the wing root, a smaller thickness chord ratio in aeronautical parlance, the effective sweep back of the wing, important for reducing drag rise at a high subsonic mach number, was greater than would be expected by just measuring the geometrical angle of sweep on the leading edge.

There were of course some handling concerns in choosing a delta, not an unusual situation in aircraft design generally where the manufacturer is looking for the maximum performance from an aircraft whilst trying to ensure that it meets the safety requirements. Many questions needed to be considered. Would the elevators on the trailing edge of the wing have sufficient power without a tailplane? Would the aircraft oscillate uncontrollably up and down, in other words would there be sufficient damping in pitch? Would the fin and rudder have enough directional stability and would the rudder be able to deal with differential asymmetric power from the engines? On the other hand it was expected that there would be some handling benefits at slow speed, since the delta design did not seem to have any of the nasty stalling characteristics of some of the other high performance aircraft flying at the time.

One might speculate what name Chadwick would have favoured for his aircraft. Certainly, deciding on a name for the new aeroplane took some time but, as Vickers had already called their aircraft the Valiant, the then Chief of the Air Staff, Sir John Slessor, requested that the new aeroplanes should also have names starting with the letter V. Handley Page chose Victor, hoping perhaps that the name would ensure success, whilst Avros, typically pragmatic, chose Vulcan, the name of the Roman god of fire and machinery, to reflect the powerful role envisaged for their new bomber; thus the era of the V Bombers was born.

Of the three V Bombers, the more conventional Valiant was the first to fly, the prototype Vickers 660 taking off in May 1951, whilst the first production Valiant flew in December 1953. By 1954 Gaydon in Warwickshire was reactivated and extensively rebuilt as the first V Bomber base. Then by 1955, 138 Squadron was equipped with Britain's first operational nuclear weapon, Blue Danube and the V Force was finally under way, less than ten years after the original concept. However, by 1964 serious fissures were discovered in the rear spars of a number of Valiant airframes, caused by the extra stress of low level flight when the V Force was made to fly at low altitude because of the new high altitude Russian anti-aircraft missiles.

All structures have a 'fatigue' life if they are continually shaken and so if an aircraft is flown for long periods at high speed and low altitude the fatigue life is rapidly consumed due to the extra buffeting and vibration from the turbulent air. The V Bombers were not designed to have a particularly long fatigue life because it was not anticipated that they would have to fly at low level; the specification was for a high altitude bomber. However, the Valiant had the lowest fatigue life of the three V Bombers whilst the Vulcan, with its stiff structure, had by far the longest life. The damage to the rear spar therefore brought the whole Valiant programme to an abrupt close. The last Valiant sorties were flown in December 1964, making the active life of the Valiant barely twelve years and so, rather unexpectedly, the most traditional, safe design proved to be the least successful.

The first flight of the Victor was on 24th December 1952, the first production aircraft arrived in early 1956 and the Victor Mk 1 entered RAF service in November 1957, to be reinforced less than five years later by the Victor Mk 2. Sir Frederick Handley Page died in 1962; one wonders what he would have thought when his firm was forced to close down in February 1970 and his great enemy Avros took over the design responsibility for the Victors and, after large scale and expensive modifications, converted twenty-four of the Victor Mk 2s to tankers as replacements for the Valiant tankers, thus preparing them for their role in the Falklands War. In fact, my first task as chief test pilot at

Woodford was to ferry these aircraft to Woodford from Radlett, ably helped by Handley Page's chief test pilot, Johnny Allam.

The first prototype Vulcan VX770 took to the air on 30th August 1952, some three months ahead of the Victor and, as will be seen later, this time advantage of the Vulcan over its competitor was increased by well over a year by the time the RAF received its first Vulcan in July 1956, partly as a result of a disastrous crash of the first prototype Victor in July 1954 whilst carrying out low level high speed position error measurements at Cranfield.

As planned by the Avro designers, the delta design really did have some distinct performance advantages over the more conventional aircraft of the time. The broad delta wing being used solved some significant structural challenges by allowing short and straight wing spars to be used. An additional bonus was that it permitted a larger wing area to be achieved. Although unusual in appearance, the Avro design was structurally conventional. The engines, undercarriage, fuel and bomb load could be enclosed in the low drag shape and there seemed to be no reason why the aircraft would not have good high altitude and high speed performance. The four engines were located in pairs and fed by two large 'letter box' inlets, one in each wing root leading edge. A single large vertical fin provided directional stability.

Leading edge extensions were used on the wing to improve the stability of the leading edge flow. Whilst under most conditions the wing operated with an attached airflow, at high angles of attack a separated conical-vortex flow was triggered and these vortices, induced in a controlled flow separation, helped to increase lift generation and give stability at low speed. Another notable feature was the use of boundary layer splitter plates at the engine air intakes; these were fitted on the Vulcan to ensure the induction into the intake of undisturbed high speed air. Without these devices, the maximum mass flow rate of air induced into the engines would have been significantly reduced. In fact, the Vulcan was able to gulp twenty-five tonnes of air per minute through these intakes and it turned out that in the event the Vulcan engine air intake, suitably enlarged, was big enough to accommodate the requirements of the Olympus Mk 301 engine producing 21,000lbs thrust.

In order to try to reduce the development risk associated with the innovative design, it was proposed to build two one-third scale models

for low speed development and two half-scale models for high speed work. In the end, however, it was agreed that only one-third scale models would be built, which Avros called the type 707. To save time and money, components from existing aircraft were used; the engine was a Rolls-Royce Derwent and the aircraft had a sharply tapered nose with a canopy from the Gloster Meteor; the air intake was very unusual as it was a split dorsal one which was never really satisfactory due to turbulent flow off the canopy. The first 707, VX784, flew on 4th September 1949 from Boscombe Down and was on static display a day or so later at the SBAC show, setting the precedent for Avros having to rush their aircraft through in time for the SBAC show, a very necessary publicity platform.

Very unfortunately, the aircraft crashed on 30th September 1949 and the pilot, Ric Esler, was killed. No convincing reason was ever found for the accident, though it was conjectured that there was a problem with the ailerons overbalancing, compounded by the air brake design on the aircraft, causing a stall; this accident is discussed in detail in Appendix 1. The loss of this 707 delayed work on the second aircraft, but then it was re-started at high speed and Avros managed to get another 707 flying a year later. The nose was made longer and thinner, the wing sweep was changed, and both the elevators and the air brakes were redesigned. The Hawker P1052 nose leg was used with an Avro Athena main undercarriage and the aircraft, re-designated the 707B, had its maiden flight a year later, on 5th September 1950. However, the dorsal intake on top and only just in front of the fin caused engine problems because of its position and its inability to cope with disturbed air; the intake was repositioned but, even after modification, it was never really satisfactory because of the turbulence from the canopy. One of the immediate contributions from the 707B to the 698 test programme was that it showed the need for a long nose undercarriage to ensure a high wing incidence for take-off.

The definitive 707A, WD280, flew from Boscombe on 14th June 1951 and was designed to fly at high subsonic speeds. It had wing root intakes, cropped wing tips and hydraulic power controls. Like the 707B, a lot of the flying was needed just to develop the aircraft itself but its great contribution to the 698 programme was to test the modified kinked and extended leading edge, plus vortex generators which were to become the standard on the Vulcan Mk 1. Eventually, in 1956 when its test programme was complete, the aircraft was shipped to Australia for test work at Laverton by the RAAF. It is now in the RAAF Museum at Pt Cook, Melbourne.

Two more 707s were ordered on 13th November 1951, a 707A WZ736 and a two-seater 707C, WZ744, but in the event they were never needed in the Vulcan development programme. Aeroflight took over the two aircraft and the 707A was used for auto-throttle work, which I had occasion to fly some years later when I was developing the auto throttle on the Vulcan. The 707C was employed for fly-by-wire experiments.

The first flight of the prototype Vulcan, VX770, which took place on 30th August 1952, was flown by Roly Falk. The Mk 100 Bristol Olympus engines destined for the aircraft were not ready in time and the aircraft was fitted with four Rolls-Royce Avon engines of 6,500lbs thrust. Later these engines were exchanged for four Armstrong Siddeley Sapphire engines of 7,500lbs thrust. As described in Chapter 2, Roly took the aircraft up to 10,000ft but when he lowered the undercarriage for landing, air traffic control informed him that two bits of the aircraft fell to the ground. A formating aircraft reported that it was only the fairings behind the main undercarriage legs that had fallen off which was not a major problem and the aircraft landed uneventfully using the brake parachute to avoid the need for excessive braking.

Besides the normal development of the aircraft systems, there were some handling features which needed to be improved and dealt with, to ensure that the Vulcan would be acceptable in squadron service. The second prototype, VX777, was the first Vulcan to have the Olympus engine, initially with 9,750lbs thrust; it flew from Woodford on 3rd September 1953 but had an accident at Farnborough a year later when the rudder went to full travel; Roly had to land at high speed and the aircraft was badly damaged; the accident is discussed in detail in Chapter 7. When it flew again on 5th October 1955 it had the revised drooped leading edge on the outer part of the wing which reduced the aircraft's sensitivity to buffet at high subsonic mach number. I never flew VX777 when it had the straight leading edge but flew it later, both in the Mk 1 and again in the Mk 2 leading edge configuration.

The first production aircraft XA889 flew on 4th February 1955 with the original straight wings and, after modification to the production leading edge, was delivered to Boscombe Down for acceptance in March 1956. This was the Vulcan used by Avros to obtain CA release and on which I had my first flight, described in the Prologue. The first delivery, XA897, to the RAF was on 20th July 1956. This was the aircraft that tragically crashed after a world tour when trying to land at London's Heathrow airport in bad weather. Altogether there were 45 Vulcan Mk 1s built between 1955 and 1959. They went to five squadrons: Nos 44, 50, 83, 101, and 617. The aircraft were gradually upgraded and fitted with in-flight refuelling capability, Olympus Mk 104 engines and electronic counter measures; this latter equipment was fitted in a revised tail fairing and the aircraft so fitted were designated Mk 1A. The last squadron with the Mk 1A finished in 1968.

The early Vulcans, both Mk 1 and 1A, were painted white for their high altitude bombing role, described in Chapter 8, but in 1960 a U2 high altitude reconnaissance plane was shot down by the Soviets, thus demonstrating that their anti-aircraft missile technology was working rather earlier than had been expected; it had been anticipated that the high altitude bombing threat of the V Bombers would have lasted into the mid 60s. As a result, the role of the V Bombers, including the Vulcan, had to be rapidly altered from high altitude to low altitude operation. The white anti-flash paint was changed for camouflage and the crews had to learn their new role in a hurry.

The RAF placed a development contract with Avros in 1954 for an improved Vulcan called the Mk 2 and the second prototype aircraft VX777 flew with the new wider thinner wing and bigger intakes on 31st August 1957. The first production Vulcan Mk 2 flew on 19th August 1958 and a few weeks later Jimmy Harrison, who by then had taken over from Roly Falk and was chief test pilot, demonstrated the aircraft at Farnborough. Vulcan Mk 2 deliveries commenced in July 1960 when I delivered Vulcan XH558 to Waddington. The Mk 2 aircraft had an improved aerodynamic design and higher powered Olympus 201 engines of 17,000lbs thrust each, enabling the aircraft to go to much greater altitudes than the Mk 1. It had eight elevons instead of separate elevators and ailerons and a much improved electrical system compared with the Mk 1, having 200V 400cycle constant frequency AC plus an auxiliary power unit, AAPU, for ground running and emergency supply in the air and also an emergency Ram Air Turbine, RAT to produce electrical power at high altitude. There was a new flight system, an improved automatic pilot with automatic landing capability and, later, a terrain following radar. Subsequently some of the Olympus 201 engines had Olympus 301s fitted with 21,000lbs of thrust. These later engines had a rapid start capability and if necessary all the engines could be started simultaneously so that four aircraft could be airborne within two minutes as part of a squadron scramble. This facility allowed instant reaction to the cold war threat from nuclear missiles; the concept was that the aircraft could not be destroyed on the ground but would be able to respond immediately with their own nuclear attack thus providing a deterrent and maintaining the raison d'être of the whole V Force project.

The usual weapon was still a free fall nuclear bomb but some aircraft carried the Avro Blue Steel stand off weapon with its designed high level maximum range of one hundred miles reduced to fifty miles when released at low level. There was a plan to carry the Douglas Air Launched Ballistic Missile, the Skybolt, and a large number of the Vulcan Mk 2s had their wings strengthened and modified to be able to carry the missile. The programme was finally cancelled in December 1962 but the strengthened wing proved invaluable in increasing the fatigue life of the aircraft.

The Vulcan then flew in a low level role using terrain following radar. Fortuitously, the pylon fitting for the Skybolt also enabled the carriage of jamming pods for the Black Buck operation to the Falklands and air sampling pods for a few maritime reconnaissance Vulcans. The final Mk 2 squadron was converted into tankers.

Arguably, the Vulcan was the RAF's prime V Bomber, being able to deliver both a nuclear or conventional payload. During the cold war, the fear of reprisal from the Vulcan fleet helped to prevent the Soviet Union from attacking the Western allies. Eighty-nine Vulcan Mk 2s were built and were operated by seven squadrons – Nos: 9, 12, 27, 35, 50 and 617 – until the Vulcan finally went out of service in 1984. No other aeroplane, except perhaps Concorde, has captured the public imagination as much as the Vulcan, possibly the greatest and certainly the most innovative aircraft flown by the RAF with its very important role in the cold war. It is because the Vulcan is regarded as such a technical achievement and such an outstanding contributor in the success of the cold war that the Heritage Lottery Fund was prepared to fund the current project at Bruntingthorpe preparing a Vulcan to fly again fourteen years after the last aircraft landed and so, unlike Concorde, hopefully the Vulcan will live to fly another day.

Though the Vulcan finished its squadron flying in 1982 when its operational role was taken over by Polaris, the RAF realized its potential as a recruiting device because of its flying characteristics and formed a display flight which carried on until 1992, the last aircraft in the flight being XH558. If one can imagine an aircraft the size of an Airbus A320 being thrown around the sky as if it was a Spitfire, then it is possible to have some idea of what flying and displaying a Vulcan was like.

The aircraft was bought privately by David Walton and ferried to Bruntingthorpe in 1993. Hopefully XH558 will again demonstrate to the youth of the United Kingdom what a superb aircraft the Vulcan is and inspire them to follow a career in technology. At the time of writing, early 2007, the aircraft is being prepared for flight later on in the year.

The Vulcan was, and still is, a most remarkable aircraft. The fact that it was designed and built in the 1950s makes the technical accomplishment of the design team even more astonishing. The Avro Vulcan has often been compared with the USAF Boeing B52 Stratofortress strategic bomber, since both aircraft were in service simultaneously. Since the Vulcan was smaller and lighter, it was much more agile and marginally faster than the B52 with a much higher service ceiling. It was designed for the European theatre and did not require a trans-continental range. However, its four Bristol Siddeley Olympus 301 turbojet engines could not compare with the B52's eight Pratt and Whitney TF33 turbofans, which allowed the aircraft to have a much higher take-off weight and a trans-continental reach. It is a sobering thought, though, that whilst the Vulcan was retired from service more than twenty years ago, the B52 is still going strong.

CHAPTER 2

THE EARLY YEARS

Roy Chadwick's decision to have a delta design was based on the need to meet the exacting performance requirements of OR229. It meant that the design aerodynamicists at Avros and in the rest of the country for that matter were entering a new world. No longer did they have the comfortable forces on the elevator and tailplane, which they well understood, to balance the lift forces on the wing. It really was a case of back to the drawing board and in some ways a bit of a gamble.

It was absolutely vital to discover the flying characteristics of the delta as quickly as possible, hence the decision to build one-third scale models of the Avro 698 to see if any urgent changes were required in the design of the basic aircraft was an absolutely vital one. Some of the key questions that needed to be answered were as follows:

Performance
1.   How efficient was the delta wing in producing lift and what would be the drag of the wing during the cruise?
2.   How much load would the Vulcan wing be able to carry and what would be the approach and landing speeds?

Handling
1.   What sort of stall would the delta have and would that affect the approach and touchdown speeds?
2.   How sensitive would the flying qualities be to the centre of gravity position?
3.   Without a tailplane, what centre of gravity range would the delta be able to have?
4.   With such powerful engines would the fin and rudder be able to control the asymmetric power with two engines out on one side?
5.   Would it be possible to have manual controls on the full scale aircraft?
6.   What size did the integral wing mouth air intakes need to be and how much loss would there be down the long intake pipes?
7.   How difficult was it going to be to get effective air

brakes which would not give a large change of trim when operated?

8.   Would there be any unexpected behaviour?

Clearly the Avro and RAE wind tunnels were very useful in getting the design parameters roughly correct, but it had been judged that it would be far too big a risk to commit to the design of the Vulcan without doing some test work on the smaller 707s. These aircraft used existing components wherever possible, such as the Derwent engine being used in the Meteor and the canopy of the Meteor landing gear, to ensure that there was as much lead time as possible between the 707s flying and the first prototype Vulcan.

Vulcan flight testing began on 4th September 1949 when the first 707, VX784, took to the air in a 10 to 15 knots crosswind. It was flown by Ric Esler, deputy chief test pilot of Avros. After a couple of short flights Esler took the aircraft to Farnborough where the annual Society of Aircraft Constructors Show was in full swing but it was only shown in the static park. After the show VX784 carried out a few handling flights adjusting the controls and Esler reported that there were no significant problems. Sadly however, on 30th September the 707 crashed in the vicinity of Farnborough and Esler was killed; in those early days aircraft were not fitted with ejector seats nor were there flight data recorders. The likely cause of the accident was not clear. The airbrakes were found to be fully extended and Avros decided that this was probably the cause of the accident since, up to that time, only partial extension of the air brakes had been tried. However, I managed to find in the National Archives an RAE internal memo suggesting that as a result of an adjustment made by Avros before the flight, the ailerons were trying to move by themselves, over correcting, when they were displaced slightly, overbalance being the accepted term to describe the phenomenon. Overbalance, if it occurs, is very dangerous since the pilot has to work very hard the whole time to prevent the controls going to full travel and causing the aircraft to crash. The RAE based their opinion on the way the aircraft was flying before it hit the ground. The RAE memo is displayed in full in Appendix 1. Interestingly however, both the likely causes of the accident, the airbrake configuration and the aileron control balance, were questions that later required to be answered before freezing the design of the Vulcan.

At this point Roly Falk, a key figure in the Vulcan success story, appeared on the scene. Roly was an amazing man and a brilliant pilot with a flying experience which belied belief. His career is particularly interesting and I believe very relevant to this story since it shows clearly his dedication to flying and how his experience made him so effective in the development of the Vulcan. His flying spans one of the most exciting and innovative periods of British aviation history. From his starting as a student at the famous de Havilland Technical School in 1928 to the glorious demonstrations at Farnborough rolling the Vulcan in 1955, a total revolution had taken place in less than thirty years.

After leaving school and studying at Hatfield, Roly found time to obtain his A and B licences at the London Flying School and, incredibly, before leaving he had acquired over 1,400 hours flying including thirty-seven hours at night. He then did a variety of commercial flying jobs including flying newsreel cameramen to Abyssinia in 1935 to cover the war and to Spain to cover the start of the Spanish civil war. By 1939 he had 3,300 hours to his credit and he was doing jobs for the Air Registration Board, at that time responsible for certificating aircraft. In fact he became the ARB's first test pilot doing one job after another. The tremendous variety of aircraft he flew and the diverse places he visited gave Roly the total mastery of flying he so often displayed later.

At the outbreak of war in 1939 he volunteered for the RAF. During his refresher course his wing commander recognised that he was above average as a pilot and he was sent to do work at the Royal Aircraft Establishment, Farnborough where he stayed throughout the war. He flew every conceivable type of aircraft and nearly all the Luftwaffe aeroplanes, including the twin-jet-engined Messerschmitt fighter. At the end of the war he was demobbed and became a test pilot for Vickers at Wisley. After a lot of testing he had a very severe accident on 4th July 1946 in a Wellington fitted with the new de Havilland reversible propellers. Despite two broken legs, a broken arm, a fracture of the spine and metallic fragments in his head he managed to start flying again in April 1947. I met Roly for the first time nine years later at Boscombe, when he recruited me to work for Avros and I noticed that he walked rather stiffly, but it was only years later that I realised how lucky he was to be walking at all. As a matter of record, in all the years flying up to the accident, Roly had had eleven near misses of one sort or another but seemed to bear a charmed life. Perhaps it was inevitable that eventually he would be caught out.

Roly managed to keep flying on various jobs but the key moment for him and the Vulcan was when he saw Esler flying the 707 at Farnborough. By that time he had flown over 300 types of aircraft and had a total of 5,545 hours, 3,500 hours testing. Of course he knew Esler very well because he, and for that matter Jimmy Nelson another Avro test pilot, had worked for him at Aeroflight during the war. Apparently he told Charles McClure, then in charge of Aeroflight and previously a student of No 3 Empire Test Pilots School course: 'I'm going to fly that beautiful aircraft soon.' Inevitably he and Esler must have had long discussions during the week, particularly as Esler wasn't flying at the show, and so Roly would have learnt all about the flying qualities of the aircraft.

When Roly had first seen Ric in the 707 he had realised straightaway that he wanted desperately to be involved in the programme and test fly the Vulcan, but there did not seem to be an opening for him at that time. Ric by then was deputy to Jimmy Orrell, the chief test pilot, and had the extra qualification of being trained on No 2 course at Empire Test Pilots School. Furthermore, Jimmy Nelson had been on No 1 course so that Avros had two recently trained experimental test pilots. Consequently, though Roly was much more experienced than either Ric or Jimmy Nelson, there was no obvious place for him at Avros; though he had learnt his flight testing the hard way by experience, he had not done the ETPS course which was becoming increasingly important in the development of the new generation of aircraft with complicated systems, as well as demanding aerodynamics. The days of the test pilot landing and telling the chief designer what do were rapidly coming to an end; flight development was being done by a large team with a lot of instrumentation and the new breed of test pilots had to learn to be a part of that team. Indeed, Roly's lack of test pilot school training was a handicap when later it came to the necessary careful, time consuming development work which was increasingly required; he liked to be at the frontier of test flying, always doing something new and not repeating tests scrupulously, again and again to establish exact parameters or performance carpets. However, Roly realised what the programme needed as test flying the Vulcan began to be routine, if that is not a contradiction in terms, and he was smart enough to recruit Jimmy Harrison in 1954 to take over the detailed testing work and, two years later, he also invited me to join the team.

Ric's death changed the whole scene and Roly wrote to Sir Roy Dobson, the managing director of Avros, applying for the job. The application came at just the right moment for Sir Roy as Avros had built a brand new advanced trainer, the Avro Athena, in competition with the Boulton Paul Balliol which, unfortunately for Avros, had been the one selected by the Royal Air Force. Sir Roy recognised that Roly was a great salesman as well as a superb test pilot, up to date with testing modern jets and, typically, he made a deal. If Roly would take the Athena on a sales tour to India he would then be given the job of flying the next 707 on his return. Roly accepted what was clearly going to be a difficult sales trip and thus he became an Avro test pilot.

The tour went ahead with Roly flying the Athena as far as Delhi and the whole trip took three months. In fact no aircraft were sold as a result of the tour but knowing Roly, I am sure it was not for want of trying.

On his return he did not take part in the routine test flying on the many aircraft that Avro were building and developing like the Canberra and the Shackleton but, unusually for that time, became in effect a project pilot purely involved with the forthcoming 707B. There were significant changes being made to this aircraft compared with the first 707. An ejector seat was being fitted, the airbrakes were being redesigned to extend both above and below the wing, and the elevators were being redesigned to give better balance and effective control. The air intake for the Rolls-Royce Derwent engine was not changed at this stage, but was altered later to try to get rid of the buffet from the canopy spoiling the airflow into the engine. The aircraft, VX790, was finally completed and taken by truck down to Boscombe Down, as usual just before the SBAC show at Farnborough! It was reassembled on 4th September 1950, taxied with short hops on the 5th and finally flew on 6th September. Roly then made another flight and delivered it to Farnborough to be exhibited in the static park. There was no way the aircraft could be flown at the show because there had been no time to adjust the manual controls.

The moment the show was over work started on getting the aircraft to fly safely throughout the speed envelope. As mentioned, the controls were the main things to be sorted out and for a relatively high speed aircraft without power controls, adjusting flight controls for balance is always challenging. The stick forces have to be light but the forces must not reverse, or overbalance, as otherwise the aircraft becomes uncontrollable. In the case of the 707B, the rudder was found to be very light and the balance tab had be geared the opposite way to get the forces correct. The ailerons proved to be straightforward but the optimum gearing on the elevator meant that at very slow speeds there was a tendency for the elevator forces to reverse. By then it had been decided that the Vulcan was going to have fully powered controls so that the work on the 707 controls did not read across directly to the Vulcan. However, such testing had to be carried out so that the aerodynamics of the delta wing could be explored.

Roly was also involved in advising the design office on the vital task of Vulcan flight deck design. The instrument panel and all the supporting controls and switches had to be arranged with the greatest care, not just so that the pilots could fly the aircraft in normal flight but also so that they would be able to take the correct action in the event of an emergency. During my years in the pilots' office we spent a lot of time trying to ensure that as new systems were introduced into an aircraft, the controls of these systems were carefully thought through, to prevent incorrect pilot reactions in the event of a malfunction. Of course in those days there were no computers. Everything was analogue in design and it was the size of the electrical signal that mattered, not the digital bits. There was not a lot of sophistication, which was not all bad, since it prevented excessive complication, but great care was still required to get the optimum layout. When the Vulcan design started there were no simulators to practise flying and emergencies, but crew drills were just as important then as they are to-day. As I mention later, the initial cockpit modification adding the auto throttle to the Vulcan, made without pilot consultation, was a classic example of how not to install a new system.

In the past the pilots were often blamed if accidents occurred when systems malfunctioned, but nowadays it is realised that incorrect design of the systems and bad flight deck layout can be just as much a cause of an accident as the resulting action of the pilot when things go wrong. My maxim when considering flight handling and flight deck layout was always that an aircraft had to be able to be flown safely by the poorest pilot in the squadron, or in the airline for that matter.

Originally, it had been expected that the Vulcan would have manual controls but, later, the decision was taken to go for fully powered controls because otherwise it would have been impossible to get the pilot's control forces acceptable throughout the speed range, particularly at high mach numbers. The flight deck was being designed with a control wheel as was customary at the time, but Roly realised straightaway that with the fully powered controls it would be possible to have a fighter type stick. Despite Roly's pleading, the design office opposed what would have been at the time a very unconventional change for such a large aircraft, probably because a change at that time would have delayed the first flight.

Whilst the control column/stick discussion was very important, it was also vital that the power controls could be controlled on the flight deck. One of the most innovative features, copied by Concorde years later, was an instrument which represented the tail view of the aircraft. All the control surfaces were shown in the correct position as if viewed from the back of the aircraft, so that when the control column was moved all the surfaces could be seen moving as signalled by the pilot. This meant that the pilot could see instantly if a control was 'stuck', that is if the surface was not moving correctly. This instrument was elegantly simple in concept but vitally important as a contribution to flight safety.

Unlike modern aircraft, the electrical system was not controlled by the pilots but by the air electronics officer in the rear cabin, rather akin to a flight engineer in the old piston-engined aircraft. This meant that

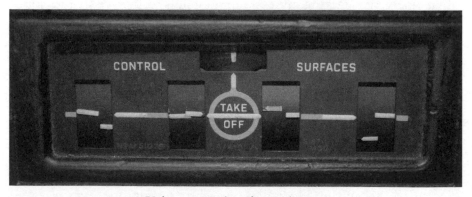

Vulcan control surface indicator.

there had to be a very good understanding between the pilot and the AEO, as the power controls were all electrically driven as were the flight instruments. The captain had to rely on the AEO to tell him if a generator was not on line, particularly as on the Mk 1 the control surfaces were controlled by pilot-operated switches without power indication, unlike the Mk 2.

There was a time when people used to wonder what a pilot did when he wasn't flying. There can be little doubt what Roly was doing; he was working with the design engineers to make sure that the flight deck was being laid out correctly. I speak with some certainty on the subject, having been involved myself in new aircraft design and I know that it is a very lengthy and time consuming task.

A typical design decision which was required was how the pilot was to control the fourteen fuel tanks. It was important that the pilots could check the indication from the tanks and control the feeding if things went wrong. On VX770 there was just one fuel tank initially but Roly had to advise on the way the production aircraft should be controlled with so many tanks to be 'supervised'. In fact using this fuel system was to be my first task on my first flight in the Vulcan from Boscombe Down.

The fuel tanks had to be arranged so that the pilots could visualise the layout of the system and be able to control the feeding of the tanks. In addition it had to be easy for the pilot to control the centre of gravity. There were going to be five tanks in each wing, Nos 3, 4, 5, 6, and 7, this arrangement being chosen so that it would be possible to fit the tanks between the wing structure; in addition there would be four tanks in the fuselage, Nos 1 and 2 on each side. The contents of Nos 1, 4, 5, and 7 tanks were approximately the same as the contents of Nos 2, 4 and 6 tanks and so it was decided that on each side Nos 1, 4, 5, 7, should feed the outer engine and Nos 2, 4, 6 should feed the inner engines. There was considerable anxiety as to the best way to feed the engines from the tanks, since it was imperative to keep the centre of gravity, cg, of the aircraft within the permitted range and, at this stage, the possible limits of the cg were not known and awaited the results of flight tests. The correct cg position was vital since the flying controls would only be able to balance the aerodynamic forces within a fairly narrow range of cg position.

After some debate it was agreed to have a fairly simple scheme, which was to have two sequence timers, one on each side of the aircraft which took fuel out of each tank in turn by switching on its booster pump. This proved to be a very effective system. Provision was also made to transfer fuel between the two front and back tanks to adjust the cg as required. In addition, Roly agreed that the system would allow manual control of the fuel tanks in the event of a sequence timer failure or other malfunction.

Fuel gauges.

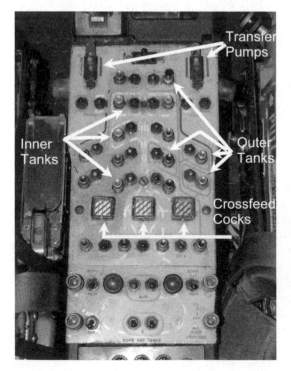

Fuel controls.

Back in the flight test hangar, having got the controls of the 707B to a safe and usable standard, work started on examining the aerodynamics of the delta wing. Roly found that he could fly VX790 right down to 80 knots maintaining lateral control, despite the fact that cine film shots of wool tufts in front of the wing showed that the air flow over the whole wing was completely stalled. However at 80 knots the elevators were fully up. Significantly, the aircraft did not show a tendency to spin provided sideslip was not allowed to build up and so the behaviour of the 707 proved to be very similar to

Top: The prototype 707 VX784.

Middle: 707B VX790, used only for low-speed handling.
Bottom: 707B VX790 with revised intake.

Top: Roly Falk flying Vulcan 707 in pin-striped suit. *(Leysa Falk)*

Middle: 707A WD280, high mach number development aircraft.

Bottom: Unusual shot of 707A WD280.

the Vulcan itself. At the higher speeds up to 350 knots the aircraft behaved normally with satisfactory longitudinal static stability.

Taking off in the VX790 proved to be unusual in that there was not sufficient elevator power to raise the nosewheel properly except at extreme aft centre of gravity positions. Roly found that he had to pull the stick right back to get the nosewheel off the ground but then, as the aircraft rotated, it became airborne immediately which was very disconcerting in that he was forced to push the stick rapidly forward again to prevent the aircraft climbing away too steeply. This was clearly unacceptable and a very crude fix was made to the nosewheel leg by adding a piece of rolled steel joist, so that the ground incidence was increased from $0°$ to $3^1/2°$ and Roly was then able to raise the nosewheel in the air at 10 knots or so before the aircraft got airborne, without pulling the elevator very far back. This meant that the aircraft would then fly off cleanly from the ground without the need to make further rapid elevator movements. Again this characteristic was evident in the Vulcan, once more justifying the decision to have the one-third scale models.

Roly then turned his mind to the optimum way to land the aircraft. Initially, he had been using a very slow approach speed which meant that the attitude of the aircraft was very nose-up during the approach. The advantage of this method was that very little braking was required after touchdown, which reduced the wear and tear on the wheels and brakes. However, while Roly had no problem approaching at these low speeds because of his innate flying ability, it became apparent that the aircraft was much easier to fly on the approach at a faster speed and $10°$ approach incidence was chosen as the optimum instead of $12/13°$. Using these higher speeds the anti-spin parachute was then streamed on touchdown, simulating the tail parachute which was planned for the real Vulcan. In the Vulcan itself it was possible to come in at a sensible approach speed, not too nose-up, and still get plenty of aerodynamic braking after touchdown thus minimising the use of the wheel brakes by keeping the nose wheels in the air. This was my preferred landing technique, but the records do not show whether Roly used this braking technique on VX790.

Because the handling of the 707B was so good it was felt that some flying should be done at high subsonic mach numbers, but as explained the engine air intake was not adequate for this task because of buffet from the canopy. Consequently, the aircraft was grounded for an intake change and in February 1951 it flew with the flush dorsal intake removed and a twin air intake fitted on either side of the dorsal fin. Unfortunately the new intake was still not satisfactory due to the disturbed air off the back of the canopy. In fact the 707B was not used much more by Avros in their Vulcan development programme. In September 1951 it was handed over to A&AEE and later to Aeroflight for aerodynamic testing, having flown 130 hours and 380 flights; of that total Roly had done all the key testing totalling nearly 100 hours. Fortuitously, Jimmy Harrison, who was to become Roly's successor, was already at Aeroflight and managed to do some flying in VX790. Jimmy did a lot of the tedious development work that was so necessary to make the Vulcan a successful aircraft and it is interesting to look at his background, very different to Roly's.

Jimmy left school in 1934 at the age of sixteen and was very interested in aircraft. He managed to persuade his father to let him sit the Halton Apprentice School examination and he became one of 'Trenchard's brats'. He then served on several squadrons, went to France at the start of the Second World War and was one of the last units to be evacuated from Dunkirk. He finally managed to persuade one of his COs to send him on a pilot's course and he went to Canada for training. He was clearly an exceptional pilot and was kept in Canada as a flying instructor for most of the war. The war ended just as Jimmy was posted to a Mosquito squadron in Belgium. He stayed on in Germany but managed to get on No 8 Empire Test Pilots School Course. He had Group Captain Leonard Snaith as his CO, an ex-Schneider Trophy pilot in 1934; Snaith was a splendid man and I had the good fortune to meet him on Jimmy's introduction some years later at Farnborough. Predictably, Jimmy passed out with a 'Special Distinction', as in fact I did some years later from No13 Course, but my award was not really for brilliant test flying but for coming top of the Ground School and possibly for giving 'out of hours' instruction for those who needed it, since I was an RAF education officer teaching maths and physics before volunteering to be taught to fly!

Jimmy was posted to Aeroflight in 1950 and very conveniently in October 1952, 707 VX790 arrived from Boscombe. He examined the handling of the 707B in great detail and even went up to Woodford to have a flight in the 707A after it had been fitted with power controls in November 1952. Clearly by this time he and Roly must have had frequent discussions about the 707s and Roly would have recognised that Jimmy was a superb test pilot. Consequently, when Jimmy Nelson retired in April 1953 and there was a vacancy, he was invited to lunch by Sir Roy and asked if he would like to join the Avro test team. Jimmy accepted on the spot and a deal was made.

There was no gap in the delta flying when the 707B came to the end of its useful life with Avros, as another 707 had been being constructed, the 707A. This aircraft was significantly different from the 707B in that the wing was altered aerodynamically so that it more nearly represented the projected 698 design, the Vulcan itself. This alteration included the leading edge engine intakes. The controls were changed so that instead of simple geared tabs, each control had a sealed balance with a spring tab. The elevators were moved outwards to leave room for the jet pipes that would be there on the full scale aircraft. However, for safety reasons it was felt necessary to fit dive recovery flaps in the free space vacated by the elevator in case the elevators were unable to pull the aircraft out of a high mach number dive; should the pilot lose control at high speed, it was hoped that operating the flaps would slow the aircraft down sufficiently for the elevators to become effective again and, therefore, for the pilot to be able to regain control. The air brake design was changed as well to more nearly represent the 698. The air brakes came out at first without the air brake surfaces rotating until the operating arms were fully extended; operating in this way, the change of trim using the air brakes was minimised.

Roly flew the 707A, WD280, from Boscombe on 14th July 1951 and, like the 707B, the first job was to sort out the controls. The elevator control was poor and there was a change of lateral stability with speed. The elevators were found to be misaligned and, laterally, the aircraft was right wing heavy due to the weight of instrumentation in the starboard wing so that 200lbs of ballast had to be put in the port wing to maintain balance. Once these problems had been sorted out, the aircraft was used to examine the high speed characteristics of the delta and it was operated most of the time from Boscombe Down. Roly did all the flying and he and Zbigniev Olenski, a Czech ex-fighter pilot and ace aerodynamicist from Woodford flight test, worked together analysing the flying and ensuring that the high speed characteristics of the airplane were fully understood.

It was during this flying that Roly encountered the three key characteristics of the Vulcan design at high subsonic mach number. The first feature was that the aircraft was longitudinally unstable as the limiting mach number of about .95M was reached; this meant that instead of the pilot having to push the stick forward to make the aircraft go faster as in most aircraft, it was necessary for the pilot to pull the stick back to prevent the speed increasing uncontrollably, potentially a very dangerous situation. In aeronautical terms the aircraft was longitudinally unstable and the situation was compounded by the fact that at the limiting mach number the elevator was almost at its limit of travel, fully up, so in effect the aircraft was out of control. The next feature of the delta was that the aircraft tended to oscillate uncontrollably up and down as the limiting mach number was approached, .95M; the rate of oscillation was so fast that the pilot was not able to stop it and, in fact, trying to stop it made the oscillation worse. This is called a short period pitching oscillation but luckily in the case of the 707s and the Vulcan the oscillation did not get out of control; the size of the oscillation or the amplitude did not increase or in other words, it was not divergent. The final feature of the delta was that at mach numbers of about .85M and higher, the local flow of the air on the top surface of the wing went supersonic despite the swept back design of the wing, causing shaking or buffeting and what was more serious, the drag of the aircraft increased unacceptably at the desired cruise speed so that the performance of the aircraft was adversely affected. Furthermore, this buffet increased severely if the aircraft was manoeuvred in any way from level flight, the buffet margin as it was called was far too small.

The instability of the delta and the short period oscillation were potentially dangerous since they affected the handling of the aircraft but, luckily, not the performance. The buffet was not dangerous but it did affect the performance of the aircraft and of course it was the performance of the aircraft that the customer was buying. Consequently, the buffet problem had to be solved or the Vulcan would be virtually useless in the war scenario that was envisaged.

Avros decided that the way round the handling problems could be solved by using artificial stability aids which were just becoming available at the time and this task was given to the flying control designers. Clearly the problem that had to be solved as quickly as possible was the performance; how to stop the buffet occurring and thus prevent the whole programme being cancelled.

Roly flew the 707A until May 1952 when it was grounded to have power controls fitted; by then it had flown 92 hours and 197 flights. It was next flown by Jack Wales the following February to assess the controls. Jack was a very experienced pilot and had done a lot of jet flying in the RAF. He had been with Avros for several years and was in the RAF auxiliary 613 Squadron flying both Vampires and Meteors.

In February 1954 Jimmy Harrison left the RAF and joined Avros to become Roly Falk's eventual successor as chief test pilot and took over the testing of the Avro 707A. The aircraft eventually finished up in Australia with the RAAF, but not before Jimmy had completed some very important aerodynamic testing of the proposed Vulcan wing design which is discussed later in this chapter.

It is interesting that Jimmy Nelson, who had lost a leg at Farnborough in a Mosquito accident after he had finished No 1 ETPS Course, managed to carry on flying. However, though he flew the 707s he did not fly the Vulcan prototype because of the high rudder forces. Unfortunately, I never had the pleasure of meeting him since he had left Avros before I joined.

At the time that Roly stopped flying WD280, the 707A, the first prototype Vulcan VX770 was getting close to flight. The three main challenges of designing a new aircraft were no different then than they are now; the handling of the aircraft must be acceptable, the systems must be adequate to control the aircraft and the performance must meet the design specification. Clearly the way these challenges were being met was open for negotiation with the customer, bearing in mind that the Vulcan was being designed right at the limit of the known technology at the time.

As a result of the 707 flying, both at high and low speed, Avros had taken the decision, already mentioned, that it would not be possible to have pilot-operated manual controls but to use motors to drive the surfaces. This immediately simplified the design of the controls but made the system design of the electro-hydraulic motors, which powered the controls, absolutely fundamental to the safety of the aircraft. The control surfaces still had to have some aerodynamic balance in order to help keep the required operating forces from the motors down to a reasonable value; without any balance the size of the motors would have had to be very large in order to operate the control surfaces. It was decided to have one electrically driven hydraulic motor for each control surface and to have eight control surfaces at the trailing edge of the wing, four ailerons and four elevators. In addition, the rudder was a single surface but had two motors. The design of the electrical system became a key milestone for the designers; the total weight of the system had to be kept to a minimum and the optimum solution at the time was for a 112V DC system to drive the motors. The aircraft had four engines and there would be three busbars and, to ensure safety in an emergency, there would be another 'battery' busbar driven by a bank of four 28V batteries connected in series to provide emergency control power. For the record, a busbar maybe defined as 'an electrical conductor in the form of rigid bars that serves as a common connection for two or more electric circuits'; in the case of the Vulcan, a busbar was a common point or points joined together to which electric motors, pumps and other facilities were all connected. It was very important from a safety viewpoint that all the electrical loads were shared between the busbars so that if a busbar became faulty or lost its supply the aircraft could still continue to fly safely.

Having powered controls simplified one problem but introduced another, since on manually controlled aircraft the airflow over the control surfaces made the control forces very high and prevented the pilot from applying too large control deflections and breaking the aircraft, providing, it must be said that the controls were set up correctly. Since the aircraft was going to have power controls, artificial feel was required to prevent the pilot over controlling or breaking the aircraft by applying excessive control angles since the amount of force to operate the control motors would be very light. Roly had a great influence on deciding the optimum solution for the control forces and it was decided that for the ailerons a simple spring would be satisfactory, but the permitted range of the controls would have to be reduced with a mechanical limiter as the speed of the aircraft was increased, since the application of full aileron at high speed would damage if not break the aircraft. For the elevator, the feel forces were arranged as for a normal aircraft without power controls and varied with the square of the speed; this was done by changing the power of the spring as the speed varied by moving the fulcrum of the lever arm which connected the pilot's stick to the spring. The rudder feel was again a spring with a moving fulcrum on the operating arm, but this time the geometry was arranged so that the foot force required to apply rudder was even greater than the natural aerodynamic force, increasing as the cube of the airspeed instead of the square. Roly was helped enormously in all this flight deck design work by a brilliant mechanical design engineer, Bill Stableford, with whom I worked a few years later sorting out, amongst other things, all the installation problems of the many flavours of Vulcan autopilots.

The aircraft systems all needed to be tested before flight and so rigs had been designed and manufactured for the flying controls and the fuel systems. In addition there were other systems that needed to be ground tested, namely the hydraulics for the undercarriage, the pressurisation and air conditioning system, the engine installation and a full scale structural test specimen. Interestingly, at this stage there was no complete electrical system test rig, unlike with the Mk 2.

The engines were going to be Bristol Olympus but these would not be ready in time for the test, so instead four Rolls-Royce Avon engines were fitted to VX770. One of the key decisions was the size of the engine intake and this was determined after considerable help from the specialists at RAE; the design cleverly allowed for the larger intakes that would be required as engine power was increased.

The main design had been decided by September 1949 and only vital changes were permitted, necessitated by safety or performance reasons; in other words the design had been frozen. However, continual pilot input from Roly and later from Jimmy Harrison and myself had to be made to the systems and flight deck as a result of the rig tests, to ensure that the systems could be controlled satisfactorily. In fact there were even more changes which were required as a result of flight tests which affected production aircraft, but those sorts of problems are routine in flight development. The actual wing design for VX770 was not frozen until late 1949 so that the basic dimensions of VX770 were not settled until February 1950 and detailed drawings were not issued until later in the year in May.

The aircraft started to come together in early 1952 and, after a lot of ground running checking of the engines and all the systems, the aircraft was finally ready for flight at Woodford on 30th August 1952, just before the SBAC show as usual. The wing fuel system had not been tested at this time and a temporary bomb fuel tank was fitted to supply the engines. In addition, Roly had agreed that it need only have one pilot seat but it should be an ejection one! The first flight was successful in that the aircraft landed safely, though both undercarriage fairings blew off. Jimmy Nelson in the 707A was immediately scrambled to inspect the aircraft but he was incredibly short of fuel since he had already been flying and hadn't been refuelled; after a quick inspection to check that there was nothing seriously wrong he had to land immediately. Jack Wales then took off in a 613 Squadron Vampire for a closer look and pronounced all was well.

As there was a speed restriction on the aircraft for the first few flights it was decided not to refit the fairings immediately. The aircraft flew to Boscombe Down and then did five flights at the SBAC show at Farnborough totalling about ten hours.

Avros ensured that there was maximum publicity for the first flight and the flying at Farnborough to demonstrate to the world, and to the Ministry of Defence in particular, the potency of the aircraft and the fact that the programme was going well. Sir Roy's remarks were particularly effective:

> Every claim and theory we have advanced in favour of the delta design had been conclusively proved in the research programmes laid down for our other deltas, the Avro 707A and B, which were ordered by the Ministry of Supply so that we could substantiate our somewhat revolutionary claim for a bomber. This has been done and the full size aircraft will soon be handed over for official trials.
>
> The new Avro bomber marks a further development of the delta wing to military purposes.... Given the necessary power the bomber could undoubtedly fly faster than sound! [Author's exclamation mark.]

Duncan Sandys, then Minister of Supply also weighed in, presumably justifying the government's expenditure:

> The advent of this huge four-jet Delta-wing plane may well have a profound influence upon future development, not only in warfare but also in civil development. The Government decided recently to order an appreciable number of these new bombers without waiting for the prototype to carry out the usual flying trials. I am confident that both on military and economic grounds our decision will prove to be justified.

Roly no longer wore a white flying suit to fly but instead a grey suit, pin striped I seem to remember, with immaculate shirt and tie. Certainly this made the engineers keep the flight deck very clean. I think Roly was unique in flying in this attire and it surely cost him a fortune since he always seemed immaculate. It must have saved him a lot of time at Farnborough since he used to talk to the VIPs in the firm's chalet and then dash to the aircraft and, no matter how well he had lunched, he always flew superbly. He certainly earned himself a great reputation as a flamboyant character and he was a great demonstration pilot. He would chat up the VIPs as if to the manner born and in my experience they lapped it up.

When the aircraft returned from Farnborough it had to be grounded to be finished, a not uncommon occurrence at Avros when an aircraft had been prepared in a rush for the SBAC show. The undercarriage fairings were refitted so that they stayed in place, the second pilot's seat was installed and more instrumentation was fitted and tested. It was at this point that the decision on how the pilot would control the aircraft was re-examined. Up to this time all large aircraft had control wheels fitted in the flight deck since considerable force was necessary to move the aircraft controls, particularly at the higher speeds. However, with the advent of control surfaces completely powered by hydraulic or electric motors there was no need for the pilot to apply large forces to move the controls; the pilot had merely to signal to the motors to move and the motors would do the work. Consequently, Roly suggested that the engineers should take advantage of this situation and use a stick which would take up a lot less room. There would be another advantage of using the stick since, with a control wheel it was necessary to remove the wheel before ejection to avoid breaking the pilots' knees. Roly being well over six feet tall was particularly sensitive on this subject. His view finally prevailed and a stick replaced the conventional 'pair of spectacles'. It was of course this decision, virtually made by Roly alone, that made the Vulcan such a distinctive aircraft from the pilot's point of view, almost handling like a fighter. As an aside it is interesting to note that nowadays Airbus aircraft don't have a control column at all but use a little stick by the side of the pilot so that the instrument panel is completely unobstructed whilst Boeing still have the conventional control wheel.

Roly then started on the basic testing to determine what were the immediate problems to be solved, bringing other Avro test pilots into the programme. With Jimmy Nelson he investigated the low speed handling of the aircraft, lateral trim curves and rate of roll, checking that there was positive elevator angle per g as well as basic longitudinal stability. Roly then checked the effectiveness, trim changes and loads on the electrically operated air brakes. Speed was gradually increased to 400 knots and then 415 knots, the maximum design speed. Having established that the aircraft was flyable at low altitude he went up to 30,000ft and up to .92 IMN, indicated mach number. Speed was then increased flight by flight to a maximum of .98 IMN. On the way it was necessary to examine the short period pitching oscillation that had been found on the 707s. This oscillation was still there on the full scale aircraft and occurred above .96 IMN but luckily, though the frequency of the oscillation was still too fast for the pilot to control, the amplitude did not diverge dangerously.

All mach numbers quoted are indicated mach numbers, written IMN, which is what the pilot saw on his machmeter. It was getting pretty clear from early rough formation flying alongside other aircraft whose true mach numbers were known, that the indicated mach numbers were significantly higher than the true mach numbers and so it became very important to try to judge the size of this mach number 'position error'. The normal method of doing this at the time was to use a so-called 'trailing static' behind the aircraft, the idea being that if the pressure was measured sufficiently far from the aircraft itself then the reading it produced would be an accurate one, unlike measurements made at the aircraft itself. Unfortunately, the trailing static would only work at relatively slow speeds and the mach number limitation of the device was significantly below the mach numbers possible in the Vulcan, despite modifications to the static itself to make it more 'aerodynamic'. Consequently, it was decided to try to measure the errors by using a specially calibrated Meteor 7 from Aeroflight. The Meteor's maximum speed was about .78M, well below the Vulcan's speeds, so that the Vulcan had to 'fly by' the Meteor at different speeds and the readings of the two aircraft were then compared. The results showed that the mach number error got larger and larger as the higher indicated mach numbers were reached and John McDaniel, the deputy head of Avro Flight Test department, who developed a special method of determining position error on the Mk 2 described later, reckoned that the Vulcan Mk 1 at 1.0 IMN was probably flying at .93 true mach number which agreed with the tests we did later at A&AEE.

Ever mindful of the need to market the Vulcan and a possible civil variant, Roly took the managing director of the British Overseas Airways Corporation on a flight up to 350knots and .86 IMN on 20th February 1953. In addition, the RAF had appointed Squadron Leader Charles Calder as a liaison officer based at Woodford to fly in the Vulcan test programme and he had had his first flight in 770 a day or two earlier. As a point of interest, it was always a matter of judgement when to ask any RAF liaison pilot to fly on a particular test since sometimes problems occurred which the firm wanted to keep to itself until it had decided how to tackle them, for example measuring aircraft performance.

The preliminary testing was completed in thirty-two hours and it was then decided to ground 770 in order to fit the more powerful Sapphire engines, the Olympus engines still not being ready; the more powerful engines were needed so that the aircraft could get as high as possible in order to carry out tests in the corners of the design flight envelope, that is at the maximum indicated airspeed and mach number. In addition, the proper fuel system was made operative instead of the bomb bay tank. Roly started the next phase of flying in July 1953 but not before taking part in the RAF Review on 15th July at Odiham by the Queen, which necessitated two earlier practices. I took part in those practices and the review myself but I was in a Venom squadron nine places behind Roly and his Vulcan which was number six in the flypast. Of course at that time I had absolutely no conception that only three years later I would not only be a fully qualified test pilot but flying the Vulcan myself.

Roly started flying the second prototype Vulcan VX777 on 3rd

September 1953 and so he was forced to delegate some of the test work on VX770 to Jack Wales. However, Roly decided to do the low level position error measurements at Boscombe Down with VX770 himself and on 12th August he carried out forty-nine runs in two flights before returning to Woodford. These measurements were vitally important to determine the error in static pressure readings at different speeds, since the accuracy of the altimeter reading depended on the static pressure error, remembering that an altimeter shows height but actually is only measuring pressure, relying on the fact that pressure drops as the height is increased. In particular, the size of this error had to be accurately determined at approach speeds, so that any errors in the measurement of altitude could be allowed for when making bad weather approaches.

Finally, VX777 was ready, fitted with the Olympus 100 engines delivering 10,000lbs thrust and the first few flights were devoted to snag clearance of the air brakes and then flying to Farnborough where on 7th September 1953 the famous flypast took place of the two Vulcan prototypes, the 707B, two 707As and the 707C. These flypasts were repeated during the week. Then Roly, as always mindful for the need to sell the Vulcan, flew the Chief of the Air Staff, Air Chief Marshal Sir J. Boothman, for fifty-five minutes including a touchdown at Boscombe before returning to Farnborough. Later that day the Vulcan formation flew along the south coast when the famous pictures were taken. Roly then flew the aircraft back to Woodford where it was grounded to have the full pressurisation system installed. This system was urgently required but could not have been fitted earlier until the cabin compartment had been exhaustively tested in a water tank. A representative cabin structure had been fitted in a water tank and had been pressurised and unpressurised, called cycling, to simulate a Vulcan doing many flights. In addition the opportunity was taken to fit the latest Olympus engine control system so that representative engine handling could be carried out at the higher altitudes that would be available with the new pressurisation system.

VX770 meanwhile was carrying out all the routine tests so essential to produce a safe aircraft, such as detailed measurements of manoeuvring stability, steady trim points to establish stability and control margins, asymmetric handling with one and two engines throttled back, flight with power control motors switched off and a host of other detailed measurements.

In February 1954 VX777 flew again and because of its capability to go over 50,000ft it was clearly necessary for the crew to wear pressure clothing. The approved equipment was a modified American-designed outfit, but the helmet was designed by the RAF School of Medicine and made by that aptly named firm Frankenstein. Roly announced that he was not going to wear the equipment as it would 'hamper his movements' and so an agreement was reached by which Calder, the RAF liaison pilot, flew with Roly when going to high altitude, suitably trussed in with the pressure clothing, the idea being that if pressurisation was lost, Calder could bring the aircraft down to a level where Roly would regain consciousness! Two years later when I joined Avros I was kitted out with the same equipment, so I know the phrase 'trussed in' is entirely appropriate. In the back, Pete Rivers, who was responsible for the aircraft pressurisation system, flew in the aircraft also wearing the kit until all the bugs were worked out of the system.

On the first flight after the grounding Roly climbed the aircraft to 45,000ft and the engineers noticed that the engine bay temperatures were very high. Roly took up Godfrey Auty, the chief test pilot of Bristol Engines, on the next flight and between them all they discovered that the air extractors from the engine bays were choking. The problem was fixed and testing continued steadily combined as always with Roly doing demonstration flying. This time it was the turn of Air Marshal Pike, the Deputy Chief of Air Staff, and he was flown to 48,000ft and .98 IMN though history does not relate what flying and pressure breathing equipment they were wearing.

Meanwhile, Sir Roy Dobson had decided as a result of the development and sales work being carried out by Roly that it was time to update the test pilots' organisation. Jimmy Orrell was still chief test pilot but was approaching retirement. He still had a few years to go but clearly all visitors to Woodford on Vulcan business went to Roly who was doing the work and not to Jimmy. Dobbie's solution was to make Roly Superintendant of Flying over Jimmy Orrell and this situation lasted for a couple of years until Jimmy withdrew from the programme and took over the Blue Steel flight testing organisation.

As the aircraft flew to higher and higher altitudes, the early onset of buffet became more and more of a problem. The starboard outer wing was wool tufted and Roy Ewans, then chief aerodynamicist and later chief engineer succeeding Stuart Davies, occupied the right hand pilot's seat for a couple of flights to observe the flow breakdown. No sooner had this technical observation been carried out than another sales flight took place, this time with the minister himself, Duncan Sandys, in the right hand seat and Air Marshal Sir John Baker sitting in the centre navigator's seat. They were treated to the 'above 50,000ft' experience and no doubt took their impressions back to MOD as Roly intended. Between demonstration flights, Roly managed to investigate the buffet boundary more carefully, applying g at different speeds, weights and altitudes. While doing this he experienced some engine surging and flame outs, a development problem with which I became very familiar myself a few years later as the Olympus engines were uprated first to 102s, then 103s and finally 104s. However it was much more serious then than it was for me as I was flying a developed airframe whilst he was trying to develop the aircraft at the same time.

About this time it was realised that the change of trim with airbrake extension could be improved by removing the outboard lower airbrake plates and so after confirmatory tests this change was carried out. While this was going on Roly flew General Gerrity, a USAF general, and two accompanying colonels at high altitude and mach number to make sure that news of the Vulcan's successful development would get spread across the Atlantic.

In April/May 1954 VX777 was grounded to have its navigation and bomb dropping system made operative and to have the new air brake configuration made into a production system. The other prototype, 770, was still being used for various tests, high mach number drag, trim and measuring the effects of aileron movement as g was applied with the elevator. This effect, called aileron float, was important since it affected the elevator control power because less elevator angle was needed than expected since the ailerons, in effect, helped the elevators. This aileron float was undesirable and the designers tried to minimise it by adjusting the connection between the stick and the aileron motors. Another new task was to check how easy it was for the aircraft to be seen by radar and some tests were carried out with the Radar Research Establishment at Malvern. Jack Wales was doing some measured take-offs to check that the length of the RAF Bomber Command runways were going to be adequate and then 770 was also grounded to undertake a varied programme of amendments.

Roly started flying 777 again in July doing bomb door measurements and dropping a few small practice bombs at Orfordness. Then on 27th July while demonstrating low speed manoeuvres to an RAE pilot the aircraft suddenly dropped a wing and Roly had a problem with the rudder, almost certainly just after he had applied full control. He found he had to bank and apply asymmetric power to try to prevent the sideslipping. There were no periscopes, as in later aircraft, to enable the crew to inspect the rear of the aircraft and Roly was worried that the fin or rudder might be damaged, so he returned to Farnborough with great care. He flew past the Farnborough tower and the controllers confirmed that the fin was still in its correct place with no obvious damage. In fact there had been failure in the rudder control linkage so that a special 'spring strut' had jammed and the rudder was kept hard over with the pedals central. He landed faster than usual, using bank and asymmetric power to hold the runway centre line before touchdown, but the chute failed when it came out, presumably due to excessive speed. The aircraft could not stop on the runway but finished up in the approach lights and the gear got trapped in a ditch so that the undercarriage collapsed. Frank Burke, the observer in the back said that it seemed to take an age before they came to rest and the bomb aimer's window was broken so that grass, soil and stones were scooped up into the rear cabin.

Roly, Frank Burke, the RAE pilot and the AEO had to get out of the aircraft by removing the pilot's canopy but at that time there was no way it could be lifted except by brute force. Roly therefore released the canopy and held it up on his shoulders for the other three to escape, but it is not clear how he managed to get out himself since he didn't want to damage the canopy by throwing it onto the ground. This accident is described in more detail in Chapter 7.

Roly got into hot water with Dobbie over this, since it was concluded that if Roly had given the rudder pedals a big clout the rudder would have come free; as usual the armchair experts after the event knew what they would have done had they been flying. Dobbie, as remarked earlier, was reputed to be a great 'hire and fire' man and he called Roly to Chadderton to give him a 'bollocking'. Roly reckoned he had better let it be known that, after examining the Convair delta-winged Hustler bomber at a USAF base in East Anglia, he had been invited to go to the USA to fly the aircraft. He hoped that the possibility of his leaving Avros and getting a job with Convair might deter Dobbie from doing anything rash.

In fact 777's incident coincided with a Victor being destroyed, as mentioned in Chapter 1, doing position error measurements at Cranfield. The problem was due to one of the Victor controls vibrating uncontrollably at high speed and causing the structure to break up; this phenomenon is called flutter and every new aircraft has to be checked to ensure that it does not occur; Dobbie in considering the 777's crash was looking at the wider view and was afraid that the politicians, always short of money, might think that both V Bombers were unsafe and start pressurising the Air Ministry to cancel both programmes. Therefore he flew down to Farnborough twice and got a very rapid temporary repair done so that it could be flown back to Woodford. While repairs were being completed the opportunity was taken to fit the production Olympus 101 engines and some strengthening modifications were also incorporated following the results of tests that had been carried out on the structural test specimen. The aircraft did not fly again until February 1955 when it then carried out tests on the production engines, drag measurements and some checks on the short period damping at high mach number. In addition A&AEE were invited to carry out preview handling.

While the second prototype was being repaired the design office was wrestling with the problem of how to get a better buffet boundary, because unless something could be done the Vulcan would be unusable. VX770 consequently carried out more buffet tests at high altitude and the results confirmed measurements that had already been made by Roly earlier in the 777, so that it was clear that some improvement to the wing design had to be made on production aircraft.

In February 1954 Jimmy Harrison, who had now joined Avros, was flying the 707A WD280, continuously doing g stalls and buffet boundaries, establishing the basic characteristic of the delta with the straight leading edge. Various tricks were tried to increase the buffet margin, like fitting vortex generators and wing fences to the wing, but all to no avail. Jimmy flew the aircraft 130 times between February and October. Interestingly, the only other flying he did was one flight in 770, an initial flight in a Canberra and two flights in 777. The three Vulcan flights were all with Roly and both the 777 flights were examining buffet boundaries, showing how important it was to solve the problem.

It is interesting to look at an extract from one of Jimmy's flight test reports for two thirty-minute flights on 20th February 1954. In these two flights Jimmy covered the range from .83 IMN to .96 IMN:

> Buffeting
> High frequency low amplitude buffeting started early, between 1.5 and 2.5 g, and, with one exception, remained throughout the spiral at a level which would constitute no handling limitation or cause any alarms to the pilot. In fact this degree of buffeting was lower by far than in Meteors or Sabres in a comparable flight condition.
>
> The one exception occurred at the highest speed tested, .96 IMN, when it is considered that the aircraft closely approached its C_L max (maximum lift coefficient). Superimposed on a moderately severe buffeting, similar to that experienced in the aircraft quoted above, was some slight lateral rocking which culminated in a sharp left wing drop through some 10°-15°. The maximum reading needle of the Kollsman accelerometer indicated 5.6g after this spiral, but buffeting may have caused a false reading. Even in this case, however, it was interesting to note that the buffeting increased only in the very late stages of the spiral.
>
> If the flying hours can be spared, it is suggested that one or two separate flights be devoted to determining the buffet boundary. Accurate results could quickly be obtained by taking the aircraft to the buffet threshold at each Mach No, instead at hoping to pick the exact moment when buffet starts during the tests described in this note.

In the middle of July the aircraft was grounded for two weeks when a projected production drooped leading edge was fitted. Jimmy then flew the redesigned wing on 14th July 1954 comparing the new configuration with the straight leading edge. However this modification was not entirely satisfactory. After the results had been analysed there was a meeting between RAE, the National Physical Laboratory and Avros; after the meeting had been going on for some time, a quiet boffin from NPL got up and said words to the effect 'this is what you want' and sketched another drooped leading edge design which at the time was called conical camber. Avros went away after the meeting and it was decided to alter the outer portion of the wing, increasing the chord by 20% over the outer 20% of the wing and 'washing out' the increase by about a semi-span as suggested by the scientist from NPL. This increased sweep at the tips delayed the shock stall and almost removed the buffeting problem completely. Jimmy tried this shape on WD280 a few months later. The results were a great improvement on the first drooped leading edge.

The wind tunnel predictions of the effect of the conical modified leading edge were confirmed by Jimmy's flights in WD280 at the beginning of February 1955. In fact we have Jimmy's flight test report on 2nd February, attached as Appendix 2, with the new 'final' leading edge fitted, covering three consecutive flights all on the same day. He checked that there was no deterioration in the low speed and low altitude handling and then had a look at the buffeting:

Buffet Threshold
At nominal 300 knots EAS the usual technique was used to record the buffet threshold between .94 and .70 IMN. The threshold varied from about 2.5g at the highest speed to 5.5g at the lowest. This compares with about 2.2g and 4.7g respectively for the last configuration.

At the medium and low mach number it seemed that the threshold is now not very far removed from the lift boundary, since very slight right wing drop coincided almost exactly with the buffet threshold. Also there was a very noticeable increase in the intensity of buffeting just beyond the threshold, whereas in the past, a substantial increase of g beyond the threshold gave little change in the level of buffeting.

The 'last configuration' quoted above refers to an earlier modified leading edge which was an improvement over the straight wing anyway, so the enormous improvement noted in the report over the straight wing must have been a great relief to all concerned. The report makes it clear that buffet was in fact delayed until almost the stall was reached which was an incredible change compared with the straight wing. As a result of these flights combined with the wind tunnel tests the wing modification was authorised for production aircraft. In fact Jimmy carried on flying WD280 doing buffet boundaries until August 1955. It should be noted that this wing design change was made with as little redesign as possible; all alterations were made in front of the main spar because by then some nine production wings had been built. When the Mk 2 came along the wing was redesigned, not only to improve the aerodynamics of the delta shape but also to make the modifications more structurally efficient and therefore lighter.

The second prototype VX777 was grounded in July 1955 for fitting the modified leading edge. Meanwhile VX770 was being used for carrying out equally vital but less glamorous tests such as cabin pressurisation, engine bay temperatures, nosewheel steering, opening of the escape door in flight and also flying with the canopy removed to check that there was no undue turbulence which would prevent the pilot flying the aircraft safely.

In February 1955 the first production aircraft XA889 made its first flight. It had the Olympus 100 engines and a straight leading edge. On 4th October 1955 Roly made the first flight in VX777 with the production leading edge and the modification proved to be an instant success.

On 11th October he took up Sir William Farren, by then Avro's technical director, to demonstrate that the programme was now firmly back on the rails. In the same month 889 was grounded to have the production wing fitted but not before Jimmy Harrison had done some testing of the mach trimmer, though of course it was impossible to finalise the desired 'shaping' of the mach trimmer without the correct wing and the ability to fly at maximum altitude. Getting the best 'shaping' was not a trivial task; the extension of the mach trimmer had to be very carefully arranged so that the aircraft was stable right up to 1.00 IMN as the speed was increased. The basic problem was that the mach trimmer strut had a limited range or 'authority', and the way the strut extended with speed needed to be 'tailored' to match the basic instability of the aircraft. If the strut extended too quickly then the aircraft would be excessively stable around .90 IMN to .93IMB but then the strut would be fully extended before 1.00 IMN was reached and the basic aircraft instability would be felt by the RAF service pilot. If the strut was extended too slowly then the aircraft would feel unstable at the lower mach numbers, become rapidly very stable at about .98 IMN and then shortly afterwards, if the speed was increased further, the strut would be fully extended and stability would suddenly change from being too stable to being very unstable. Not surprisingly 'optimising' the mach trimmer extension, the shaping as we called it, took a lot of flying and hard work and I did a lot of the testing after I joined Avros.

After Roly's first flight in VX777 in the final configuration, he gradually allowed Jimmy Harrison to take over the testing responsibility for the Vulcan. Jimmy flew 777 almost continually from October onwards testing the buffet boundaries, the pitch damper, finalising the vortex generator configuration, checking the position error with an A&AEE calibrated Venom and the mach trimmer 'shaping' which had been fitted in December. In addition a yaw damper had had to be fitted to the rudder controls because at the cruising mach number the aircraft tended to oscillate slowly from side to side and roll at the same time; this was clearly unacceptable for a stable bombing platform and the yaw damper's mechanical strut, controlled by a rate gyro, damped the movement out.

Jimmy's new role was in effect confirmed when on 26th March 1956 he demonstrated 777 to Air Marshal Sir Harry Broadhurst, then C-in-C of Bomber Command and AVM Bufton. Interestingly, that was the day that Roly flew Vulcan XA889 to Boscombe Down for CA release trials, the day I first met Roly and the day I had my first flight in a Vulcan, a remarkable coincidence.

During the next few months Jimmy was doing the urgent outstanding work of mach trimmer runaways just ahead of my flying the aircraft at A&AEE to confirm his results and the acceptability of the mach trimmer malfunctions for CA release.

Roly by now had virtually finished flying, his last Farnborough show being in 1957. On 1st January 1958 Jimmy became chief test pilot, Roly retired to a sales job at Chadderton and I became deputy chief test pilot.

CHAPTER 3

BOSCOMBE DOWN

It was March 1956. The V Bombers were the main UK defence project and, though I could not know it at the time, I would finish up not only having tested the Valiant and the Victor as well as the Vulcan but amazingly seeing two of the aircraft which I had tested and cleared, the Vulcan Mk 2 bomber and the Victor Mk 2 tanker, being operated successfully in the Falkland campaign in May 1982.

The legendary test pilot Roly Falk had finally arrived at Boscombe Down from Avro's test airfield at Woodford with the Vulcan aircraft we had been waiting for and expecting for many months. I was part of the Royal Air Force evaluation team deciding whether this first production Vulcan was safe to fly and had met the performance requirements specified in the original operation requirement OR229 when the contract was awarded eight years previously.

Boscombe Down was the Ministry of Defence establishment where all aircraft and armaments had to be evaluated and tested before the equipment could be released to the relevant service, hence the name Aircraft and Armament Experimental Establishment, A&AEE. It had two huge runways, and many hangars including a vast white one called The Weighbridge which could be seen for miles around. There were also a large number of offices where the scientists and engineers checked the results of the performance and handling tests which were carried out on the aircraft which we flew. Its role today is basically the same, though Qinetiq carries out a lot of the functions for the Ministry of Defence.

The establishment was split into four test squadrons, A Squadron for testing the latest fighters, B for bombers and transport aircraft, C for naval aircraft and D for helicopters. I had been posted to B Squadron with Wing Commander Roy Max in charge who, unusually, had not attended a test pilot's course. However, shortly after I arrived Wing Commander Saxelby, who had been on No 7 Course of the Empire Test Pilots School, took over the Squadron. Sax was a very far seeing man and perhaps realised more than Roy Max the strategic importance of the V Bomber programme to the defence of the United Kingdom. He had a great sense of humour but it tended to be hidden somewhat by his intellectual approach to most things.

50

Sax was an excellent boss and organiser. On his arrival he formed two teams to evaluate the flying qualities of the new aircraft we were expecting, one for the Vulcan and one for the Victor. Naturally, he himself headed both teams with Squadron Leader Paddy Harper and myself on the Vulcan team and Squadron Leader 'Tommy' Tomlinson and Graham Moreau on the Victor. This simple decision by Sax in fact determined the rest of my working life.

The Valiant, the first of the three V Bombers, had just received approval from Boscombe to enter Royal Air Force service, Controller of Aircraft (CA) release as it was called. Of course this release was only an initial one, enabling the Operational Conversion Unit at Gaydon to start flying the aircraft and training the squadron crews. Before the Valiant could be considered to be fully operational, many more clearances would have to be given, including the carriage of bombs which had to be tested and dropped by B Squadron before the RAF squadrons could use the equipment and the weapons. Consequently, there were other pilots on B Squadron, not on the Victor and Vulcan programmes, flying the Valiant and carrying out tests to extend the Valiant clearances.

The Vulcan and Victor had already had preview tests carried out by B Squadron test pilots at Woodford airfield just south of Manchester, where the Avro Vulcan was assembled and tested, and at Radlett just north of London, where the Handley Page Victor was built. The rivalry between the two firms was intense and had been so for many years, especially with the Handley Page Halifax and the Avro Lancaster war time bombers; in fact there was a well known adage at the end of the war that 'Avros had three enemies, Handley Page, the Ministry of Defence and the Luftwaffe, in that order'. Clearly, even with the war over, nothing had changed.

Frederick Handley Page was still running his company but A V Roe had sold his company back in 1928 and Avros was now part of the Hawker Siddeley Group and 'Dobbie', Sir Roy Dobson, was very much in charge. Both men were legends in their own time, but were very different. Handley Page was an engineer whilst Dobson had a reputation as an industrialist whose 'hire and fire' employment practices would not be tolerated in the present day environment. Apparently he would go round the factory floor watching what was going on and if he didn't like something he would tell the person concerned in no uncertain terms that his/her services were no longer required – 'you're fired'; I suspect that at the shop floor working level the person concerned would probably have remained at Avros notwithstanding Dobbie's remonstrations but would have kept out of sight for a bit, but at the higher levels things might have been different. I do remember one managing director at Manchester, after Dobbie had moved on to London to take charge at Hawker Siddeley's headquarters in Kingston, who left rather earlier and sooner than was expected.

I only met Dobbie a few times. The first time was when he interviewed me as I was about to join Avros and I tried to improve the salary that I was being offered; if my memory serves me right I managed to get an increase of £50 per annum to reach the princely sum of £2,000 a year. Another time was in the Thieves Neck, a pub in Woodford, which was conveniently placed at the back entrance to the airfield and also at the bottom of Church Lane where my wife and I had bought a house. At the time, the pub had sawdust on the floor and Dobbie's north country brogue matched the environment of the pub perfectly. I can remember now the chat that I was having with Roly Falk, who was by then my boss; our received pronunciation accents stood out like a sore thumb from the conversations of the rest of the people taking refreshment in the pub, mostly locals, who Dobbie knew by their first names.

The Vulcan which Roly had brought to Boscombe had the RAF registration of XA889 and, unlike the two white Vulcan prototypes, was painted silver. It was the first production aircraft and had initially flown with a 'straight' wing, the original pure delta shape. The preview handling of the Vulcan had confirmed the firm's tests on the prototype Vulcans, VX770 and VX777, namely that the aircraft buffeting at the cruise mach number of .85 and above was unacceptable due to excessive drag and lack of manoeuvrability. These first two Vulcans were initially 'pure' deltas in shape in that the leading edges were absolutely straight, though VX777's wings had recently been modified to what was hoped to be the Mk 1 production standard with the extended and drooped outboard leading edges; in fact a year or so later VX777's wings were modified yet again to the Mk 2 standard so the aircraft turned out to be a real workhorse. Of course we had read in detail the reports of the Boscombe pilots who had done the preview flying and therefore knew all about the buffeting, the associated increase in drag at higher speeds and also that, if the aircraft was turned or manoeuvred in any way, the intensity of the buffet steadily increased. An aerodynamic fix had obviously been urgently required before the Vulcan could go into squadron service and, of course, before it could be delivered to Boscombe for CA clearance.

We knew that Avro's solution to the buffeting, discovered at first in their wind tunnel, was to modify the wing and we understood that the work which had been carried out initially on VX777 was now considered by the firm to solve the problem. XA889, the first production aircraft, had been fitted with the new wing, checked by the Avro test pilots and, finally, it had arrived at Boscombe Down for us to evaluate. In fact the modification, once it been agreed that it should be the production standard, had actually been incorporated in a very short time scale, just over a year, but to us, anxiously waiting for the aircraft, it did not seem that way. This was the only aerodynamic change that Avros had to do to the Vulcan original design, which tended to prove the excellence of the delta concept.

However, we knew that Avros had had to solve other problems, the most important being the fact that the aircraft was longitudinally statically unstable at speeds above .88 IMN. This meant that instead of the Vulcan tending to pitch up as the speed increased, as on all stable aircraft, it was more likely to dive and had to be restrained by the pilot pulling back the stick further and further as the speed increased. Roly told us that above 1.00 IMN the aircraft felt dangerously unstable; if the speed was allowed to go only slightly higher then a very large extra pull force was required and the elevators were very nearly fully up. Avros therefore did not want us to go faster than 1.00 IMN, since the aircraft was virtually out of control at any higher speed. This feature was completely unacceptable for the RAF and would have been dangerous if nothing had been done; we had visions of pilots losing control and aircraft diving out of the sky. Avros had explained to us that the way they had dealt with this problem was to introduce a mechanical extendable jack or strut, called the mach trimmer, which was controlled by the speed of the aircraft. They had arranged the strut extension so that above .88 IMN the jack applied up elevator automatically. The magnitude of the extension had been chosen so that the aircraft nose tried to rise as the speed increased and it therefore felt stable to the pilot; apparently the Vulcan was now like all normal aircraft, in that the pilot had to push the stick forward to prevent the aircraft pitching up as speed increased. Of course the aircraft was still basically extremely unstable at high mach numbers and once the mach trimmer was fully extended with the elevators nearly fully up, it could only go down; one of our jobs at Boscombe, therefore, was to find out how serious this was going to be for the RAF.

Roly warned us that although Avros felt that this modification was very effective in that it was now possible to fly the aircraft accurately at the cruise speed, he emphasised to us that if the speed was greater than 1.00 IMN then, despite the mach trimmer being fully extended, the four elevators at the trailing edge of the Vulcan would be nearly fully up and the pull forces to prevent the aircraft diving out of control would increase very sharply. Clearly Roly and Jimmy Harrison, his deputy, felt that this instability was acceptable for the RAF up to about .98 IMN and they presented the aircraft to us at Boscombe to get our views, not only on the effectiveness of the mach trimmer but also on how acceptable it was for the aircraft to be flown without a mach trimmer should it fail.

There were two other less serious problems with the Vulcan which Avros had told us that they had had to deal with. The first was that the aircraft tended to oscillate directionally, albeit quite slowly, accompanied by a rolling motion at the cruising mach number of .85 IMN, which they realised was completely unacceptable for what was meant to be a stable bombing platform. To obviate this they had fitted another mechanical jack, this time connected to the rudder, and this 'yaw damper' damped the oscillation out.

The other problem on the Vulcan, of which of course we were aware, was that at about .96 IMN the aircraft was poorly damped dynamically in the pitching plane, that is the aircraft oscillated up and down in pitch at a frequency greater than the pilot could control, as previously explained. Roly told us that the oscillation did not increase in size, in other words it was not divergent; had it been, the aircraft could have broken up since the oscillation was far too rapid for the pilot to correct. Avros had fitted two pitch dampers which were mechanical jacks controlled by pitch rate gyros which, like the yaw damper, sensed the oscillation and moved rapidly to damp the oscillation out. My memory says that when we started flying the aircraft, not only was the oscillation not divergent but that the other saving grace was that it only occurred in a very narrow speed band between about .96 IMN and .98 IMN; however, my memory may be playing me false as the Boscombe Down CA release graphs which I helped to compile at the time suggest that the oscillation did not damp out as the speed increased.

These three modifications, the mach trimmer, the yaw damper and the pitch dampers, were fitted to XA889 to obtain A&AEE's agreement that, with their fitment, the handling of the Vulcan could be recommended for CA release. However, the situation was definitely more complicated than just judging whether the modifications worked and had the right performance. There is a down side to all autostability aids; the modifications have to be assessed not only for their effectiveness but also consideration must be given as to what might happen to the aircraft structure if any of these actuators malfunctioned, before we could decide whether they were acceptable or not.

My first flight in the Vulcan was on 26th March 1956 with Sax in command and myself as co-pilot. In order to prepare for this flying it was necessary for us first to be fully briefed on how to fly the aircraft. In those days there were no flight simulators to practice at the design firm's location. There were no pilots notes either, since these documents were written by Handling Squadron, which was based at Boscombe though not part of the A&AEE testing establishment; the notes could only be completed and published after CA release had been given and our task completed. There was a lot for us to learn, not just in order to fly the aircraft but, more importantly, to know what to do if anything went wrong. The days of the conveniently small pilots notes which could go into one's pocket were disappearing fast. The Harvard on which I did my flying training had just twenty-four pages in a small booklet which fitted into my flying jacket. The Vulcan Mk 1 Pilots Notes when it finally came out was a large thick volume with 210 pages and didn't fit conveniently anywhere.

The main problem we faced was that new aircraft had many

'systems', particularly on the larger aircraft, to control the electrics, the hydraulics, the pressurisation, the fuel, flying controls, the autopilot, the instruments etc; so in the case of the Vulcan when the pilots notes eventually materialised there were actually twenty-one chapters describing all the systems. These were designed to be simple and straightforward to work for normal operation but also provision had to be made for the aircraft to continue to fly safely should anything go wrong. The problem with large aircraft, then and now, particularly with modern airliners, is that for 99.9% of the time everything is very simple and the systems don't require any attention once the initial flight settings have been made. The pilot therefore is sitting comfortably, fully relaxed, but at any moment he or she might suddenly have to take emergency action which he has to remember and get right. Obviously these days a pilot can practice in a simulator but not then; anyway a pilot in a simulator knows that there is going to be a malfunction so the realism is spoilt, though practising the drills is very important. As an aside, the really dangerous malfunctions are the ones that haven't been anticipated and haven't been practised in a simulator, such as a control surface dropping off or a system failure due to faulty maintenance.

For the Vulcan we had to learn all about the systems I mentioned above and much more. Though there were no notes as such, there were lots of Avro documents which we had been studying intensively, but these were not very easy to assimilate without having a flight deck to look at. The situation was compounded by the fact that the electrical system was not under the control of the pilots but controlled by the AEO. So though we learnt all about the electrical system and the way the flying control motors were connected, it was the AEO who had to take action on his control panel at the back and advise the captain if anything went wrong. And, of course, since the power controls were operated by electric hydraulic motors, complete failure of the electrics would mean an almost immediate bale out, so crew emergency training and co-operation in flight was a must to enable the captain to decide the correct malfunction or emergency procedure to be followed.

Sax had flown previously with Roly Falk so he was already checked out, but it was all new to me. Just getting into the aircraft for the first time was an amazing experience. The Vulcan crew compartment was unique, not like any other aircraft I had ever flown. The rear crew compartment had operational seats for two navigators and an air electronics officer. There was also provision for two other seats for supernumerary crew such as the ground support engineers. None of these rear crew members had ejection seats, unlike the pilots, since the concept was that in an emergency necessitating abandoning the aircraft, the rear crew would slide down the escape hatch and then use their parachutes. Since the entrance ladder was fixed to the escape hatch it was essential for the ladder to be stowed once all the crew were in the aircraft. The nose undercarriage clearly had to be up if the rear crew were going to bale out since the escape chute was in front of the nose landing gear; if the nose gear was down the crew had very little chance of escape. We were all aware of the escape procedures and the associated drills but at that time we did not practice escape drills with the rear crew as we did in later years. One good feature was the fact that the AEO had a periscope which had a limited visibility over the rear of the aircraft, both upper and lower surfaces which proved to be a great help when the Vulcan went into service and engine emergencies accompanied by fire occurred.

The next move for me on this first flight was to get onto the flight deck, by climbing yet another ladder just behind and between the two ejector seats. When I reached the top I only just managed to avoid hitting Sax who was already seated, such was the restricted size of the flight deck. Interestingly, by the end of the Boscombe trials I was able to race up and down the ladder between the seats without giving it a thought but this first time it seemed a bit of a challenge. I settled into the right hand seat, strapped myself in and then the safety inspector armed the ejection seats and climbed down both ladders to leave the aircraft. We were finally ready to do the start up checks.

Looking around I was immediately struck by the poor view out of the front of the aircraft through the three very narrow windscreens. The only good and clear view was sideways out of the circular windows just next to the pilots' heads. The flight deck was small by any standards and I could almost reach across Sax to touch his side panel. Of course, because the flight deck was so small it would have been almost impossible for Avros to have put a conventional control wheel in front of each pilot and we were both delighted with their decision to have a fighter type stick for each pilot with a combined elevator and aileron trimmer switch mounted on the top; we realised that this was only made possible because the flying controls were fully powered, unlike the Valiant which had a manual control capability in case of failure of the power controls. Up to then large aircraft had to have control wheels so that the pilots had sufficient strength to move the controls. However even with fully powered controls, some aircraft still had wheels because the pilots were more comfortable with them; for example the Victor had a wheel in front of each pilot even though a stick would have been adequate. In my view the human being is very adaptable and will get used to anything, providing it is safe.

With fully powered controls the pilot had to be prevented from inadvertently using too much force and breaking the aircraft and so our tests had to evaluate whether the protection that Avros had provided with the artificial feel springs and stops was adequate to prevent the pilot overstressing the aircraft by trying to use too large a control angle at high speeds.

Again because of the small flight deck, Avros had decided very sensibly just to have one set of throttles, situated centrally between the pilots; both the Valiant and the Victor had two sets of throttles located on the side consoles. The Vulcan throttles were conveniently placed so that either pilot could reach them. The forces needed to move the throttles were quite low and consequently they were delightful to use. The combined effect of having a stick and four small throttle levers easily held in one hand made the aircraft feel like a fighter and, having trained as a fighter pilot, in later years I was accused of flying the Vulcan as if it was one. However, I wasn't the first to be accused of that; Roly beat me to it by quite a few years.

The actual instruments were very conventional, but I really liked the special instrument between the pilots which showed the position of each of the nine control surfaces, four elevators, four ailerons and the rudder[2]. This instrument was incredibly useful since it made it possible for us to see not only that all the surfaces were moving correctly on the ground during pre-flight checks but it also enabled us, and of course all Vulcan pilots, to diagnose control faults. If a surface malfunctioned due to an electrical or a hydraulic motor failure, it was easy to spot the control that was faulty by moving the stick and watching if all the controls moved. Interestingly, despite the fact that the position of the controls could be seen as the stick was moved, careful sense checks were always made with the ground crew, probably I suspected because of the terrible accident to the Tudor at Woodford all those years ago when the chief pilot, Bill Thorne and the chief designer, Roy Chadwick, were killed when taking off with the aileron controls connected incorrectly.

One feature that needed getting used to was the aircraft's fuel system, controlled by a retractable fuel panel located under the throttle console. As described earlier, the Vulcan had fourteen fuel tanks, seven on each side and it was important that the fuel was fed correctly from each tank in order to keep the centre of gravity of the aircraft from moving unexpectedly. There were two fuel proportioners, called sequence timers by the RAF, which ensured correct feeding from the tanks by switching the booster pumps on and off in turn at predetermined timings. The fuel tanks were arranged in four groups, one for each engine, and the contents of each group were displayed on four gauges just in front of the throttles. The pilots could see that all was well by checking the individual contents of each tank by pressing a button next to each booster pump switch on the fuel control panel. The contents would be displayed on one of the four fuel gauges, depending on which tank was being checked[3]. The centre of gravity of the aircraft could be altered using transfer pumps which pumped fuel from the number one tanks to the number seven tanks and vice versa.

---

[2] See picture Chapter 2.
[3] See pictures Chapter 2.

A fuel cg slide rule was provided for the pilots to check the centre of gravity of the aircraft; by reading the individual contents of each tank and entering the contents of the tank in turn on the rule it was possible to discover where the cg was located.

Sax spoke to the ground engineer who was supervising our starting procedure on the interphone and got permission to start the Olympus 101 engines from the Houchin ground rig, which provided 112V DC to the aircraft until the aircraft's own generators could take over. As Sax pressed each starter button we could hear the engine winding up with a characteristic whining sound; he opened the relevant fuel high pressure cock by lifting throttle levers over a mechanical gate and we watched the jet pipe temperatures start to rise and then stabilise. The noise level even with all four engines running was very quiet. The AEO confirmed that he had brought all four generators on line and Sax then started the power control motors. After completing the after start up checks which, as I've already mentioned, included checking the flying controls, he asked the engineer to unplug his intercom and clear the aircraft. We taxied out slowly; the view wasn't very good ahead but the side porthole windows made the whole thing possible. I called out the take-off checks and air traffic gave us permission to enter the runway. Sax opened the throttles, the engines slowly spooled up to a very satisfying roar and he released the brakes. The aircraft leapt forward and we were soon airborne climbing at what seemed like a very steep angle; unlike a conventional aircraft there were no flaps or slats to be retracted, only the undercarriage, which meant that there were no changes of trim to be dealt with as these surfaces moved, as occurred on most aircraft.

For this, my first flight, we were tasked to examine the behaviour of the Vulcan with the centre of gravity of the aircraft at the rear limit. Like all aircraft, the Vulcan had design limits for the most forward and aft positions of the centre of gravity so that the aircraft elevator controls could keep the aircraft flying safely; for example if the cg was too far forward the elevators would not have sufficient power to be able to control the aircraft. The Vulcan would have to be able to carry a variety of weapons and it was necessary to ensure that all the specified weapons could be carried and dropped in such a way that the centre of gravity remained within limits. On this flight we looked at the low altitude longitudinal stability of the aircraft when speed was increased from the low end of the speed range to the limit of 415 knots. We also looked at the force required to apply 'g', normal acceleration, since at an aft centre of gravity the force to apply g always reduced and it was important to ensure that at the extreme aft limit the force was not so light that the pilot might actually apply too much g and break the aircraft despite the artificial feel. There was also another aspect we were looking at, which was checking that the stick force required to apply g did not suddenly reduce as the g increased; a sudden reduction of the force required as the stick is pulled back occurs on quite a few aircraft and in extreme cases the aircraft 'pitches up' and the pilot has to push the stick forward very rapidly to prevent too much g being applied and, on a large aircraft, almost certainly breaking up, clearly a very dangerous feature.

It was my job on this first flight constantly to check that the centre of gravity was in the correct position by reading all the gauges, using the cg slide rule and then pumping the fuel backwards and forwards between the number one and seven tanks as required. Of course all the fuel gauge readings were repeated on the photo panel in the bomb aimer's position but the information was only available post flight, after the camera film was developed, so that all that could be done was to check that the fuel and, therefore the cg, was where it should have been. This instrumentation photo panel on XA889 consisted of about 120 mechanical instruments including the fuel gauges, with two cameras for redundancy. The cameras took pictures of these instruments four times a minute but the rate was increased to about once a second when we were doing tests and taking measurements. There were also trace recorders which ran at high speed and were switched on just before we carried out certain tests which required high speed analysis, for example doing a pull out at a particular speed and g, called stick force per g. The flight test observer occupied one of the navigators' seats and kept a record of the whole flight including precise timing and event marking. On this first flight and indeed on most of the flights I did at Boscombe, we had Brian Ramsdale or Wason Turner, who was head of the B Squadron office, operating the instrumentation; it turned out to be a great advantage having the engineers who did the analysis flying with us as well, so that they understood the critical issues as we the pilots saw them. Wason and Brian a few years later on took over the technical management of the Blue Steel programme in Australia when the Vulcan/Blue Steel programme was getting CA release.

Sax made rough and ready measurements of the forces he was applying when making the tests using a small spring balance called a 'meat hook' which was hooked onto the stick at one end while Sax pulled the other end to apply the g. He then read the value of the force he was applying. It was of course only a very rough measurement but Sax had sufficient experience to know whether the forces were satisfactory or not. To enable definitive measurements and analysis after the flight, the aircraft had been fitted with strain gauges so that the pilot's forces on the stick could be measured with all the other parameters such as normal acceleration and, important on these particular tests, the fuel gauge readings to double check the cg position and make sure that I had kept the cg in the correct place. All the transient forces such as stick force, g, altitude and airspeed were measured on the trace recorder and it could be argued that it was not

necessary for Sax to try to measure the force as well, but experience
showed that it was always a good idea to get a personal impression of
the forces and how the aircraft felt at the time.

On this particular flight which lasted one hour forty-five minutes we
did not encounter any problems and I flew again the next day with Sqn
Ldr Harper, repeating the tests at aft cg, this time at high altitude.
These tests at the greater height were much more demanding and
harder to fly, particularly at the higher mach numbers. The aircraft had
to be dived so that the speed increased and then the stick pulled back
at the target mach number to pull the aircraft out of the dive. Clearly,
at the maximum mach number of approximately 1.00 IMN the test
was very difficult to carry out since the pull forces were high and the
elevators seemed almost fully up; if the angle of dive before the pull out
was too great the aircraft might dive out of control because the
required pull forces would be too high with very little elevator left. This
didn't happen to us but it did happen to Milt Cottee on a later test at
Boscombe and this event is described in the next chapter.

Later that day Sax put me in the left hand seat, in effect to check me
out as captain of the aircraft. It was a big moment for me actually to
be in the left seat though in fact in the Vulcan there was very little
difference between the two positions. However, being left handed I
always felt particularly comfortable flying the aircraft from the left
seat. As I taxied, I found manoeuvring on the ground was a delight
compared with other aircraft I had flown, as the rudder pedals
operated the nosewheel steering if the nosewheel steering button at the
bottom of the stick was depressed. The only other aircraft at that time
that I had flown with such a system was the North American Sabre; all
the UK aircraft of that era relied on differential braking for steering on
the ground and in the aircraft I had flown, like the Canberra, the
Hunter and all the older aircraft like the Valetta, the system was very
imprecise and jerky.

It was a great thrill taking off for the first time in the Vulcan,
opening the throttles, releasing the brakes and pulling the aircraft up
steeply after getting airborne to prevent the airspeed climbing too fast.
We carried out some more aft cg tests at high altitude so it was a good
test for my flying abilities as well as for the aircraft. We also examined
the engine handling of the Olympus; we tried slamming the throttles
open at various altitudes and speeds and there was no surging or flame
outs. In fact the engines worked perfectly throughout the flying that we
did. I only learnt later when I was at Avros how much testing and work
was required by us and by Bristol Siddeley to ensure that the engines
had such superb handling qualities, because invariably a new mark of
engine always had problems such as flaming out as the throttles were
moved rapidly forward at high altitude.

In fact, Avro's confidence in the behaviour of the aircraft handling
was justified and its behaviour at aft cg seemed acceptable. The

analysis of the results supported our rough measurements and our opinion, namely that the aircraft was safe to fly at the proposed aft centre of gravity.

My next flight, mentioned briefly in the Prologue, was my first in command and I had Graham Moreau as second pilot, since the Victor had not yet arrived; I was required to measure the elevator position through the speed range and therefore to check whether the aircraft was stable at low altitude. As speed was increased between each measurement point, I had to push the stick forward to stop the aircraft climbing; I used the trim button on the top of the stick to retrim the stick forces to zero before going on to the next speed. Consequently, I knew the aircraft was stable without having to wait for the analysis of the instrumentation which would show that more and more down elevator was needed as the speed was increased to restrain the aircraft from climbing. We then climbed to high altitude and I repeated the tests with and without the mach trimmer working. With the mach trimmer I had to push the stick forward as the speed increased until we reached 1.00 IMN. In fact I then dived slightly and increased speed to marginally over 1.00 IMN and found that I had to pull the stick back very rapidly to prevent the aircraft increasing speed further; however the pull force was very high and the stick was very nearly fully back which definitely alarmed me, so from then on I was very careful to avoid losing control. I realised that Roly's warning was fully justified. Though the Vulcan felt definitely stable up to 1.00 IMN it was clearly very dangerous to go there as a matter of routine, particularly as the calibration of the mach trimmer and machmeters could not be guaranteed to be accurate within about .02 IMN.

Without the mach trimmer working I had to pull the stick back all the time as the speed increased above about .88 IMN, trimming back constantly to keep the force zero; this time there was no discontinuity at 1.00 IMN, but the increase of pull force and stick position was very high above .95 IMN and at about 1.00 IMN the aircraft wanted to dive in an unacceptable manner and again it felt as if the stick was nearly fully back with large pull forces. This instability was definitely unpleasant and the aircraft felt as if at any moment it could dive out of control. However, I considered that any competent pilot would be able to control the aircraft up to about .98 IMN so that this could be the limiting speed for the RAF and the extra .02 IMN which we were flying to, 1.00 IMN, would give an adequate safety margin. This type of decision is one of the many that a test pilot has to make to determine what is safe enough. Nothing in this life is absolutely safe and judgement is always required on where to draw the line. We referred to the speed as IMN all the time, indicated mach number, because that was the important speed as far as aircraft handling behaviour was concerned, since that was what the pilot could see. The true mach number, however, as explained earlier, was a lot less than the indicated mach number.

Wason Turner very kindly has made available for this book some of the results of our tests which justified the CA release for the aircraft. I have included the longitudinal instability measurements at high mach number with the mach number position errors, and the steep drop of the curve at the top indicated mach number clearly shows the instability of the aircraft.

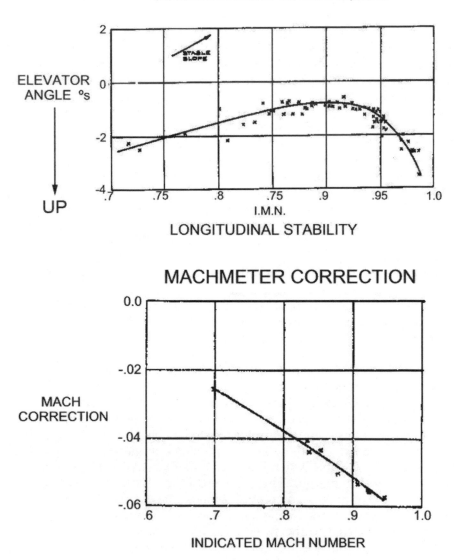

ELEVATOR ANGLE TO TRIM 40,000ft.

LONGITUDINAL STABILITY

MACHMETER CORRECTION

INDICATED MACH NUMBER

STATIC ERROR PRESSURE CORRECTION

I slowed the aircraft to .97 IMN and flew for a few minutes at this speed. Then I switched off both pitch dampers and the aircraft started bouncing up and down at a frequency of less than one a second. It was quite difficult to keep the aircraft oscillating in this manner as the speed had to be kept accurately between about .96 and .98 IMN or the oscillation would stop. This lack of longitudinal pitch damping was not particularly alarming in my opinion and the effect completely disappeared when I switched on either one of the two dampers. As can be seen from the damping factor, the damping never quite reached zero which meant that the oscillation was uncomfortable but it never went divergent.

Pitch Damping Mk.1

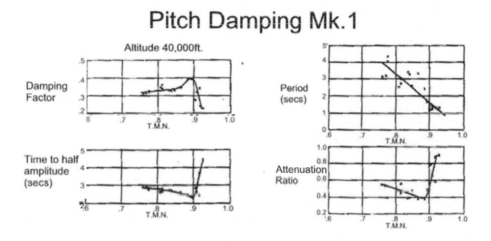

PIn fact my next flight was with Wason Turner in the right-hand seat. Wason was not a pilot but being in charge of the B Squadron technical office he was responsible for submitting the results of all our tests to the UK Government Procurement Executive, with a recommendation of all the conditions for a CA release so that the RAF could accept deliveries, initially for crew training.

Up to this point all the flying we had been doing was concerned with making sure that the handling of the Vulcan was satisfactory and that the RAF pilots would be able to fly the aircraft through its speed range safely without having an accident. However, an aircraft is bought, be it for commercial service or for military purposes, not because it flies nicely but to carry out a particular task; in other words it must have the performance required by the customer and specified in the design requirements. The flight therefore that we were about to do was part of a series to check the performance of the aircraft; how fast would it go at a particular weight and altitude and, equally important, how much fuel the engines were using, since the fuel consumption would determine the maximum range of the aircraft.

Measuring the ultimate cruise performance of a jet aircraft is quite a lengthy and painstaking job. With a commercial airliner, the aircraft flies at constant height and airspeed, so that as the aircraft gets lighter the throttles gradually have to be closed. For a military jet flying for maximum range, the aircraft is allowed to climb at constant mach number and constant engine rpm as the weight is reduced, called constant W/p. Once a steady rate of climb has been established, it is possible to determine the cruise performance at that one particular throttle setting and speed. The problem is that the atmosphere is seldom static, so it may take half an hour or more for an aircraft to be stabilised at a steady rate of climb and therefore for one point to be established. Many, many points have to be measured to be able to plot a carpet of an aircraft's performance; consequently, establishing the full cruise capability is a very time consuming and expensive business. At that time, I was doing a lot of theoretical performance work on range flying and in fact an article of mine was published in the RAF magazine *Air Clues* called 'Flying for Range in the V Bombers' which introduced pilots to the concept of cruise climbs, W/p (aircraft weight over ambient pressure), $n/\sqrt{\theta}$ (engine speed over the square root of the absolute temperature) and the rest of the jargon.

The Vulcan rate of climb on a cruise climb was thirty feet per minute and on my first Vulcan performance measuring flight with Wason I think we managed to measure just one point in a flight of one hour and forty-five minutes, but we also measured the climb performance of the aircraft. In addition, we assessed how easy it would be for the pilot to fly at the cruise speed with the mach trimmer switched off, an important handling assessment since with a single mach trimmer it would be possible that the Vulcan would have to be flown on quite a few occasions without the benefit of it providing longitudinal static stability. In fact there was no problem flying the aircraft at cruise speeds round about .85 IMN without the mach trimmer since luckily the instability was really only noticeable above .87 IMN.

My next flight was with a visiting squadron leader from the Superintendent of Flying's office at MOD(PE) where all the civilian test flying was controlled. The tests were handling ones and we had to examine closely the behaviour of the aircraft at minimum speed when the wings are unable to provide any more lift because of the high attitude of the wing to the airflow; in other words we were looking at the stalling performance. Stalling speed and behaviour is a very critical matter on every plane, be it military, commercial or general aviation. The stalling speed determines the speed at which an aircraft should be landed; clearly there has to be an adequate margin above the stalling speed to enable it to be landed safely. If the pilot lets the speed get too far below the recommended landing speed then the aircraft may stall

Top: Twin-seater
707C WZ744.

Middle: First
prototype VX770
at Farnborough,
September 1952.

Bottom: VX770 at
Farnborough
missing its
undercarriage
fairings, same show,
September 1952.

Top: Under the wing of VX770 at Woodford, September 1952. Left to right: Jimmy Kay, Roly Falk, William Farren, 'Cock' Davies, Dobbie, Gilbert Whitehead, Teddy Fielding. *(Leysa Falk)*

Middle: 1953 Farnborough formation. Roly Falk leading.

Bottom: 27th July 1954. VX777 comes to grief after landing with full rudder jammed on.

and some, if not all, of the lift will be lost from the wings; the aircraft will then hit the ground very hard, possibly causing structural damage, known as a heavy landing.

There is another aspect of stalling behaviour which is very important; when the aircraft stalls there should not be a sudden roll which the pilot cannot control or, even worse, it should not enter a spin. Strict rules are laid down in certification, be they civil or military, on how an aircraft should behave as it stalls or reaches maximum lift from its wings. It is important that an inadvertent stall should not result in immediate loss of control and an accident result. Ideally, the stall should be evidenced by a distinct nose drop which causes the aircraft to increase speed and reduce incidence away from the stall.

The nature of the stall varies with the configuration of the aircraft and there is one particularly unpleasant type of stall which usually occurs if the tailplane and elevator is set high above the fuselage. When the aircraft stalls and the wings lose lift, the disturbed wake from the wing goes over the tailplane and elevators so that pushing the stick forward, and therefore the elevators fully down, will not get the aircraft out of the stall, with catastrophic results; this stall is not surprisingly called a deep stall and is highly undesirable. The Victor was forecast to have such a stall in some conditions and therefore the way the Vulcan stalled was being watched with great interest. In fact there was very nearly an accident in Australia with a Victor Mk 2 on the Blue Steel programme when there was a malfunction of one of the airspeed measuring systems and the aircraft went into a deep stall but luckily streaming the tail parachute enabled the aircraft to recover.

In the case of the Vulcan, we found that the stall proved to be very straightforward in that as speed was reduced the aircraft started to buffet and this buffet got larger and larger until the stick was fully back and I had applied full up elevator, though the shaking of the airframe was a little bit disturbing and the rate of descent was very high due to the drag of the wings. There was no obvious rolling moment though there was a very slight tendency to sideslip. I carried out a large number of stalls on the flight but the Vulcan did not exhibit a clear cut stall speed when lift was lost. The only point that had to be watched was that it was important to prevent the aircraft yawing from side to side and thus stop the sideslip building up. Applying aircraft ailerons at these low speeds not surprisingly did not produce a high rate of roll; the ailerons were very ineffective but tended to generate sideslip, so with the stick fully back it was necessary to use a lot of rudder as well as aileron to keep it from diverging and the wings level. However, the aircraft was judged to be controllable at the stall without any alarming side effects.

On this flight we also looked at stalling the aircraft while turning. Again this was a very sensitive handling test as some aircraft 'pitched up' at the stall so that the pilot would lose control and excessive g would be applied which could cause it to spin or possibly break up during the manoeuvre. I tried pulling g throughout the speed range and also at different centres of gravity but the aircraft was 'honest' without any problems, the pull force increasing steadily as the g was applied. In fact the stalling behaviour of the Vulcan which we had tested was one of the plus points claimed for deltas.

In all the slow speed flying that was done then and in later years there was only one case of the Vulcan going into a spin and that occurred during a very long, slow speed stall which resulted in an accident to Vulcan Mk 2 XH535 described in Chapter 7.

We got a lot of visitors all mad keen to fly in the Vulcan and my next flight was with a visiting group captain; this time we examined the Vulcan's rate of roll through the speed range. The Vulcan had fully powered controls and though the motors were probably strong enough to apply full aileron up to 415 knots, the ailerons themselves and the structure were not strong enough at these high speeds if full aileron was applied and the aircraft would be liable to break up. Consequently, as mentioned earlier, the Vulcan's artificial feel system was designed to protect it from having these excessive control deflections being applied. The lateral stick forces were supplied by a simple spring and the mechanical stops reduced how far the ailerons could be moved as speed was increased. The system worked well and the aircraft felt very pleasant to fly; one was not conscious of the aileron stick travel being restricted. However, at the lower speeds when it was possible to apply full aileron, the rate of roll was very much reduced and lateral sideslip built up; in order to get a smooth rate of roll it was necessary to use the rudder at the same time but I felt that this was very instinctive and would not cause an RAF pilot any problem.

Of course, making judgements on how easy it would be for a pilot to fly an aircraft in certain circumstances is always a very difficult job. As has been already mentioned, an aircraft must be capable of being flown by the worst qualified pilot, be it on a military or a civil aircraft. I've always felt that it was hard for really first class natural pilots such as Roly Falk, who first flew the Vulcan, to judge what was acceptable or not, because they found flying so easy. I was never a particularly skilled natural pilot, so in some ways my judgement of handling acceptability was probably more valuable than one from an instinctive pilot.

On this flight I also investigated the buffet boundary of the aircraft at the higher mach numbers. We were evaluating the effect of the modified 'cranked' leading edge, which had been introduced when it was realised that the buffet and drag was unacceptable with the original straight wing. XA889 had no buffet in the cruise and very little right up to the maximum mach trimmer speed of 1.00 IMN. It was possible to turn the aircraft at cruise mach numbers without buffet occurring though this depended on the altitude; at high altitude the buffet margin, that is the amount of g that could be applied before buffet commenced, was reduced. At the higher mach numbers this margin was further reduced but I felt that the margin was more than adequate for RAF operational use.

I did a total of twelve performance flights at Boscombe establishing the capability of the aircraft, including one with Wason when we flew for very nearly six hours to ensure that our sample measurements were confirmed over a long flight.

As mentioned earlier, one very important safety aspect of the stability devices which Avros had introduced was the way the aircraft behaved when they malfunctioned. This is always a very important issue, much more so nowadays with the very sophisticated control regimes which are used to enable aircraft to be flown way outside the normal stability requirements, in order to get the most performance out of them. Consequently, I had to do some flying to assess the malfunction of the autostabilisers. The yaw damper mechanical strut could only apply a small amount of rudder angle so that applying full stroke to the yaw damper servo at maximum speed did not overstress the fin and rudder; the aircraft yawed, but not by much and the sudden yaw was not too unpleasant. Malfunction of the pitch dampers again presented no problem when tested at the maximum speed of 415 knots, because of the small amount of elevator they could apply.

The critical failure was with the mach trimmer, since the mach trimmer strut could apply about one third of the full elevator range and so it was vital to stop the strut extending to full travel due to a fault and, in so doing, causing damage to the aircraft and possibly causing it to break up. It was not possible to rely on an instinctive pilot reaction to push the elevator forward to counteract the 'runaway'. Therefore an altitude switch had been fitted to the system set at 20,000ft which removed all power to the mach trimmer below that height preventing it from 'running away' at high speed. The critical failure case above this height was considered to be at 'the corner of the flight envelope', when the aircraft was flying at 27,000ft, 1.00 IMN. Because the pilot could not be relied upon to counteract the 'runaway', two g switches set at 1.7g and .7g had also been fitted so that if the pilot was not quick enough to prevent the mach trimmer runaway pitching the aircraft up or down, these switches would cut out the power to the mach trimmer system. Summing up the safety provision of fitting the altitude switch and g switches, it was assumed that the pilot would normally take instinctive action to prevent the mach trimmer runaway breaking the aircraft, but if there was any lag on the part of the pilot then the g and altitude switches would protect the structure.

VX777 flight deck – note round non-production throttle levers. (*A V Roe*)

I remember Avros being particularly interested in the flights I did checking the mach trimmer runaways. We had to do the tests using the second prototype, VX777, since it had been fitted with the special instrumentation that was needed. Understandably, Avros were very nervous about the way we conducted these tests since the whole CA release depended on the correct evaluation of the runaways. We had agreed the methodology with them and we started doing the tests. I can't remember the details now but I seem to remember that on the first flight which Paddy Harper did there was a problem in the way the tests were carried out. We had a post flight briefing and then it was my turn to have a go which luckily produced the results that Avros were expecting. Of course, while all this was going on I was starting to get to know Jimmy Harrison, by now Avro's deputy chief test pilot, who had taken over the responsibility for the Vulcan getting a CA clearance from Roly. Jimmy had done the original test work on the mach trimmer design and also its malfunction behaviour and he was trying to ensure that we did the job properly, but without seeming to be interfering too much. Once I had understood what Avros had done and had completed the tests, I felt that the runaway behaviour with the protection that Avros had provided was acceptable.

Another phase of the Vulcan acceptance tests was flying the aircraft on instrument approaches. As I mentioned, when I first got into the pilot's seat I was appalled by the poor visibility out of the front. We had received one lecture when on the test pilots' course from a Mr Calvert of the Royal Aircraft Establishment, who was probably one of the world's experts at the time on airfield lighting, explaining what the pilot needed to see in bad weather in order to land the aircraft safely. Clearly the Vulcan met none of Calvert's requirements, but somehow we all got used to the poor visibility on the approach and landing.

I did not learn how to land the Vulcan to the best advantage while I was at Boscombe; I used to touch down at the recommended speed and stream the tail parachute, an enormous device which was incredibly effective. Landing in this manner meant that the nose of the aircraft was not particularly high, which helped my forward view. There was a distinct 'ground effect' with the Vulcan if the touchdown speed was too high; the aircraft tended to float just above the runway so it was important not to try and touchdown too early. Looking back I think that Avros got the correct approach speeds for landing but encouraged pilots to touch down rather faster than was really necessary and then to stream the tail parachute. Later I learnt, as did the Bomber Command pilots, how to use the enormous drag of the Vulcan for landing and not stream the chute at all, but it all took time.

Bad weather instrument approaches on the Vulcan were carried out at first using GCAs, ground controlled approaches, and later using the ILS, instrument landing system. The two methods were completely different in that the GCA relied on two radars, lateral and vertical positioned by the runway. Two radar operators were needed, firstly the tracker who watched the aircraft on the vertical radar; any displacements from the correct glide slope were shown on a meter situated in front of the controller. This controller observed the position of the aircraft relative to the centre line of the runway on the lateral radar. He then passed to the pilot the necessary heading changes to regain and hold the centre line and also passed the glide slope deviations as shown on his meter. The pilot then had to judge the

ILS Indicator

Transmitter   Localiser

RUNWAY   Touchdown Point

Transmitter

Glide Slope

Note how narrow the glide slope beam
is at the touchdown point, compared with
the localiser, due to being so close to the
transmitter.

necessary changes to the rate of descent to keep on the glide slope, as well as steer the aircraft to maintain the runway centre line.

The ILS system used two radio beams, localiser and glide slope and there was a meter on the instrument panel which showed the deflections from the centre lines of the two beams. At that time there was no computer to help the pilot make the necessary corrections to regain the centre line of the two beams; he had to compute mentally the changes needed to keep on the localiser and glide slope allowing for both the distance from the runway and the wind, not a particularly easy task. Both the radio beams were conical; the localiser antenna was positioned at the far end of the runway but the glide slope antenna was located at the touchdown point. This meant that the glide slope beam was very narrow as the aircraft approached the desired touchdown point and, consequently, it was much harder to keep on the glide slope than on the localiser centre line. The faster an aircraft flies the harder it is to fly the ILS beam manually and, unfortunately, at the time the Vulcan was specified there were no simple computing instruments like the zero reader to make the pilot's task easier.

At Boscombe we had to make a judgement on how low the Vulcan could be permitted to descend when making an instrument approach, without taking too big a risk of the aircraft hitting the ground. The pilot had to be able to see the runway in plenty of time, in order to adjust the flight path of the aircraft to land at the correct speed at the right touchdown point on the centre line of the runway. There clearly was a height below which it would be impossible for the aircraft to remain on the glide slope even if it was on the localiser. We had to recommend a decision height at which, if the runway could not be seen, missed approach action had to be taken.

At the time we reckoned that the pilot would be able to descend safely to 300ft above the ground on a GCA as judged by the altimeter. However, an altimeter does not read physical height above the ground; a radio altimeter can do that but the Vulcan then, and most aircraft still today, use an altimeter which displays height, but based on the ambient pressure, since the higher an aircraft is above the ground, the lower will be the pressure. The actual height indicated to the pilot with a pressure altimeter, will therefore depend on the combination of the aircraft's pressure height and on the manual setting that the pilot makes on the instrument; this manual setting in turn relies on the atmospheric pressure at the time of landing which is passed to the pilot by the air traffic controller or broadcast on the radio. If the pilot wants the altimeter to read zero when the aircraft is on the ground then the pressure setting on the altimeter is called QFE. Alternatively, the pilot might want the altimeter to read the height of the airfield above mean sea level when the aircraft touches down, in which case the setting for the altimeter is called QNH.

Unfortunately, the situation is more complicated when measuring static pressure in the air because when an aircraft is flying the pressure which the altimeter uses to indicate height, called the static pressure, is, not surprisingly, affected by the aircraft itself as it moves through the air. The difference between the true outside pressure and the static pressure is called the static position error and this error is determined very carefully and accurately by the aircraft manufacturer; the manufacturer always tries to find a measuring position on the aircraft which has the minimum static error; however at that time, on the Vulcan, there was no way that this error could be fed automatically to the altimeter. Furthermore, in spite of many attempts, Avros could not find a really suitable place to measure the outside pressure and the Vulcan Mk 1 used two pitot static booms placed at the wing tips. On the approach, the static pressure error was slightly over 50ft so that the aircraft was always at least 50ft closer to the ground than the reading on the altimeter. After we had made quite a few GCA approaches, we recommended an indicated decision height of 350ft for the Vulcan when making a GCA approach, which was therefore 300ft above the ground.

In addition, at that time there was a frictional lag on the altimeter so that the reading of height could be up to 50ft above the correct pressure height, but this error was not measured or covered in the initial CA release. This frictional error was corrected by fitting a vibrator on the altimeter, soon after the aircraft entered operational service.

I did one flight doing ILS approaches with Sax assessing the difficulty of controlling the aircraft using the 'raw' deflections on the ILS indicator. However, when the first CA release was given in August 1956 there was no official ILS release. This was because we had not come to a decision on the height to recommend and the situation was complicated by the fact that Bomber Command airfields had the localiser beams offset by 3° to the runway, for reasons explained in the autolanding discussion in Chapter 4. This meant that even if the aircraft was perfectly located on the localiser centre line it was necessary for the pilot to turn the aircraft to line up with the runway when it could be seen. It would be pointless to choose a decision height that was so low that the aircraft would have crossed the runway centre line while still on the localiser centre line.

The subject of instrument approaches has been covered in some detail because it was absolutely vital for the Vulcan to be able to fly safely in bad weather and because of the terrible accident, discussed later in Chapter 7, which occurred to the first Vulcan which was delivered to the Royal Air Force.

Altogether, between 26th March and 24th July I did thirty-six flights on the Vulcan including two on the second production aircraft, XA890, which had straight wings and was being used for radio trials; I was checking out Geoff Fletcher, and Peter Baker who had joined us from D Squadron, both of whom had been on No12 course.

During my stay at Boscombe, responses were received at B Squadron from the UK industry for a specification issued by the Procurement Executive for the design and development of a Mach 3 supersonic bomber. We were asked to evaluate these responses and I remember reading these documents at length. Wason sent a considered review comparing the different design proposals back to London and in due course the aircraft design selected was one proposed by Avros. The aircraft was called the 730 and was to be made of steel and used television to enable the pilots to fly it; there were no windows to enable the crew to see the ground. Like the Vulcan, it was proposed to build and fly small-scale models of the 730 to aid development. The programme was a very lengthy one and Avros realised they needed a pilot who would be able to follow the programme from initiation to first flight and longer. Both Roly Falk, then chief test pilot, and Jimmy Harrison his deputy would have been too old to meet this requirement. By the middle of 1956 while the Vulcan acceptance trials were proceeding, I had got to know both Roly and Jimmy and, perhaps more importantly, they had got to know me. Consequently, Avros asked me to join them and, incredibly, after only being at Boscombe nineteen months I left the safe haven of the RAF and joined the commercial world. Perhaps even more amazingly, my first flight at Woodford for A V Roe and Co Ltd was on 8th August 1956 and somehow between 26th March when I first flew the Vulcan and joining Avros in August, I had managed to arrange my employment terms with Avros, resign from the Royal Air Force and be released.

The supersonic bomber project was cancelled soon after I joined Avros but I didn't regret my decision to leave the Royal Air Force and go into industry for one moment.

CHAPTER 4

DEVELOPING THE VULCAN MK 1

My arrival at Woodford to start work with Avros was inauspicious to
say the least. It was August Bank Holiday Monday which, in those
days, came at the beginning of the month, which seemed a strange day
to begin a new career. I had seldom been further north in England than
a straight line joining Bristol to the Wash except on a brief visit to the
English Electric factory at Warton, Lancashire, where the Canberras
were being built, while I was on the Empire Test Pilots School course.
Consequently, I found the environment at Woodford just south of
Manchester very strange. It took a little time for me to be able to
understand the local accent which souded very strong, though
nowadays when I hear it, I feel I am coming home; luckily everyone
was very friendly and didn't mind repeating what they had just said so
that I could understand. I had no home but was in digs right opposite
the factory gate so that every morning while I was still in bed I saw the
night shift going home and the day shift commencing. My landlady was
very kind though I wasn't overly keen on her cooking.

Margaret, my fiancée, was still education officer at Boscombe Down
and was not due to leave the Womens Royal Air Force, or the WRAF
as it was called then, until the following January and one of my first
jobs was to find a home for us. However I suspect I gave that a slightly
lower priority than settling in to the Woodford pilots' office.

Woodford aerodrome was divided into two halves. On the north
side of the runway were the assembly sheds where the components
from Chadderton, at the time the main Avro factory to the north of
Manchester, arrived by lorry and were assembled into the completed
aircraft. On the south side of the airfield were the flight sheds where
the aircraft were prepared for flight in the hangars. Built on the side of
one of the hangars overlooking the airfield were the offices for the
flight test engineers and the pilots. Also on the south side, not too far
from the offices but on the other side of the tarmac was the club house
where important visitors used to stay.

At the time of my arrival, Avros had just won the contract for the
Blue Steel air launched stand-off missile and the design work was being

carried out next to the assembly sheds. Jimmy Orrell had become chief of flight test operations for the Blue Steel project and he held this post until he finally retired. This was not a trivial task since there were to be a lot of carriage and dropping trials on a Valiant based at Woodford, WZ375, plus a Vulcan Mk 1 XA903. The range for this work was at Aberporth and a lot of liaison was required to ensure successful flights. The pilots to fly these aircraft were to come from the Woodford pilots' office and Jimmy Orrell had a stroke of luck there as I was already qualified on the Valiant. However, he had to recruit two more pilots from the RAF, Dave Haskett and Tony Jones, to fly the aircraft locally and then go out to Australia. The actual firing of the weapons was to take place on the Woomera range in South Australia and the aircraft were to be based at the Royal Australian Air Force base, Edinburgh Field. Aircrew had to be found for the Australian part of the operation and Jimmy carried out all the work for these trials very meticulously.

After I joined Avros, Roly very rarely appeared at Woodford. At this time, I had absolutely no idea of Roly's amazing piloting background which I've recounted earlier. It was very clear that he seemed to spend a lot of his time at Chadderton talking to the senior management and very rarely appeared to fly. However, when he did fly I was amazed to see that he really did fly in his grey pin-striped suit, whereas we poor mortals changed into our flying overalls, apart from anything else to avoid ruining our clothing. I later got to know Leysa Falk, Roly's wife, very well and she told me that Roly used to wear his suit because he was making the point that he felt that a plane should be as clean as his car. I did wonder perhaps if he simply couldn't be bothered to carry all the gear and find somewhere to change.

I do remember, though, that shortly after I joined Avros, Roly suddenly wanted to fly one of the Shackleton Mk 3s which were still being built and tested at Woodford. The aircraft was being delivered to Boscombe for testing, which suited me because I wanted to be with Margaret over the week-end. The weather at Boscombe was not brilliant but, in my opinion, no problem for landing. However, when we got to Boscombe Roly announced that the weather was not good enough and we returned to Woodford, much to my disgust. It did not take us long to work out what Roly's problem was. At the time, for some strange reason I never understood, a test pilot only needed a private pilot's licence to be able legally to carry out the job of a test pilot with a civilian firm, notwithstanding that test pilots were flying for hire and reward. To keep the private pilot's licence current it was necessary to do at least five hours flying a year. The SBAC show was coming up at the beginning of September and Roly had decided he was going to fly XA892 there. However, he must suddenly have realised that his licence needed renewing and that he had not flown for five hours in the preceding year, hence the need to fly to Boscombe and back. I managed to go to Farnborough on one day to watch the flying display and, despite his lack of flying practice, the Vulcan display was superb. There were also wild stories of Roly going from the company's chalet after a good lunch and being poured into the pilot's seat but these were almost certainly apocryphal. All I did know was that he was able to fly anything immaculately without any practice, a truly larger than life figure. It is only now as I write this book that I have come to realise what a fantastic flying career Roly had had.

Because Roly seldom appeared very much at Woodford, Jimmy Harrison was in reality in charge of the Vulcan development programme, working with Cyril Bethwaite who was in charge of the technical flight test office. Together they had had the task of developing the aircraft. There must have been at least fifty people directly responsible to Cyril including some very able aeronautical engineers. Zbigniev Olenski, no longer in his first flush of youth, was still very much in evidence and he made an enormous contribution to the successful installation of the mach trimmer, so crucial for the successful operation of the Vulcan. I worked with him a lot on later Vulcan developments. His English was not too good and his pronunciation was appalling, but it was always worth the effort to try to understand what he was saying since he had a tremendous grasp of the critical issues.

There were two other Avro test pilots when I joined Avros, Jack Wales and Johnny Baker. Unfortunately, Jack was killed flying a Shackleton in the November after I joined, when the aircraft entered a spin doing stall warning tests just above cloud and the aircraft never recovered. Johnny Baker was in charge of the Shackleton development but had not had any formal test pilot training. I flew with him a bit helping to develop the Mk 3 including the autopilot installation. He was a local boy and very blunt in his remarks. He took over the flight development of the Blue Steel in Australia a few years later and changed his accent to broad Australian before he died. Unfortunately, he had a problem with a Victor flying from Edinburgh Field when the right pitot static system failed; the aircraft went into a spin but he managed to rescue the situation by streaming the tail parachute. However he got into trouble for the way he handled the Australian press, which was a great pity.

Avros managed with such a small number of test pilots because there were often visiting RAF pilots staying with us who would fly in the right hand seat and when I joined, Squadron Leader 'Podge' Howard had been flying with Jimmy Harrison for many months, in preparation for accepting and captaining the first Vulcan to go into RAF squadron service. Furthermore, it was accepted practice for flight test observers from the technical office to fly in the front of the aircraft, as well as the back, because it helped the pilot doing the tests at the time to know exactly what was expected from an instrumentation point of view. In fact I helped two of the observers, Dave Pearson and

Kevin Moorhouse, to become pilots; Kevin actually became an Avro production test pilot but sadly was killed demonstrating a Mosquito at an air display. The regular flight test observers were Stan Nicol, Dicky Proudlove, Ted Hartley and Frank Burke and they were as often in the right hand seat as they were in the back.

The Avro 730 supersonic bomber programme was well under way and a 'blow down' supersonic wind tunnel had been constructed at the end of our hangar, next to the other conventional low speed wind tunnels. The new wind tunnel worked by pumping up a huge spherical container to a very high pressure and then exhausting the air through a very tiny aerodynamic chamber, so that the local speed could be adjusted up to mach 3; in the chamber was a highly instrumented airplane model of the 730. The noise while this was happening could be heard all over the flight sheds if not on the other side of the airfield and in the neighbouring village of Poynton; it only lasted for a few seconds while the measurements were being made but it was very disturbing and a warning horn was always sounded a few seconds before the test. All conversation or logical thought had to stop while the tests were being carried out.

Initially, the head of the wind tunnels was Lionel Leavey and then his place was taken by John Scott-Wilson, who I had known at Cambridge and with whom I later worked for some years on the Airworthiness Requirements Board where John was chairman and I was on the Board of the Civil Aviation Authority. Of course we were all very interested in the 730 tests at the time and since both Lionel and John used to have lunch in the same room as we did, we got to know them very well discussing all the issues. In fact, when I first joined Avros there was not too much flying taking place and so these conversations were very useful, as we were deluged with the design details of the supersonic bomber. Jimmy and I spent hours poring over all the graphs and discussing the proposed flight deck layout before it was cancelled. Poor Jimmy had been through all this before as he was hired by Avros to fly the Avro 720, a rocket fighter in competition with the SR53. Though the Avro aircraft was ready for flight well before the Saunders Roe aircraft, the people in the ministry decided that the SR53 would be a better bet, cancelled the project and would not let the 720 fly.

My first flight with Avros was six days after my last flight at Boscombe, but my role was very different. At Boscombe my job was just to evaluate and criticise. The RAF might be crying out for the aircraft but if it did not meet the requirements, Aviation Publication 970, then the job of the Boscombe pilot was to say so. At Avros I had become a manufacturer's pilot, my bread and butter depended on the success of my firm and if the aircraft didn't meet AvP 970 requirements then it was my job to say so and make suggestions to the designers so that the aircraft could be improved. It was a difficult tight rope to walk because the last thing the firm wanted was the expense of having to make changes. Quite understandably, the chief designer wanted to be sure we were not gilding the lily. Of course nothing is ever black and white and sometimes judgement was required to decide if the aircraft would meet a particular requirement and whether it was possible to persuade the Boscombe pilots that the handling was alright. There was no point in making the aircraft better than the requirements, since safety costs money and there is no such thing as absolute safety. Is it safe enough? Does the aircraft meet the requirements? These were the points I was always stressing with my team when I became chief test pilot, but it was a lesson I had to learn when I started with Avros.

This first flight was in the second prototype Vulcan, VX777, and the object was to increase the flight envelope to some design point at high mach number. I remember thinking at the time how strange it was to be asked to carry out the test without any check flight; I have a feeling that Jimmy Harrison was on holiday. Avros kept to the RAF rules and had an authorisation book in which each flight was entered and authorised but as, right from my first day, I was allowed to authorise myself there did not seem much point in it. In fact all the flying that we did on RAF/ministry aircraft was supervised by a team in London in MOD(PE), Ministry of Defence Procurement Executive, which had replaced the Ministry of Supply; it was headed by the Superintendent of Flying, an air commodore, initially Sidney Hughes and then John Brownlow with whom I worked later on the board of the CAA. The supervision was pretty light when we started but, as accidents and incidents started to take place throughout the industry, the inspection regime became much stricter. In retrospect, it was just as well we didn't have an accident that first day.

In the right hand seat on that occasion was Stan Nicol, who was Avro's chief flight test observer, and Ted Hartley was in the back controlling the cameras and the trace recorders. In addition Eric Burgess, a very experienced radio operator, was controlling the four 112 Volt DC electric generators which drove the flying control motors. Since the electrical generating system did not require any special handling once all the generators were on, assuming that there were no malfunctions, Avros had realised that the AEOs could spend their spare time usefully navigating the aircraft or, to be more realistic in my case, telling the pilot where he was. We used a wartime hyperbolic fixing aid called Gee which worked very well. In the RAF the AEO had other equipment to control dealing with electronic counter measures and of course there were two specialist navigators, but for our test work the AEO/navigator was an ideal solution.

As mentioned, the electrical system normally required no attention at all once all the generators were online. Redundancy and safety features were built in, in case of any failures of the generators, by having separate busbars with automatic coupling so that the power controls would keep on running. However, after the aircraft went into service an accident occurred, described in Chapter 7, and some incidents which showed that the 112V DC system was not as reliable as it might be, due to busbar and other failures. The Mk 2 200V 400 cycle per second constant frequency system using Sundstrand constant speed drives and alternators was a distinct improvement in reliability, though still not immaculate. Luckily, at Woodford the only electrical failure we had was not due to the Mk 1 system but occurred when developing the Mk 2, so the judgement of giving the AEO a second role as navigator proved to be a good one.

The Vulcans that we tested at Woodford all belonged to the government and were controlled by the Procurement Executive. I was always surprised that the Superintendent of Flying and his team allowed us to fly without a qualified pilot in the right hand seat and that we were permitted to use a technician. The decision, like the AEO dual role decision, was a good one for us as we never had an accident due to only having one pilot on board, but I'm sure if there had been an accident due to an incapacity of the test pilot there would have been a lot of red faces and covering up in London. In fact there were very few switches for the person in the right hand seat to operate, the only really important two being the pressurisation switches. I later discovered that the cg slide rule was long enough for me to be able to operate the switches by pushing the end of the rule onto them, though of course I could not turn them off after landing; luckily this did not matter since it was always standard drill to open the DV, direct vision, window after landing to make sure the pressure was zero before the entrance door/escape chute underneath the nose of the aircraft was opened. This meant that for non-test simple delivery trips, I could fly the Vulcan without anyone in the right hand seat. Incidentally, I was not the first pilot to fly a Vulcan by myself in the front; Roly Falk did it as a matter of routine on VX770, initially because only one seat was fitted.

Since the aircraft were controlled by the Procurement Executive, there were government inspectors based at Woodford to 'clear' the aircraft for flight; they were called AID inspectors. The drill was for Avros to carry out all the preparation work required for a particular flight which had been specified by Flight Test. When this had been completed, the company's inspection department would check the work and then clear the aircraft for flight; they would then take the paperwork to the AID inspector. He, in turn, would then check all the paperwork, go and function all the flying controls, look round the plane and clear it for flight on a form 1090. Only then would we be allowed to fly. Checking the controls always seemed to take a long time and since the Avro inspection had already done it and we were going to do it all over again I always felt the AID check was completely unnecessary. However, my frequent suggestions that there was no need for an extra AID flying control check were completely ignored.

The AID inspector I remember, and who I think was there throughout my stay at Avros, was Len Lee and he was always being blamed for not letting the aircraft fly when, in reality, in most cases it was not ready and had not been cleared by the company inspection department. I can remember his internal telephone number to this day, it was 13; I often wondered whether he had been given that number by someone with a droll sense of humour. However, I still begrudge the time he wasted functioning 'my' flight controls.

There was a rather poorly furnished room without windows on the ground floor where the crew would assemble before a flight. It was full of steel cabinets, one for each crew member, and it was here that we got changed into flying suits. I never flew with Roly in a Vulcan so I don't know what he did; he certainly didn't have a cabinet. When Roly flew Sir Anthony Eden in the Vulcan at Farnborough he was definitely wearing one of his favourite pin-striped suits.

The rear crew members, who did not have ejector seats, had to carry their parachutes, so usually the emergency ambulance would arrive to take us from the flight sheds to the aircraft, normally about 150 yards away on the sloping tarmac. By this time, as a result of my Boscombe flying, I had become pretty adept at getting into a Vulcan. It was said in later years that I held the record for getting from the ground, into my seat and getting all the engines running while everybody else was still strapping themselves in. I have no idea if the story is true but I did find I could reach the engine starter button of number 1 engine on the side console as I was climbing up the second ladder! I was never noted for my patience and it always seemed to me that it saved time as the engines took such a long time to crank up.

On this first flight from Woodford I took time to look around the cockpit and at the instrument panel of VX777; because I had flown it twice before doing mach trimmer runaways at Boscombe, I knew that it was not identical to XA889 and the other production planes. There were some special instruments, the most prominent one being the accelerometer, to enable the tests to be carried out accurately without damaging the aircraft. However, the production indicator with deviation bars for the nine flying controls, shaped like the back of the aircraft, was on the centre instrument panel so that as the four elevators, four ailerons and the rudder were moved, the mimic controls moved in turn on the indicator. The starting drill was for the pilot to select each engine in turn, press the start button and lift the throttle from its rearward, closed position, forward over the gate thus opening the engine high pressure cock; the rpm would slowly increase with a reassuring whine, there would be a rumble as the engine burners started and the jet pipe temperature gauge would begin to rise from its stop. Normally the temperature would stabilise as the engine rpm reached flight idling; however it was always advisable to make sure that the temperature was stabilising before asking the AEO to bring that engine's 112V generator on line.

Once all four engines were burning and turning the controls would be functioned and checked for correct sense with the ground crew. Again I was reminded of the terrible accident to the Tudor when the ailerons were assembled in the wrong sense, when Roy Chadwick the Avro chief designer and Bill Thorn the chief test pilot were killed.

The chocks were removed and I slowly opened the throttles and steered the aircraft through a narrow gap between the grass verges onto the short runway and then taxied down the hill to turn right onto the main runway which was about 2,500 yards long, a lot shorter and narrower than the 3,000-yard huge runway I had got used to at Boscombe. It was necessary to be a bit careful at Woodford as the main road from the assembly sheds to the flight sheds crossed the runway and so traffic lights had been installed at the intersection. The drill was for the crash vehicle to be stationed on one side of the runway and the ambulance on the other to try to stop recalcitrant vehicles crossing the runway when they thought they could just make it, even though the lights were red. The lights of course were controlled by Air Traffic which at the time was situated on top of one of the flight shed hangars. The chief controller was Ken Cook, an ex Avro test pilot who had been trained on No1 ETPS Course with Jimmy Nelson; he had had an amazing RAF war time career flying Hampden bombers for forty-three missions into Germany. He used to say that he volunteered for the course because he reckoned test flying had to be a lot safer than dropping bombs over Germany. Ken died quite recently, aged ninety-four, cheerful to the end.

The main runway in fact had been extended for the Vulcan programme so that it reached almost into the very large village of Poynton to the east of the airfield. It had virtually no approach lights because of the proximity of Poynton, which didn't make flying in bad weather any easier. We used to have to come in very low over Poynton to touch down at the beginning of the runway and, to the best of my recollection, there were no warning signs for unsuspecting drivers on the main road through Poynton. I'm told that after I left, the bungalow nearest to the runway was sold and the new owner got the Civil Aviation Authority to make Avros use a regulation touchdown point way down the runway. Presumably that still allowed large aircraft to take off but probably not to return.

Woodford airfield was situated in the Manchester control zone and no movement could take place without the permission of Manchester's Ringway Airport controllers. The standard departure procedure was for the aircraft taking off to be cleared to the south east after take-off, but it would not be allowed to climb until it was clear of the airway which went over and well to the east of the airfield. Since Avros had no approach radar at the time, all recovery after test flying could only be made by their controllers getting clearance from Manchester. In fact the Ringway controllers using their approach radar often helped us back to the airfield, though Eric Burgess and Bob Pogson, our other AEO, were very adept at navigating back to Woodford using Gee.

I taxied down to the far end of the runway, turned round in the turning circle at the end and waited eagerly for the take-off clearance to come from Ringway. I was lucky that day as the clearance came through quickly; as I learnt later, generally it was necessary to wait for quite a long time for clearance because of the need for the Manchester controllers to deal with their own traffic to which they gave priority. I opened the throttles quickly and we got airborne without using much runway since we were flying at quite a light weight and then rapidly turned left; there was normally no need for the test aircraft to carry a lot of fuel but the long runway was always available if we needed to take off or land at higher weights for some reason. Once clear of the airway we shot up to over 40,000ft and started work. Stan Nicol in the front and Ted Hartley in the back had to ensure that each test we did was clearly marked in flight time after take-off, and each test event numbered, so that the film when developed and the traces could be synchronised and the results calculated. On this flight, the task was to apply up to 3g normal acceleration at slowly increasing speeds until we reached the pilots notes' limiting speed of .98 IMN, observe how the mach trimmer behaved and measure the stick forces. It was quite difficult to fly the tests to ensure that, for each desired event, the g occurred at the correct speed; the aircraft had to be committed to a dive and then the pull out started with the speed increasing but still below the target speed so that, as it went through the horizontal at the bottom of the pull out, the g and speed were correct. Since we were operating near the maximum speed where the Vulcan had its greatest instability, it was necessary to be very careful because the elevators were almost fully up. Luckily, as far as I remember, we did not have any unplanned excitements. It occurred to me later that the crew barely knew me and were taking a lot on trust.

Like most test flights, the total duration from take-off to touch down was quite short, in this case one hour and forty minutes. I soon learnt not to waste time getting back to Woodford when the tests were complete: I tried to keep to the east of the UK, often in the Lincoln area, so that we were ready for a quick recovery. Later when I became chief test pilot, I was always having to remonstrate with some of my pilots who seemed to like 'boring a hole' in the sky after their tests were over, thus wasting the firm's time and money as well as precious flying hours.

My first landing at Woodford was not a success. I tried to come in slowly because the runway was shorter than I was used to and the aircraft thumped the ground in a very definite manner. I streamed the 'chute, taxied up the short runway and then down the hill between the two hangars. It took me a little time to work out the optimum way to land the Vulcan, which was to approach at the correct speed but to start the flare a little bit early, not letting the aircraft touchdown. The nose of the aircraft would rise steadily until the wing ran out of lift and the eight rear bogey wheels, four on each side, would touchdown gently with the nose way off the ground. The trick then was to keep pulling the stick back and the nose in the air until the speed dropped so low that the nose could no longer be kept in the air and the nose wheels would touch the ground. The drag with the nose in the air was very high so only minimal braking was required to stop and there was no need to stream the parachute, which probably pleased the fire crew who had to pick up the parachute from the runway if it was used. If the cg was aft, the nose could be kept in the air almost as long as one liked and one of my party tricks was to turn left up the short runway with the nose wheels still in the air.

Approaching the flight test hangars one had to be a bit careful as there was not a lot of room between them for the Vulcan to go through. The Vulcan Mk 2 which came a year or so later had even less room; still as far as I know we never had a taxiing accident coming in. Once parked, Derek Bowyer, the inspector in charge of our safety equipment, climbed up between our seats, inserted the ejection seat safety pins and we then climbed down, had a shower and got dressed.

The results of flight tests could not be assessed immediately as happens today. The trace recorders could be examined straightaway but the flight conditions for each event could only be checked after the film had been developed, which took at least twenty-four hours, and then it was painstaking work correlating all the parameters and working out all the results.

My first flight set the pattern for the next few months, when we were tidying up all the loose ends that remained for the initial CA release of the Mk 1 Vulcan and for establishing in more detail the cruise performance of the aircraft. The behaviour of the yaw damper needed optimising, measurements of the amount of unusable fuel in each of the fourteen tanks were made, the shaping of the mach trimmer extension against mach number was refined and many other handling and engineering tests were undertaken.

I have included a rough picture of the elevator circuit and a graph of the mach trimmer extension and stick position at 40,000ft up to the limiting mach at the front and aft centre of gravity positions, courtesy of Wason Turner but modified for readability, just to give a taste of the enormous amount of work that was required to test each mark of Vulcan so that it could be cleared for CA release. In this particular graph it can be seen that the stick is moving forward as the speed increases and the mach trimmer extends. However, it is very clear that as 1.00 IMN is approached the aircraft is getting very unstable.

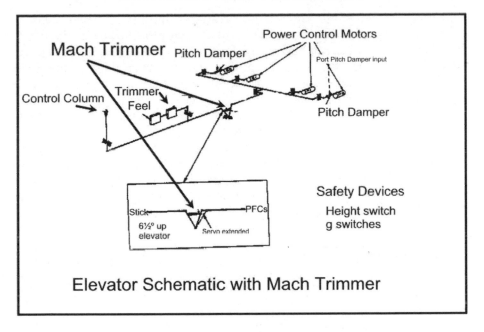

Elevator Schematic with Mach Trimmer

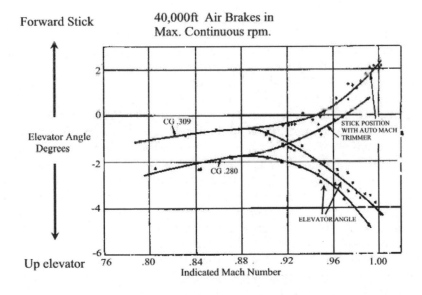

Vulcan B1 longitudinal stability.

We also had to check the engine handling of the various marks of the Bristol Olympus engines. The Bristol Engine Company at that time did not have a flight test organisation capable of developing the engine and consequently Avros had to carry out the engine handling tests. On each side of the aircraft there was only one engine intake for both engines and this caused some significant problems. Firstly, if there was a compressor failure of one engine the blades would initially go forward into the common part of the intake and then some of the blades could be sucked into the other engine, causing significant damage or possibly a failure of the second engine. Luckily, I never had this experience and as far as I know such failures never caused an accident. The second most common problem with the shared air intake was that any engine surging at high altitude would cause the adjacent engine to surge and this was very undesirable. Consequently, I found I was spending a lot of time on engine handling tests, trying to determine if and when the engine surged. The procedure was to stabilise the aircraft and engines at the desired test point and once there the throttle or throttles would be slammed open. My concern was that in doing these tests, if surging and flame out occurred, it was very difficult to relight both engines immediately, hot relights as they were called. In these cases, if the hot relights were unsuccessful the aircraft had to be allowed to descend to below 30,000ft so that cold relights could be carried out. The aircraft had then to be climbed back up to the next test point to check once more for surging.

Clearly Bristols were modifying the engine fuel system as a result of our tests to prevent the surging, but the engine had a very complicated analogue fuel system and it was a very tricky and time consuming task both for Bristols and for ourselves, checking the improvements that they were making. In the end the engines worked extremely well and we very rarely had a handling problem in flight.

When I had been at Woodford for about a month the Royal Air Force took delivery of their first aircraft, Boscombe having given the RAF an initial CA clearance for crew training. Podge Howard took XA897 away to Waddington and prepared it for a round-the-world flight, showing off the RAF's brand new shiny strategic bomber. The flight took place with Air Marshal, as he was then, Sir Harry Broadhurst, Commander-in-Chief of Bomber Command in the right hand seat and was hugely successful, but it all ended in disaster as the aircraft crashed on the approach to London's Heathrow Airport on 1st October 1956. This accident is discussed in Chapter 7. Obviously the effect on all of us at Avros was extremely demoralising. Both pilots ejected but the four rear crew members were all killed. By chance I was going by train to Boscombe Down at the very moment the aircraft must have been landing and to this day I remember the pouring rain and poor visibility as I travelled not too far south of the airport. I was sitting in the officers mess at one o'clock just after lunch when I heard the news. The room was full and the radio was turned on to listen to the headlines. As the announcer told of the dreadful disaster I could feel the effect on everyone there and, of course, a lot of them looked at me to see how I was reacting.

Back at Woodford everyone carried on with their work but it was a very difficult time for all concerned, particularly for the engineers in flight sheds since one of their experts and a very popular figure, Freddie Bassett, was in the back of the aircraft supporting the flight. To make matters worse, he was engaged to the secretary of Frank Sheehan, the head of flight sheds. By chance I barely flew at all in October which didn't help matters, but in November things seemed to recover and I was particularly busy both in and out of the office since I was getting married at the end of the month.

Looking at my log book for about this time it is clear that the production aircraft were beginning to roll out. However, most of the early aircraft seem to have been allocated for extending the CA clearance for the Mk 1 or doing development for the Mk 2. XA898 was the next aircraft to be delivered in January 1957 followed by XA896 and XA900 in March; XA896 was late because it was originally built without the modified leading edges. The missing numbers were CA aircraft 889, 890, *891*, 892, *893*, 894, *895*, 899, *903* – the aircraft in italics were doing work for the Mk 2 as detailed in the next chapter; we used them for testing aerodynamics, engines and systems.

The production schedule which we had to carry out could in theory be done on one flight lasting about two hours, but I don't believe we ever cleared an aircraft in one flight. We had to climb up to 45,000ft and check the mach trimmer, pitch dampers and the yaw damper and go to .98 IMN and make certain the handling was acceptable. Then we looked at the engines for correct settings and performance followed by slam accelerations to make certain the engines did not go out and, whether they did or not, we stopped each engine in turn to make sure the relighting was satisfactory. We had to function the bomb doors at the limiting speed of 415 knots, followed by operating the airbrakes. Then we needed to make sure that the power controls motors could be switched on and off and that, with each control switched off, the surface did not move on the control surface indicator. During the flight we monitored the fuel system to ensure correct feeding and that the transfer pumps worked; we also needed to make certain that all the fourteen gauge readings worked correctly. In addition, the pressurisation needed checking together with the temperature controls. The production schedule gradually got longer during the life of the Mk 1 as the ILS was fitted followed by the autopilot; then it was necessary to go to Bedford or some Bomber Command airfield to carry out instrument approaches to check the correct functioning of the autopilot.

When we had finished the production schedule satisfactorily, the AID inspector would go over the aircraft with a fine tooth comb and then a Bomber Command crew would come and take it away. All the Mk 1 aircraft were delivered by April 1959 though we got twenty-eight of them back to convert to Mk 1As, which was basically a Vulcan Mk

1 with a bulbous back end containing the ECM equipment and Olympus 104 engines delivering 13,000lbs thrust.

The Vulcan was now getting very well known throughout the country and we were very pleased when we heard that the Duke of Edinburgh had visited Waddington and had a flight with Wing Commander Dodd who, if my memory does not play me false, was called 'Fearless Frank'. Apparently he demonstrated the aircraft at .98 IMN and did a simulated radar bombing run at Boscombe Down.

Around the end of the year the supersonic bomber got cancelled but, though I was initially depressed, we had the contract for the Vulcan Mk 2 which gave us plenty of work. The Mk 2 had a 15ft wider wing span than the Mk 1, the Olympus engines produced 17,000lbs of thrust and the maximum take-off weight was 204,000lbs, 20,000lbs heavier than the Mk 1. The Mk 2 with its new wing was needed because the wing on the Mk 1 started to buffet at the higher altitudes and angles of attack made possible by the larger engines.

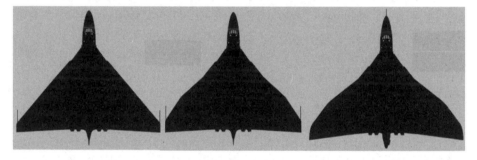

Original wing   Mk 1 wing   Mk 2 wing

During the life of the Mk 2 the Bristol Olympus engines were increased in power, initially to 19,000lbs thrust and then to 21,000lbs. The development programme was based on using Vulcan Mk 1s to develop the Mk 2. The aerodynamics and handling were to be done on the second prototype VX777, the electrics on XA893, the autopilot and automatic landing system on XA899 and the engines on XA891. Some of the other early Mk 1s were used by the Royal Aircraft Establishment to develop radio equipment and by Boscombe Down to develop some armament. A detailed analysis of the development aircraft, flights and flying hours involved will be found in the next chapter.

In parallel with the development of the Mk 2 there was still a lot of work to be carried out on the handling of the Vulcan Mk 1A, the uprated engines and the autopilot including ILS approaches. This was very time consuming, even tedious, and in no way resembled the film *Test Pilot* with Jack Hawkins and his 'daily dice with death in the afternoon'! Incidentally I am reminded of another film which was very relevant to the Vulcan flight test programme called *The Sound Barrier* with John Justin desperately trying to go supersonic in his fighter which had the same problem as we had in that he ran out of up-elevator as mach one was approached. He solved the problem by pushing the stick forward at the critical moment and the aircraft went through the sound barrier; I always felt that this was fine for Pinewood Studios but I never fancied trying it out myself.

The Olympus proved to be a very reliable engine for the Mk 1 and it was steadily being uprated. Another stage had been added at the front of the low pressure compressor and the engine was first designated Mk 102 with 12,000lbs of thrust. The engines were fitted to XA889 and we started examining the engine handling, which proved to be still very reliable achieving 3,000 hours between unscheduled removals. However, by July 1957 the design of the Mk 102 had been improved using better materials and the thrust was raised to 13,000lbs, and designated Mk 104. I did the first flight of this engine in XA889 and then we spent the next few months carrying out more handling tests on the engine and also strain gauge measurements on the turbine blades to try to ensure that there would be no failure of the blades, particularly important on the Vulcan since any blades shed would go forward and then be sucked into the adjacent engine. A pilot operated switch was introduced to change the fully open throttle power from take-off to cruise. The engine proved very reliable and did extremely well in service but there was one serious failure which caused the loss of an aircraft, XA909 described in Chapter 7.

The autopilot work was carried out on Vulcan XA894 using the Mk 10 autopilot, manufactured by Smiths Industries at their Cheltenham facility. I first flew it in March of 1957 and there were no basic problems flying at low altitude at constant height. We were able to choose the optimum gearings which determined how the autopilot interfaced with the aircraft controls without any problems. However, at cruising altitudes the aircraft presented much more of a challenge to the autopilot. Finding a gearing which enabled it to fly smoothly at constant height was very difficult since the Vulcan tended to execute a long term phugoid in pitch, that is it would oscillate up and down by several hundred feet over a period of perhaps a minute or two. The problem was compounded by the fact that the mach trimmer was moving in and out as the speed varied and we soon discovered that the autopilot could not manage to fly the aircraft at all at a constant height if the mach trimmer was switched off. Eventually we managed to find a suitable gearing, but the nearer the aircraft was to its ceiling, the poorer was the height control.

The autopilot performed better at altitude if the aircraft was allowed to cruise climb, so that it climbed steadily as the weight was reduced. This was because it was then flying at constant attitude and it was this attitude that the autopilot was controlling.

As already mentioned, with any automatic system there is always a downside, however well the automatics perform. The aircraft structure has always to be protected from any malfunctions of the automatics and, in the case of the autopilot, there had to be some means of turning off the autopilot if the servomotors went wrong and suddenly signalled the controls to go to their limit, full travel, called a hardover or runaway. In fact there were no problems with aileron hardovers or runaways, since the aileron stops prevented excessive control angles being applied and so it was agreed that should this type of fault occur, the autopilot would be disconnected by the pilot using the instinctive autopilot cut-out on the back of the stick.

An elevator malfunction was a much more serious event since in the time it would take for the pilot to get his hand on the stick and disconnect the autopilot, the aircraft structure could have been extremely badly damaged by the excessive application of elevator. The problem was solved by fitting a 'spring strut' between the autopilot servomotor and the Vulcan elevator control circuit. There was a micro-switch on the strut which in effect limited the amount of force the servomotor could apply; the moment the force applied to the strut exceeded a preset amount, the spring would compress, the micro-switch would operate and the autopilot would be disconnected. The critical case was at the maximum speed of 415 knots with a nose-up runaway. We had to ensure that the servo-motor power was strong enough to be able to control the aircraft in the most demanding case, which turned out to be during an ILS approach, while not breaking the aircraft at high speed. In fact we managed to find the setting for the micro-switch reasonably quickly, but it still took seven flights and some careful testing.

The most interesting part of the autopilot clearance was flying automatic ILS approaches. We did not realise it at first, though we soon learnt, that the localiser and glide slope beams that had been installed on Bomber Command airfields were not very good. The transmitted deviation signals were not linear and were liable to be affected by other ground objects like hangars and small buildings near the runways. This had the effect of upsetting the steering signals from the autopilot. The problem was particularly serious for the glide slope, since the beam was so narrow at the critical decision height.

In fact, in spite of the imperfections of the localiser beams, we were able to choose suitable gearings so that the autopilot controlled the Vulcan satisfactorily laterally down to 250ft. However, we wasted a lot of time trying to get the aircraft to fly a good glide slope before we realised the problem was with the beam itself. In the end we had to send the aircraft down to Boscombe without the glide slope steering working properly. A few years later when the glide slopes at the airfields were improved, the autopilot managed to control the Vulcan down to 250ft without going unstable and there was no point in trying for anything better since the localisers which were installed at Bomber

Command airfields were offset from the runway itself by three degrees and had the decision height been any lower the aircraft would have crossed the centre line, which would have meant that it needed to turn back towards the runway at a very low altitude.

We had another problem using the autopilot which was not the fault of the equipment at all. The Vulcan had a pronounced nose-down trim change when the bomb doors were opened and this was clearly undesirable. There was no way that the autopilot could hold the aircraft level as the doors were opened. It was vital to correct this problem and once again I got Bill Stableford to fly with me so that I could demonstrate what was wrong. Bill went away and in due course, after examining the tests that we had done, measuring the stick forces I used and the resulting elevator angles, he produced a mechanical design which interlinked the bomb door mechanism with the elevator control run. I flew the modification about eighteen months or so after his flight with me and, to my satisfaction, there was virtually no trim change as the bomb doors were opened.

Six months later at the end of 1959 I did the first flight of the Vulcan Mk 1A. The aircraft was a basic Mk 1 aircraft with Mk 104 engines, producing 13,000lbs of thrust and fitted with an electro counter measures, ECM, rear fuselage. I remember remarking at the time to Cyril Bethwaite, chief of flight test, that I hoped the ECM bulge at the back would not upset the bomb door trim change that we had so carefully proposed, designed and installed. He 'pooh-poohed' the idea as rubbish but my pessimistic forebodings were unfortunately correct. The aircraft pitched up as we opened the bomb doors and we had to remove the modification rather hurriedly.

In fact Cyril was a really excellent chief of flight test. He had been there during the very difficult times of the Vulcan Mk 1 development, when strict control was needed to ensure the programmes were carried out to maximum advantage. In later years we worked together very closely when he was appointed HS146 project director down at Hatfield and I was appointed project pilot, I suspect at Cyril's request. Apparently, when I was a comparative new boy at Woodford he remarked to someone in his department about me, 'He'll meet himself coming back one day', though I'm not sure whether the remark was made about my flying or the speed at which I was alleged to go up and down the flight test corridors.

During my years flight testing, I became very familiar with flight director systems as well as autopilots made by Smiths Industries for whom I later worked on their Aerospace Board. At about this time I was struggling with the problem of manually flying the Vulcan down the ILS beam and deciding what was possible, bearing in mind the fast 145 knots approach speed of the aircraft and the demanding control characteristics. The easier it was for a pilot to keep to the correct glide slope and remain on the centre line, the safer would be the approach

and it was for that reason that I liked the pilot instrumentation to compute and show the action required by the pilot to keep on the centre line as well as display the actual deviation from the centre line itself. Consequently, I started to consider better solutions and instrumentation for flying ILS approaches than just a 'raw' deviation indicator shown in the previous chapter.

I remember flying a Sperry zero reader in XA892 in preparation for the Mk 1A together with Sax, who was still in charge of B Squadron at Boscombe, in the right hand seat soon after I joined Avros. As the name of the instrument implied, all the pilot had to do was to keep the deviations on the instrument central and the aircraft would execute a perfect approach. Later, Lear demonstrated their flight system to me in a Beechcraft. There was no doubt in my mind that having an instrument like a zero reader would be an enormous help to the pilot to achieve repeatable localiser and glide slope holding, down to a low altitude and in fact, as a result of the XA892 flights, the Vulcan Mk 1A had a zero reader fitted as standard. The decision height needed to be as low as possible but not so low that the aircraft might get dangerously close to the ground without seeing the runway. With the zero reader it was possible to get down to a 300ft decision height whilst the CA clearance with just the ILS deviation indicator was 400ft, these heights being above the ground uncorrected for static position error which was taken as 50ft.

In June 1959 we had our first aircraft cleared for flight refuelling, Vulcan Mk 1 XH478. I took it down to Boscombe and did three flights with Squadron Leader Peter Bardon behind a Valiant, one flight doing dry contacts and then transferring fuel. I have to admit that I was not particularly good at making contact and Pete did rather better than I did, but then he had done it before in other aircraft. Nevertheless, I would have liked to have got it right straightaway.

While we were continuing to fill in the missing development points on the Mk 1A, Boscombe Down was still flying Vulcan Mk 1s and extending the CA release. Flight Lieutenant Milt Cottee, Royal Australian Air Force, who was on the ETPS course after me, had joined B Squadron and we flew together quite a few times, mainly on autopilot clearance work doing servomotor hardovers. I was amazed when I heard from him some years later about a flight they did at Boscombe in 1957. Milt and his co-pilot Ray Bray had been briefed to fly with the bomb doors open and a full set of twenty-one 1,000 lb bombs over Lyme Bay; the target test point was right in the corner of the flight envelope at 415 knots, .98 IMN and apparently the brief was to pull 3.0g. I can't do better than to quote Milt:

> Towards the end of 1957, Flt Lt Rus Law was selected to replace me at Boscombe Down. He was then completing the ETPS course at Farnborough. I commenced handing over my responsibilities for Vulcan flight tests to others in the squadron. Flt Lt Ray Bray was to pick up on weapon carriage and release trials. So, one day we were out over Lyme Bay in Vulcan 892 with a full load of practice bombs. One point for measurement was to be at the corner of the aircraft flight envelope with the weapon bay doors open. This was 415 Knots IAS, 0.98 IMN and 3.0g. The cross over for IMN and IAS was at about 27,000ft. Ray was flying the aircraft from the right seat. We started a spiralling descent at high mach number from above 35,000ft, aiming to reach all of the test conditions together at 27,000ft.
>
> The Vulcan had an increasing nose-down pitching moment due to shock wave effects as speed increased above 0.88 IMN. To artificially correct this instability, Avro had inserted an auto mach trimmer in the elevator controls. The trimmer responded to mach number by extending up elevator without any change to stick position or feel until it ran out of authority at 0.95 IMN. There was then little remaining elevator movement available, especially for manoeuvre.
>
> We were thus spiralling down with almost full up-elevator. I had discussed these limits during our pre-flight briefing so we were a bit wary. As it happened, Ray pulled a little too tightly into the spiral just short of our target conditions and speed dropped off. He relaxed stick back pressure to recover speed which increased too quickly just as we had reached the limit of the auto mach trimmer. The result was an abrupt increase in nose-down pitch and an attempt to control this by further back-stick. But there was no more left, the elevators were at full authority.
>
> I grabbed the stick with both hands, stopped the roll and tried to milk some more elevator. With two of us pulling hard on the stick, we found it to be very firmly against the stops. But, the nose was pitching down at an increasing rate as mach number went up past 1.0. I let go of the stick with my right hand and pulled all engines back to idle, before pondering the effects of the speed brakes if I were to extend them now at a speed well above their

maximum operating speed. There was a real risk of them failing structurally. By now we were going through the vertical with the Mach No reaching 1.04+. I was considering pushing under and slowly rolling upright.

I took the risk and slammed down the speed brake control and felt them bite. IAS and IMN started to come back and, slowly at first, the elevators started to pitch the nose up. We came back through the vertical at about 18,000ft and soon gained normal control. Continuing buffet reminded us that the weapon bay doors were still open. To my relief they closed as we continued to pull out of our dive, regaining level flight at 8,000ft. Any ships below would have received a very substantial sonic bang.

There was a residual abnormal noise and my concern about the speed brakes returned. I called base and asked for assistance from any airborne aircraft in the vicinity. A Canberra was vectored towards us as I headed back towards Boscombe Down. I found that, as I slowed the aircraft, the noise became worse. At 150 Knots the noise in the cockpit was like blowing across the top of an empty bottle. Soon we had a Canberra pilot looking us over. He spotted a small access hatch open under the nose and no other problem of external significance. The hatch turned out to be the access to the oxygen filling connections. Ground inspection revealed that the rear bulkhead of the weapons bay had been deformed. If that had let go we would have lost our tail.

This turned out to be the first time that a V bomber had gone supersonic. It was not to be a normal event. In the next year one of B Squadron's Victors ran-away nose-down after losing a pitot tube and broke up over the Bristol channel.

I've discussed this event with Milt several times. It was way beyond anything that we had done at Woodford and I cannot imagine why it was necessary to do this test point since it exceeded the RAF limitations. From my experience doing aerobatics at Farnborough I was only allowed 3g and the aircraft was very light; in Milt's case perhaps the target g was less than he remembered. I'm not sure what the court of inquiry would have said if there had been an accident and he was briefed to go to 3g; I think B Squadron might have come in for some criticism. Certainly it is not clear to me what clearance Avros would have given Boscombe and I'm not surprised the rear of the bomb bay was damaged. With regard to what true mach number the aircraft actually went, the answer has to be problematical. There was a large position error at 1.0 IMN but I don't know what it was; I asked John

McDaniel quite recently, who was the expert at the time and he thought at 1.0 IMN the error was probably .07 mach number. Apparently there was no confirmation of a sonic boom so perhaps the Victor was still the only supersonic V Bomber.

As already mentioned, Avros did not do weapons testing unless there was some special handling reason or Boscombe had had a problem. Consequently, again I think it is appropriate to quote Milt Cottee:

> On 17 June, I was to fly Vulcan 982 for the first drop of a 10,000lbs dummy nuclear bomb. The shape of the bomb was at that time highly classified. When I was doing my pre-flight inspection of the aircraft, security officers prevented me from approaching the weapons bay. I argued for a few minutes and then declared my intention to cancel the flight. I took my crew back to the squadron offices and advised the CO that I would not fly the aircraft under the circumstances. He soon had the problem sorted out and 30 minutes later, I had a close look at a nuclear shape before going off to drop it. We had weapon-bay TV surveillance anyway and I watched that huge thing fall away, gently rocking as it rapidly became a small speck. I felt a small lurch of the aircraft as it released. I dropped several of those 10,000 pounders before agreeing formally to Squadron carriage and release.

The Mk 1 development decreased steadily and by 1959 we were just tidying up loose ends. The table below shows the size of the CA fleet used for developing the Mk 1 and the Mk 1A, and the number of flights that I did in the aircraft:

Tail number	Aircraft test programme	ALB flights
VX770	First prototype	
VX777	Second prototype	5
XA889	Handling Performance Boscombe acceptance	58
XA890	Radio clearances RAE	13
XA892	Boscombe and Avro trials	15
XA894	Mk 10 autopilot	59
XA895	Handling Vulcan Mk 1A	22
XA903	Blue Steel	18
XH478	Anti-radar stores Flight refuelling	16 16

I mentioned earlier that pilots always tend to extol the virtues of the aircraft they fly and Vulcan pilots were always comparing their aircraft with the Victor. Once clear of the ground there was not a lot of difference between the Victor and the Vulcan but I personally always preferred the Vulcan because of the landing issues. The Victor in fact was probably easier to fly on the approach, requiring smaller deviations in pitch to keep on the glide slope and the approach speed tended to be more stable and required less throttle work by the pilot to hold the desired approach speed. However once near the ground the Vulcan handling was superb in that it was possible to flare the aircraft so that it touched down very slowly with the nose of the aircraft right up in the air and the rear wheels of the main landing gear just kissing the tarmac and, as I remarked earlier, very little wheel braking was required. The Victor on the other hand had to be flown on to the ground with a speed very little less than the approach speed and the parachute had to be streamed if the wheels and wheel brakes were not to be damaged.

I can't resist adding a comment, again from Milt Cottee, on the two aircraft:

> I flew the Victor occasionally. The feel of this aircraft always gave me an impression of fragility. Control reaction, wing and tail bending combined to cause one to take care with gross manoeuvres. Handley Page had tried hard with cockpit design but it seemed over complicated compared with the ruggedness of the Vulcan. Perhaps the cohesive structure of the Vulcan made the difference. The Vulcan felt like a fighter having excellent manoeuvrability. The Victor, with its lower rates of roll and pitch, was more complex in its manoeuvre characteristics. Now, as an experienced test pilot, I became very aware of these subtle comparisons and pondered about the reasons for such differences.

There was probably another difference between the two aircraft which was basic to their design. Handley Page, rather like de Havillands at Hatfield with whom I worked a lot in later years on the HS146, were a design led organisation. Systems and structure tended to be over complicated. Avros on the other hand went for simplicity and if a design was too complicated it would be changed if at all possible. A good example of this was in the modification of the leading edge to reduce buffet; the main structure was not altered when the new leading edge was fitted even though a weight penalty was incurred. The situation was only optimised when the Mk 2 aircraft was designed.

In fact the Vulcan Mk 2 was even better than the Mk 1. It flew higher and its controls felt more positive and precise than the Mk 1.

This was particularly so on the approach where it was much easier to hold the desired approach speed and fly an accurate instrument approach. Finally, it was even nicer to touch down than the Mk 1. It was these flying characteristics that helped to make it not only an effective weapon of war but also a beautiful aircraft to demonstrate.

CHAPTER 5

DEVELOPING THE VULCAN MK 2

The Vulcan Mk 2 development work was fed gradually into the Vulcan test programme, steadily taking over from the Mk 1. The second prototype VX777 was used yet again for testing the new aerodynamic configuration, the Mk 1 wing being replaced by the Mk 2 wing, though the basic structure remained the same. Besides having the new wing, which increased the Vulcan span by 15ft, there were some other very significant system changes and, as already mentioned, some of these systems were initially developed using Mk 1 aircraft. In fact, while Jimmy was doing the initial flying on 777, I was dealing with the new AC electrical system on XA893, the autopilot and automatic landing system on XA899 and the engines on XA891.

The Vulcan first flew in the new Mk 2 configuration on 31 August 1957. Jimmy Harrison, after demonstrating the new shape at the SBAC show, did the initial handling work on the Mk 2 and there were no particular new problems; however, the undesirable characteristic aerodynamic handling features of the delta wing, like instability and short period pitching oscillations at high mach numbers, were still present and had to be dealt with to make the handling acceptable. One new feature of the Mk 2 was that the ailerons and elevators had been combined into elevons, probably because the designers had anticipated that the nose-down pitch at high mach numbers would be even worse than on the Mk 1. This clever design was again done by Bill Stableford and the control of the aircraft in normal flight and on the approach was much superior to the Mk 1. However as mentioned, the basic instability of the Vulcan with its delta plan form was unchanged and even all eight control surfaces acting as elevators, fully up, could not stop the aircraft trying to dive uncontrollably at high subsonic mach numbers.

The instability of the Mk 2 seemed worse than on the Mk 1, but this feature was probably accentuated due to the change in the way the pitot and static pressures were measured; instead of pitot static booms at the wing tips there were pitot heads and static plates on the sides of the nose. The object of this change was to try to reduce the size of the

Top: VX777 in the Farnborough hangar prior to repair work.

Middle: V Bombers flying from Boscombe in 1957.

Bottom: Farnborough 1958. Jimmy Harrison landing the first production Mk 2 Vulcan XH533. Note pilots' tents in the background.

Top left: Author and Jimmy Harrison at SBAC show, 1958.

Top right: From left, Dickie Proudlove, author, Eric Burgess, SBAC show 1958.

Bottom: Author refuelling Vulcan XH478 from a Boscombe-based Valiant.

Inset: Prince Philip entering the Vulcan at Waddington, early 1959.

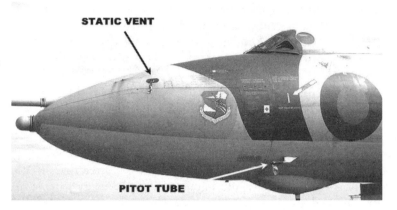

Vulcan Mk 2 pitot tube and static vent. (*Fred Martin RZF Digital*)

position error at high altitude in terms of indicated mach number. No longer could the magic 1.0 mach number be seen as on the Mk 1; instead all that could be seen safely was about .95 IMN.

One of the difficult tests I had undertaken on the Mk 1 was actually determining the size of the difference between the indicated mach number and the true mach number. However, as explained the 'trailing static' system was not very good as the static pressure source we towed behind the aircraft did not work well at high mach numbers. On the Mk 2 we used a different system and fitted a high altitude radio altimeter and calibrated the atmosphere where we were going to do our flying by using the conventional trailing static, once more towed behind the aircraft but at a comparatively slow mach number. We compared the readings of the radio altimeter with the trailing static and then wound it in and then used the radio altimeter readings to measure the static pressure errors. It was a neat system, developed by Avros and now used elsewhere. The results we obtained agreed very well with our estimates and confirmed the indicated mach numbers already mentioned for the Mk 2.

The mach trimmer was redesigned slightly so that there were two variable length struts, actuators, in series instead of the single actuator on the Mk 1. The concept was that even if one actuator failed, the basic instability of the aircraft would be reduced by the operation of the good actuator. In addition, the design of the system was such that it was only necessary to consider a runaway of one of the two actuators. There was a detection system to show if the output of the two systems did not agree. The limiting speed for the RAF was .93 IMN which was reduced to .92 IMN on later aircraft fitted with Olympus 301 engines with 21,000lbs of thrust at sea level because of the greater altitude capability and therefore the greater likelihood of exceeding the limiting speed.

The short period longitudinal pitch damping experienced and

described in the Mk 1, this time occurred at about .92 IMN and, as forecast by the design team, was much less well damped. Unlike the Mk 1, the oscillation looked as if it might be divergent, that is the pitching motion would get larger and larger and eventually break the aircraft. As explained previously with the Mk 1, the oscillation was so rapid that it was impossible for the pilot to control it. For this reason, four pitch dampers instead of the two for the Mk 1 had been installed.

The situation was complicated because the Vulcan Mk 2 had 'control float' which was similar to the aileron float mentioned with the Mk 1. This meant that as the structure deflected when g was applied, the control rod length from the pilot's stick to the electro-hydraulic motors effectively changed in length so that the elevons moved by themselves. Consequently, as the pitching oscillation took place, all eight elevons moved up and down with the oscillation and affected its magnitude. We found that if the control run was altered to remove the float, the pitching oscillation was improved but, unfortunately, the normal control forces to apply g, called the stick force per g, was reduced. As usual, Bill Stableford was called for and he found a compromise setting for the control run float which kept the pitching oscillation under control and the stick force per g to an acceptable value at aft cg, the critical case.

It was still possible to fly the aircraft with all four dampers switched off for a short time, but the amplitude of the oscillation was unpleasant and it was always a relief to finish the testing and start switching the pitch dampers on again. It felt as if the situation could get out of hand and become divergent, but I never got too worried probably because the moment the speed changed by a fraction from the critical speed to .93 IMN the damping immediately improved. However, when carrying out these tests I kept my hand on the pitch damper switches so that I could switch them back on immediately if I felt things were not under control. I tried using the airbrakes to slow down at this speed but found that it was definitely not a good idea as there was a pronounced nose-down trim change which did not improve the situation.

As usual we had to deal with the downside of having stabilisers. I've already mentioned that the mach trimmer had two actuators which solved the malfunction or runaway case; however we still had to have the g switches to protect the structure. The quadruple pitch damper installation was a much bigger challenge. It needed some careful design to guard against runaways and Newmarks, who made the servos, devised a 'voting' system so that in the event of a runaway of an errant pitch damper strut, the one that had an extension different from the other three would be shut down automatically. The RAF was limited to .90M if two dampers were inoperative, since it would not be possible to determine a faulty pitch damper if there were only two struts.

With regard to the maximum speed at which it was safe to fly the Vulcan, I personally don't remember ever going beyond about .95 IMN as the aircraft was getting very unstable by that time and the pull forces were high. Jimmy Harrison however did have a problem one day as he hit .955 IMN and found he was not strong enough to apply full up elevator; he had to ask his co-pilot to help and, understandably, he immediately asked for a modification after he had landed. The problem was that the artificial feel was designed to protect the structure at high airspeed using the standard stick force 'shaping' based on the square of the indicated airspeed; it was not envisaged that full up elevator would be needed at lower altitudes when the stick forces would be much higher due to the higher airspeeds; in fact, in these flight conditions, when the mach number was very high, it was safe to apply full elevator since it would not break the aircraft. The difficulty was solved by putting a collapsing spring strut between the elevator control run and the artificial feel set at 150lbs, so that 'in extremis' the pilot would be able to override the artificial feel; the strut was designed so that as it collapsed the force required to operate the controls did not increase significantly above the operating force of 150lbs.

As usual we had to decide before giving the aircraft to Boscombe Down for CA release the maximum speed it was safe for their test pilots to fly it and, as another issue, whether the autostabilisers we had provided protected the aircraft adequately. We took the view that what we had installed and tested provided sufficient safety and I believe we got it right. There were never any notified accidents or incidents from either the Mk 1 or Mk 2 aircraft diving and getting out of control; I suspect that that was because the drag was so high at these mach numbers that the mach number wouldn't increase much as the aircraft dived and then the speed would fall rapidly as altitude was reduced. Milt Cottee, in the previous chapter, reckoned he went supersonic but, as already remarked, the position error was very high at these mach numbers so it is most unlikely. However, there was one case of going too fast in the Vulcan Mk 2, reaching Mach 1.0 IMN, probably .975 M, which I have described in Chapter 7. Luckily it did not result in an accident but it didn't do the aircraft much good, the upper skin on the wing was wrinkled and the aircraft had to be repaired at Bitteswell. As a matter of interest our great competitor the Victor Mk 2 did go supersonic in Johnny Allam's very capable hands but, of course, it was by accident, he said!

To cope with the poor directional damping and associated long period rolling oscillation, two dampers were fitted and the system worked well though I was surprised to find when I was returning the second prototype Vulcan VX777 from Farnborough to Woodford in the middle of the 1958 SBAC show that the directional damping was poor on the approach, due to the settings of the yaw damper. We had to make some adjustments to the damper settings to rectify this. Jim, who had been flying the aircraft, had never noticed it and, I suspect, just corrected with rudder automatically; that was the problem with gifted, natural pilots, they did not always notice the difficulty.

The electrical system on the Mk 2 was a great change from the Mk 1, more reliable but more complicated in a way. Of course both marks of aircraft relied on the electrical system to drive the power control motors, ten in the case of the Mk 2, one for each control surface and two for the single rudder. However, the Mk 1 system used a 112V DC system consisting of four DC generators charging a bank of four 28V batteries in series. The system was heavy and the concept of automatic powering of the busbars in the event of power being lost on the busbar could be a threat to safety, because of the limited time the batteries could supply adequate power. On the Mk 2, the electrical power was generated by four 200V 400 cycle AC alternators running at constant frequency and it was possible to synchronise the alternators if necessary. In addition to the supply from the four alternators, there was a fuel driven auxiliary power unit, AAPU, which could provide power to the busbars and there was also an air driven Ram Air Turbine, RAT, which could be dropped into the slipstream if its emergency eject handle was pulled; the concept was that the RAT could provide enough electrical power to keep the aircraft flying but only after all non-essential supplies had been automatically disconnected.

Normally each alternator drove its own busbar; the supplies to the eight elevon power control motors were split between the four busbars. If a busbar went dead it would automatically be connected to the common 'synchronising' bar so that electrical power would be maintained on the busbar. In the event of a serious or potentially catastrophic failure of the electrical system the correct drill was to lower the RAT and, if the aircraft was below 30,000ft, use the AAPU. As a precaution, the AAPU was normally started on the ground and kept running until 30,000ft and then restarted on the way down and kept running on the ground.

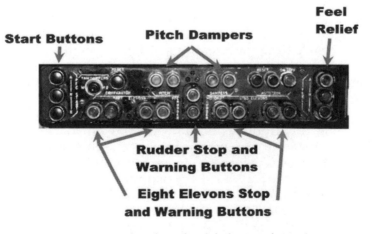

Power control and artificial feel control panel.

The switching and control of the power controls was much superior on the Mk 2. Each motor had not only a push button switch but there was a light on the top of each button. If a control motor failed its light would come on and the pilot would then cancel the master warning light by pressing the button of the failed motor; the individual light would remain on.

This new electrical system needed a lot of careful testing and so half of the system was installed on two of the engines of XA893 plus an AAPU and RAT. It was necessary to test the new alternators by simulating the Mk 2 aircraft electrical loads and so we fitted a lot of loads consisting of high resistance coils of wire which got very hot on a metal frame in the bomb bay; naturally the structure was immediately caused the toast rack. The aircraft started flying in November of 1956 and many test hours were spent operating the system and warming the bomb bay! In fact the aircraft was still flying in the summer of 1958 when the first Mk 2 aircraft, XH533 started flying with the full system.

To finish the AC development story, in 1959 when I had completed the initial engine development of the Olympus 201 in XA891, the aircraft had some of the Mk 2 AC electrics fitted, replacing some of the 112V Mk 1 electrics. Whilst I was on holiday in Spain, the aircraft was ready to fly with this new arrangement and so Jimmy Harrison had to fly it. In Barcelona two weeks into our holiday I chanced to get hold of a *Daily Telegraph* and read that a Vulcan, which turned out to be XA891, had crashed but all the crew had bailed out successfully. It turned out that Jimmy Harrison had done an absolutely superb job, because the aircraft was basically a Mk 1 with all the power controls on the DC bar. There was a complete electrical failure in the aircraft and this meant that the controls would only last as long as the batteries, which in this case turned out to be no more than two minutes. Jimmy had to depressurise the aircraft, get the three rear crew to open the escape hatch and then slide down the chute. Luckily, the rear crew had their parachutes on and managed to get out in time and then Jimmy and Dickie Proudlove, co-pilot/flight test observer, escaped using their ejection seats. I could only hope that I would have done as well as Jimmy (see also Chapter 7).

This accident explains clearly why the Mk 2 system, when it was operating correctly, was superior to the Mk 1 since, in a similar occurrence on the Mk 2, electrical power would have been maintained by the RAT and the AAPU and there would have been time for the aircraft to be positioned to a safe area or even landed.

In fact as mentioned above, XA891 had flown for the first time a year previously in June 1958 fitted with the Olympus 106 engines which were the development engines for the Olympus 201 in the Mk 2. The engines had 16,000lbs each instead of the 17,000lbs for the production engines. The aircraft was basically a Mk 1 in every way and therefore very light. The modifications had been carried out at Avro's

Langar facility near Nottingham and I remember doing a low run over the field as a thank you when I collected it, before setting course for Woodford to embark on a fairly long engine handling programme to try to get the engines to an acceptable standard.

Just before the first flight of the first production Vulcan Mk 2, 19th August 1958, we got an urgent request from our then managing director Jimmy Kay for a progress report on the Mk 2 flight test programme, as a result of the flying we had done on the aerodynamic prototype VX777 and on the engine handling aircraft Vulcan XA891. Presumably this report was required for some local board meeting or, more likely, to send to the MOD Procurement Executive. The report was in two parts, one which Jimmy Harrison wrote and one written by myself and gives a snapshot of the progress we had made so far. It must be emphasised that progress reports are the meat and drink of development work and we always had a tendency to tell our bosses of the difficulties, to prevent them reporting to the world that the development programme would be finished immediately; getting the right balance was invariably a problem particularly since management always suspected that we test pilots were trying to make the aircraft better than it needed to be.

Jimmy concentrated on handling and started his report by pointing out that we were limited to 350 knots because more ground resonance tests of the wing structure were required on the structural test rig. The pitch damping checks were going well but runaways were still to be done. The high mach number instability was worse than the wind tunnel predicted but luckily the instability did not start until just beyond the cruising mach number. Because of the severity of the instability, tuning the mach trimmer was proving a challenge and there was a lot more work to be done. The elevon float with g had been reduced but this had made the pitch damping worse; the present settings were probably a satisfactory compromise. Buffeting threshold seemed as if it was going to be satisfactory but more vortex generator work was required. The general flying of the aircraft was considered better than a Mk 1 with lower control break-out forces at the control stick and the aileron response was distinctly better than the Mk1. The conclusion of Jimmy's part of the report was that the Mk 2 programme was going well as far as we had gone, with the mach trimmer the only known problem, but the aircraft had yet to go to the higher altitudes and the higher weights.

In my part I discussed the problems we were having with the engines. Initially the engine nozzles were unsatisfactory and had to be changed to convergent-divergent nozzles because with the higher air mass flow of these bigger engines it was necessary to slow the air down to get better surge margins. After a few flights the Mk 201 production engine fuel systems had been fitted and it was then possible to go to 54,000ft (probably a record for a Mk 1) but the engine handling had deteriorated so that slam or even moderate throttle openings caused the engines to surge and flame out above 30,000ft. Bristol Engines, now Bristol Siddeley confirmed our assessment and modified fuel systems were awaited. The other problem we had with the Mk 2 engines was that the constant frequency Sundstrand drives, needed for the 200V AC generators, were getting too hot above 50,000ft.

The full report is published as Appendix 3. We never heard what happened to it but it did not matter because we now had other things to occupy us. We had come to the conclusion that it would be possible to do an aerobatic manoeuvre in a Vulcan called a 'roll off the top'; this meant pulling the stick back and applying g so that the aircraft went vertically up and over on to its back and then half rolling it so that it was the right way up again, but a lot higher than when it started. The United States Air Force were advertising that such a manoeuvre, which they called an Immelmann, was a good way to deliver an atom bomb and then turn tail quickly to avoid the effects of the explosion. John Gilder in our tech office did some sums and confirmed that we should not have a problem doing this half loop and so off we went. I did it first in XA894 starting at about 340 knots, pulling 3g which was the maximum allowed for the weight of the aircraft; the speed on our back was about 160 knots or maybe a bit more. The plan was for me to take XA891 to the SBAC show at Farnborough in September to show off the Mk 2 engines and I realised that rolls off the top would be a good demonstration. Roly Falk had done simple rolls three years previously in the Vulcan XA890, but a roll off the top would definitely be new.

The flying we did at Farnborough is discussed in the next chapter but at the time, as we were preparing for the SBAC show, we were also considering looping the aircraft, that is instead of stopping half way round as we did doing rolls off the top, we would carry on pulling the aircraft all the way back to level flight. John Gilder again did the sums and told us it should be alright but we never did risk it. The difficulty would have been ensuring that the wings were kept level during the pull out and this would have been virtually impossible because of the poor view through the windscreens. On a fighter it does not matter if the wings are not kept level because the aircraft can be banked slightly to correct this. On a Vulcan such a manoeuvre, called a rolling pull out, would almost certainly have damaged it since the maximum amount of acceleration that it was safe to apply was 3g, and then only with the wings level and at light weight.

In researching this book I found to my amazement that the first prototype VX770 had in fact been looped. The circumstances were that the RAF provided crews to help Rolls Royce at Hucknall flight test the Conway engines that had been fitted to VX770 and were being developed for the Victor Mk 2. The aircraft was normally flown by mixed RAF and Rolls-Royce crews and the pilots apparently were carrying out aerobatics at the end of each sortie. Doing rolls over the airfield was standard practice but one day a full loop was carried out, though the event was hushed up, chiefly because it was known that loops were not permitted. The significance of these aerobatics is discussed in Chapter 7.

For the next year we steadily developed the engines to achieve satisfactory handling and at the same time we carried out strain gauge measurements on the blades to make certain they were not being overloaded or resonating, and that they would therefore have a good fatigue life and not start separating from the hub with disastrous results. Unlike with the Mk 1 engines, there was a very dramatic low level surge which made a loud bang and shook the whole aircraft. I remember flying down to Filton and demonstrating the surging right over the engine design department offices, since I felt at the time that the engineers didn't really believe there was a problem. In retrospect, this was perhaps not the most sensible thing to have done but luckily no-one complained. I could not finish the engine handling work on XA891 because of the restricted altitude capability of the Mk 1 and I carried on the engine development using a Mk 2, XH534.

Unlike the Vulcan Mk 1A, the Vulcan Mk 2 was to be fitted with a flight system and not a zero reader. This was to be the first flight system

Vulcan Mk 2 flight deck with production throttles and MFS. (*A V Roe*)

fitted to an RAF aircraft and it had become possible because it was realised that it was no longer necessary, for example, to have the static pressure sensor measuring altitude situated actually in the altimeter on the pilot's instrument panel. The reading could be measured elsewhere and sent electrically to be displayed in front of the pilot. Similarly, the attitude of the aircraft could be measured on a remote gyro instead of an artificial horizon and the information relayed to the pilots' instrument panel. This technique enabled a new concept of instrumentation to be adopted, with the great advantage of being able to integrate the information being displayed in front of the pilot, thus making the task of controlling the aircraft a lot easier.

Smiths Industries made this first flight system in the UK and sold the SFS, as it was called, to British European Airways for commercial airliners like the Comet and the Vanguard. Smiths also sold the system as the Military Flight System, MFS, to the RAF for the Vulcan Mk 2 and the Victor Mk 2. The first MFS was fitted to XA899 and I flew it in March 1958. To the amazement of both Jimmy and myself the MFS displayed the heading as a moving pointer on a fixed but manually rotatable compass card and not, as was normal on every other system then flying, on a rotating card with the aircraft's heading always at the top of the instrument. It was therefore quite awkward to find out which way the aircraft was going as it was necessary to look carefully at the compass indicator to find where the heading pointer was pointing on the instrument. To make any sense of the display when flying a desired path, it was necessary to keep leaning forward and rotating the compass card to keep the correct track at the top of the instrument. We asked the designers at the Smiths factory at Cheltenham, where the system was made, why they chose to have a moving pointer and their response was that it would make it more reliable. This explanation did not really stand up since the SFS was no more reliable than the competing systems from Sperry, Bendix and Collins to name but a few.

Mk 2 beam compass.

Mk 2 director horizon.

Notwithstanding the fact that I felt that the compass display was completely non-instinctive, pilots who flew the system regularly managed it very well and were most enthusiastic, but then the pilots concerned had never had a flight system so that the MFS was viewed as an improvement. Anyway in my experience, pilots always loved the aircraft they flew and justified any deficiencies. Of course, unlike the RAF, we were never on a steady heading for more than a few minutes at a time, which made a moving heading pointer particularly undesirable to us.

There was another problem with the MFS, this time on the director horizon. The glide slope deviation needle was displayed behind the aircraft attitude pointer and Smiths' concept of flying the ILS glide slope was for the pilot to keep the attitude pointer on top of the glide slope deviation pointer all the way down the glide slope, the centre of the glide slope scale having been adjusted for the aircraft's attitude on the approach so that it would then be kept on the glide slope. However as previously explained, the glide slope beam was conical, not linear, so that the effective 'gearing' to the glide slope increased all the way down the approach. This meant that on approaching the decision height, the requested pitch movement of the aircraft to make a small correction to regain the glide slope, if the glide slope deviation pointer was followed slavishly, was far too great; the aircraft would go dangerously unstable and be unable to land. At the time, the head man at Cheltenham was a famous ex-BOAC ex-Comet senior captain and he was not at all happy with my criticisms. I persuaded him to fly with me to demonstrate the problem and after the flight I remember him saying at the debriefing, 'well, you don't have to follow the glide slope deviation exactly'. Easy to say but not practical to do.

Smiths' engineers rallied round to deal with the problem and adjusted the shape of the glide slope deviation so that it was non-linear and this helped the problem on Vulcan Mk 1 XA899 enormously. Luckily, they had built some variable adjustments into their new design because when the Vulcan Mk 2 came along the aircraft was much more forgiving on the approach when it came to pitch changes at low speed; consequently, less non-linearity was required in the glide slope deviation. In the end we made the MFS work well though we could never get round the misfortune of having a moving heading pointer. Not surprisingly, the weakness of the SFS/MFS basic design meant that Smiths never sold flight systems significantly in the commercial airliner marketplace.

In fact, when XA899 first flew after its production schedule, it was not to examine the MFS but to look at the auto throttle which was a basic component of the planned automatic landing system for the Vulcan Mk 2. Up to this time all automatic landing work, including the auto throttle, had been carried out by the Blind Landing Experimental Unit, BLEU, initially at Martlesham Heath but shortly after the start of the tests they moved to Bedford. In fact, the design authority at the start of the programme was still BLEU and they were understandably nervous at watching the first automatic landing installation being carried out by an organisation different from themselves and to which they had no input.

On 31st October 1957 we took off on our first flight of the auto throttle system. Initially we were delighted because when the auto throttles were engaged, the four throttles would move backwards and forwards to try to keep the airspeed constant. However, we soon discovered there were two problems; firstly, the pilot interface with the throttles was completely non-instinctive and unacceptable; it was difficult to engage the system at the desired speed and, more importantly, to disengage the throttles immediately, which was vital when landing or if anything went wrong with the system. This poor interface was due to the fact that the Avro engineers had taken advice from BLEU instead of asking us how we wanted to control the system; the main change I instigated was fitting instinctive auto throttle cut-outs on the number one and four engine throttles instead of having to grope around on the instrument panel trying to find the right switch to disconnect the system.

The second problem with the auto throttles when we first flew was that the performance was not repeatable. We discovered that, providing the weather was absolutely smooth, we could find gearings that enabled the auto throttle to work reasonably well but the moment there was any turbulence or we needed a large variation in pitch, the auto throttle was alarmingly ineffective. The reason was that BLEU had been developing the automatic landing system and the automatic throttle using a Vickers Varsity piston-engined aircraft; apparently the auto throttle worked well on the Varsity. However, the only sensor that was used by BLEU to control the Varsity throttle servomotors was speed error, which was good enough for the Varsity because of the rapid response from the piston engines; if the aircraft was a bit slow the throttles would open responding to the speed error and the piston engines straightaway supplied the power and the correct speed was regained. For the Vulcan, with its large pitch changes and slow throttle response it was glaringly obvious that some 'phase advance' was needed in the system; in other words when the aircraft pitched up, for example, the throttles needed to open up immediately even though the speed had not significantly fallen, in order to anticipate the inevitable fall in speed that was going to occur. Because of the slow jet engine power response to throttle opening, if the throttles were not signalled to open immediately when the pitch of the aircraft was increased, then the speed drop would be very high and, in our tests, our attempts to choose a large throttle opening to compensate resulted in wild over controlling.

Unfortunately, BLEU did not take kindly to having their beloved auto throttle redesigned and so they suggested that the problem was in the location of our pitot static system. In fact we wasted nine flights removing filters and trying different pitot static systems before we gave up and told Smiths what needed to be done. Finally BLEU capitulated and let Smiths introduce the obvious necessary design change of adding pitch rate gyros.

While the pitch rate gyros were being prepared I had a couple of flights in the BLEU 707A, WZ736, to see how its auto throttle worked. I'm afraid I found the aircraft very unpleasant to fly and it took me all my time to make it go in the direction I wanted! Its stability in all three axes was not particularly good and I seemed to spend most of my time trying to control the aircraft, rather than observing the performance of the auto throttles. In fact the auto throttle, even without pitch gyros, did work better than on XA899 but then the engine response of the Derwent was better than the Olympus because the engine was running at a high power setting on the approach which helped enormously. My memory of the two flights therefore was not of the auto throttle but of the unpleasant nature of the aircraft handling and how well Roly had done selling the Vulcan to the MOD and the RAF. In retrospect perhaps I should have just flown the aircraft to get used to it first before trying to do tests; after all the aircraft was flying regularly with the BLEU pilots and I always remember what my flying instructor once said to me: 'It can't be very difficult, look at all the other .... people who are flying it.'

The Smiths engineers of course had realised the auto throttle problem straightaway but their hands had been tied by the initial BLEU design. Authority was now given to Smiths to introduce pitch rate gyros and, at the same time as the pitch gyros were being installed, the new pilot interface was introduced so that the desired airspeed could be selected easily and the auto throttles could be switched on and off in a sensible manner. On 11th March 1958 I flew with the pitch rate gyros and everything worked perfectly. We never had a moment's trouble with the auto throttle after that. To this day I cannot understand how BLEU allowed the system to come to us without pitch rate gyros and, even worse, why they argued with us after our flight tests had demonstrated the problem. It taught me a lesson never to trust experts implicitly but to think through problems myself.

Another task that was taking place at this time was the development of the Blue Steel missile and XA903 was modified at Langar for the carriage and dropping of this weapon. I had brought the aircraft back to Woodford on 27th January and on 19th April Jimmy flew with a missile on board for the first time. The first Vulcan drop was on 9th May 1958 though I had made quite a few drops earlier from the Valiant which was based at Woodford. In fact the Blue Steel posed no handling problems on either the Vulcan Mk 1 or Mk 2.

As we came to the conclusion of the Vulcan Mk 2 handling

programme on the first production Mk 2 XH533 in late 1958, the next production Mk 2s started to appear and the first two were earmarked for development work. XH533 was delivered to Boscombe for initial Mk 2 clearance in June 1959 and on its return it was prepared for automatic pilot clearance, followed by automatic landing trials. We used XH534 for engine handling, extending to higher altitudes the testing we had not been able to do on XA891. Because of this high altitude capability of the Mk 2 Vulcan, we were outfitted with partial pressure suits in case of pressure cabin failure, good for over 60,000ft. The equipment, including a pressure jerkin and an anti-g suit, was not very comfortable and was worn over an air ventilated suit so that connecting the various pipes and then strapping in was not the quickest operation in the world and certainly had the effect of slowing my starting drill. Still, all our various pipes were connected to a PEC, personal equipment connector, as we put on our flying equipment which greatly simplified the connection to the aircraft supplies since all we had to do was to 'snap' the connector into its socket by the ejection seat. We were meant to wear the gear above 40,000ft, but I suspect we only dressed up in the partial pressure suit if we were planning some long cruises above that height. At very light weights the Mk 2 could reach 58,000ft in the cruise but later with the Olympus 301 engines it was possible to coax and zoom up to higher altitudes. The highest altitude I remember reaching was 61,000ft but I could not maintain that height.

The production schedules started in 1959 but in fact there was an enormous amount of development work to do as quite a few new aircraft were diverted to the Skybolt programme, so we were extending the Mk 2 CA clearance, developing the engines, both Mk 201 and Mk 301, carrying Skybolt, whilst still using XH539 in Australia for Blue Steel trials.

After we had got CA release for the Mk 2 there was a difficulty with high altitude engine handling and XH560 was returned from the RAF to have it fixed after we had carried out our production schedule and cleared the aircraft. The engines kept on surging and going out; Bristol Siddeley looked at this and decided to cut back the engine low pressure stators by 2% and revise the fuel scheduling in the fuel control, but it seemed to take quite a long time for a solution to be found. Interestingly, the problem was due to the fact that the inboard engine was receiving some disturbed air from the air intakes and was therefore more prone to surge; however, Bristol Siddeley decided to modify all the engines to give flexibility on maintenance. Another annoyance with the engines was the enormous amount of black smoke emitted from the exhaust. At Avros we were not involved in ameliorating this but Bristols did a lot of work trying to compromise between acceptable engine handling and no smoke before they managed a modification approved by the RAF.

We were checking and developing the aerodynamics of the Vulcan Mk 2 the whole time, as we were now able to get to higher altitudes with the developed engines. By mid 1959 we felt we were ready to deliver an aircraft to Boscombe for CA release. We had been up to 58,000ft, covered the full cg range, flown at .95 IMN or just above testing the autostabilisers and their malfunctions. I had cleared the engine handling and got the behaviour surge free; also I had made sure the MFS worked including the ILS approaches. I had checked the full scale electrical emergency ejecting the RAT above 55,000ft and then using the AAPU from 30,000ft down. It had taken Jim and I about a year from XH533's first flight to getting it ready for CA release but of course the Mk 2 wing on 777 had been flying a year earlier.

The CA clearance at Boscombe went well and I soon got the aircraft back for the autopilot clearance. However XH533 did not have the production electronic countermeasures, ECM, back end fitted but all later Mk 2 aircraft did. There was some worry that at aft centre of gravity on the Mk 2, the bottom of the ECM bulge would hit the ground on landing and so a spring loaded strut was fitted to the bottom of the ECM which operated a warning light on the flight deck. In fact, even at aft cg I never saw the light come on nor, to the best of my knowledge, did I ever damage the ECM fairing despite the very high attitudes I used for landing.

I flew and cleared the autopilot in XH533 completely, including auto-ILS, for sending to Boscombe to get CA release in a comparatively short time in the spring of 1960; in fact it only took eleven flights which I thought was remarkably quick by any standard in those days

Vulcan Mk 2 with ECM fairing. (*Fred Martin RZF Digital*)

and showed how well the Vulcan Mk 2 handled as well as the autopilot. While XH533 was doing this work and then having the automatic landing equipment fitted, we used XH536 to check out the finer points of the MFS which was now called MFS1B and had a speed lock as well as a height lock fitted. We were able to adjust the glide slope pointer shaping so that Boscombe allowed the aircraft to be flown down to 250ft with a localiser lined up with the runway and down to 270ft with the then standard Bomber Command offset localiser, though I thought the 20ft difference was rather an unenforceable refinement!

XH533 re-emerged on 24th July 1961 with the auto throttle working and we started doing de-icing work at the same time as testing the auto throttle. This mixing of different tests was a very standard procedure since it enabled the testing of minor, but necessary, system work to be carried out without extra flying. The auto throttle gearings were optimised very quickly and we started looking at automatic landings three flights later. At this point I became aware of BLEU having made another, perhaps more serious, mistake in specifying the requirements for an automatic landing system. BLEU was convinced that it would not be possible for an aircraft using just an ILS localiser to land safely on a runway; it was thought that there would be too great a 'lateral dispersion', that is on some occasions the aircraft would land too far from the centre line and could even miss the runway on touching down. Consequently, BLEU persuaded Bomber Command to install localisers offset from the runway centre lines and, in addition, install a 'leader cable' for lateral guidance on the runway. This of course meant that electrical cables had to be installed on either side of the approach lights and down the sides of the runway; furthermore, every aircraft had to have a 'leader cable' receiver. The drill then on an automatic landing was for the aircraft to hold the localiser as usual down to about 300ft above the runway and then the leader cable receiver would lock on to the leader cable's signals. At this point the autopilot would turn the aircraft, normally left, and line up with the runway. In fact the system worked very well laterally and we had absolutely no problem at all while testing it. However, the extortionate cost to the RAF of this installation probably contributed to the fact that the system was never used operationally. In fact John Charnley, now Sir John, was sent to BLEU to sort out the leader cable fiasco but by then it was too late. It would be interesting to know how much the decision to have leader cables cost the MOD. It almost certainly not only caused the cancellation of the production Mk 2 automatic landing programme but also probably caused the UK to lose its global position, which it had in the late '50s, in developing automatic landing equipment for commercial airliners. Perhaps the BLEU engineers were striving for perfection in formulating their requirement for accurate positioning on the centre line on touching down; they clearly didn't realise that it only had to be good enough to meet the requirements. Perfection, like safety, costs money.

The flare of the aircraft during an automatic landing was controlled by a radio altimeter so we rapidly calibrated the device over the Bedford runway where we were doing our trials. Once done, events moved very swiftly and after about four flights we carried out our first automatic touchdown at Bedford where the leader cable was located. Two or three flights later after one of the landings I invited Ray Bray, a BLEU test pilot to fly with me to demonstrate the whole system to him; I knew him well from when he had been at Boscombe Down. It so happened that the following week was SBAC week and I was flying with Jimmy in the Avro 748. To my surprise I heard from the Procurement Executive department that administered our flying that I had been reported by a scientist in BLEU for carrying out our first landing without their permission. Nobody paid the slightest attention to the complaint but it showed very clearly how sensitive BLEU were at the time to the work we were carrying out and, probably, to our criticisms of some of their design concepts.

In fact, achieving our first touchdown was the start of a very long programme tuning the multitude of gearings through which the autopilot controlled the Vulcan, to get optimum performance. We discovered after our initial euphoria that we had a difficult problem to solve in that, despite all our efforts, the touchdown points were too widely scattered up and down the runway, excessive longitudinal dispersion as they say in the trade. The problem was caused by the ground effect of the Vulcan in that, as remarked earlier, the aircraft tended to float if the speed was too high and the autopilot was unable to make the aircraft touchdown. Conversely, if the speed was a bit slow the autopilot could not prevent the aircraft touching down too soon. In my opinion we wasted quite a few flying hours trying to solve this problem until I finally hit on what should have been the immediately obvious solution of varying the approach speed with the runway headwind component. We rapidly discovered that all we needed to do was to add 1 knot of speed for every 4 knots of headwind and the longitudinal dispersion became entirely acceptable. I understand that allowing for the wind speed is now normal procedure on some modern aircraft but at the time the problem had not been encountered. My log book shows that we only did automatic landings on one other aircraft before the automatic landing programme for the Vulcan was cancelled, sometime in the middle to late '60s. It was a very interesting programme and I got to know the people at Smiths Industries very well. I worked with them not only on the Vulcan but also on the Avro 748, the Nimrod and the BAe 146 when I was the initial project pilot, so that after I stopped flying they asked me to join them, in spite of my rude comments about their flight system.

There was a sequel to the automatic landing trials as we sent

XH533 down to Boscombe for CA clearance. They didn't seem to have any trouble with the gearings we had chosen but decided that in order to be able to give a full clearance it was necessary to explore the behaviour of the aircraft if all the autopilot pitch gearings were not 'nominal' but were at the limit of their tolerances, all at the same time. Jim Watts-Phillips was the pilot and he has described the final flight of the Boscombe autoland trials:

On 20 June 1967 I was tasked to carry out Autolandings at Bedford with the longitudinal gearings at 150 % over-geared. I believe this was towards the end of the programme and the Release to Service had already been given. The only proviso in the release was that, when an aircraft was first fitted with the system, an experienced Autoland pilot should flight test the aircraft just to check that the gearings were acceptable. This task was to be carried out by B Sqn pilots initially but handed over to the RAF as soon as they had gained sufficient experience.

The Autoland sortie was carried out in good conditions and, as the sortie progressed, the gearings were progressively increased to the 150% value. It was observed that the longitudinal behaviour of the aircraft became progressively more oscillatory. However, the round out to touch down was a two-phase motion with the pitch motion more and more exaggerated. The touchdowns were good although the final nose-up pitch became progressively more rapid. When all the gearings were set to the over geared value the aircraft was generally less steady but the round out was more exaggerated. However, the aircraft did not touchdown after the second phase and ballooned. The aircraft then went rapidly nose-down and I cut out the automatic control and attempted to rotate the aircraft nose-up, adding power. The aircraft struck the ground firmly and did not bounce, but the increase in power accelerated the aircraft and a roller landing was carried out as normal on our Autoland trials.

The aircraft was flown wheels down to Boscombe and a normal landing was made. However, after we were clear of the runway, the control tower reported some fluid leaking from the area of the undercarriage. The aircraft was shut down and towed to dispersal. It was found that the main attachment bolts of the main undercarriage bolts had sheared and the doom and gloom merchants predicted that the aircraft would not fly again. In any case its work as an Autoland test vehicle was complete and so there was no need to repair the aircraft. On examination, it was found that the damage was not severe and the aircraft flew a few months later. Examination of the instrumentation traces showed the exaggerated behaviour of the aircraft and, also, showed a touchdown rate of descent of 21ft/sec. However, this was not confirmed as the sensor on the undercarriage had failed. At the subsequent inquiry it was decided that if one were testing to the extreme, now and then there would be accidents.

To show how quickly A&AEE could react, by five o'clock I was presented with one of the undercarriage bolts, suitably mounted, with an engraved plate reading, "Presented to Flt Lt J Watts-Phillips to commemorate his arrival in the Autoland field!" Sadly, that "trophy" has been lost in my many moves since then.

I asked Jim why I had not heard of this incident since it was clearly a heavy landing and he told me that Boscombe decided that perhaps it might be better to keep the incident 'in house'. I can well understand such a decision since the combination of the autopilot gearings all set at 150% tolerance seems extremely unlikely and perhaps the tests might have been considered not particularly sensible and therefore unnecessary.

Besides autopilot development there was a lot of other work taking place. The key one was the decision taken in the late '50s to fit the Douglas Air Launched Ballistic Missile, called Skybolt, to the Vulcan. The USAF B52s were also going to carry Skybolts and so it was very much a joint development programme. The missile weighed 15,000lbs and two were to be carried by the Vulcan, one under each wing. For this to be possible the wing had to be strengthened which, as an added advantage, meant that it had a much longer fatigue life. The first carriage flight of the Vulcan with two dummy missiles was on 29th September 1961. We had planned the flight very carefully so I was not best pleased when, almost immediately after take-off as I was heading out of Manchester controlled airspace, I was called back by the tower to do a flypast. Apparently Sir Harry Broadhurst (by then our managing director) of Bomber Command and London airport accident fame, had an important government visitor he wanted to impress. So I reluctantly turned the aircraft round and flew twice past the clubhouse, very low and very noisily. In retrospect I suppose Sir Harry knew very well that if the handling had been questionable I would have refused to come back.

In fact handling the aircraft in flight with Skybolts was fine. If I hadn't known the missiles were there I doubt I would have noticed any difference from normal, though the drag was up slightly. The only place where the handling was significantly different was when landing. As discussed previously, the standard Vulcan had only a small ground effect if the landing speed was too high, but the Vulcan with two Skybolts attached had an enormous ground effect even landing at the normal speed, so that the aircraft would float down the runway without touching down. This effect was caused by the large size of the two Skybolts underneath the wing funnelling and keeping the air underneath the wing from escaping sideways. In effect there was a cushion of air between the aircraft and the ground which prevented the aircraft touching down. However, with my normal technique of keeping airborne as long as possible before touching down, the aircraft with Skybolts landed normally and the drag slowed the aircraft down without the need to stream the tail parachute. Jimmy was worried that this would cause a problem in RAF service but in fact I didn't believe it would, because the Vulcan squadrons had learnt from the moment they got their first Vulcans what a pain it was having to repack the tail parachute each time after landing; they adopted my landing method of keeping the nose well up before touching down and then using the aircraft drag to slow down and I am sure that they would have done exactly the same with Skybolts on.

It was necessary quite early on in the programme to try flying the aircraft with just one Skybolt on, since we had quite a few dropping trials to do and we would then return with only one missile. I remember the day very well, 29th September 1961. As usual we had a full briefing, the briefing group being headed by John Scott-Wilson who by now had become chief aerodynamicist after the retirement of Roy Ewans. I was told there would be no noticeable effect at all with one missile on, except for small amounts of rudder trim being required to remove the asymmetric drag effect. We duly taxied out, I opened the throttles fully and off we went. The aircraft immediately decided it wanted to leave the runway sideways, swinging towards the Skybolt, and I found that I needed full nosewheel steering, jabs of brake and then full rudder before hauling it into the air in a rather untidy manner. Once in the air everything was absolutely fine, exactly as predicted, with a little more work being required on directional trimming as the flight manoeuvres were being carried out. Landing too was no problem and there didn't seem to be any noticeable asymmetric ground effect on touchdown, which was good.

The take-off problem should of course have been realised straightaway but somehow we all missed it. The asymmetric inertia effect of having 15,000lbs on one side of the Vulcan was very significant indeed at high accelerations and Vulcan XH537 had Olympus 301 engines. We probably only had half fuel load so the aircraft would not have been very heavy which clearly accentuated the problem. These days the effect would have been discovered straightaway with design office simulators, but they didn't exist at the time. Again I am amazed that all those 'boffins' missed the obvious and I am still not pleased with myself for not anticipating the situation.

Like so many other programmes at about this time, Skybolt was cancelled, but not before I had had the opportunity to spend a month at Long Beach learning all about the missile, and not before I had had the opportunity to take XH535 out to Edwards Air Force Base for ground radio tests. Such a trip for a civilian pilot was a very rare event and it was my first visit to the States. Dickie Martin from No 4 ETPS Course was my co-pilot. He had joined us from Glosters having concluded the spinning trials on the delta Javelin; to me that had sounded like an incredibly demanding programme and I was glad we didn't have such excitements on the Vulcan. The ferry to Edwards highlighted one disappointing feature of the Vulcan, which was that despite its thick wing it really carried very little fuel because it was contained in bag tanks. At the time, Boeing 707s were flying non-stop to Los Angeles from London but we had to refuel at Goose Bay. Since the 707 made the West Coast in a day I was determined not to have to night stop at Goose and we did a quick refuel and carried straight on. However, we did score over the 707 when it came to cruising altitude; we started from Goose Bay at about 47,000ft and the FAA controllers were clearly not interested in what altitude we were flying, so we cruise climbed for maximum range.

It was an exciting moment when we started our let down for the dry lake. At first we could see nothing significant, just a lot of brown ground indistinct in a haze because even in those days the smog from the Los Angeles basin was drifting up into the desert. Gradually our eyes became accustomed to the varying shades of brown and we could distinguish the lake bed with its huge runway from the surrounding desert. We clambered down and were glad to be able to have a shower and change out of our ventilated suits and flying clothing; we had been wearing the kit for over twelve hours. The trip made me realise the huge size of the United States; it only took us four hours forty-five minutes to cross the Atlantic to get to Goose Bay but it then took six hours ten minutes to get to Edwards.

The following morning the aircraft needed to be moved to a deserted spot on the lake bed where the Douglas radio experts could make their measurements without extraneous radio interference. I had no idea where we were going and a pilot joined me who claimed to know the way. I followed his instructions only to find that I was stuck in a cul-de-sac, no room to turn round and a pile of rough stones between the aircraft and the test area. Rightly or wrongly I taxied over the stones only to learn later that I had ruined a complete set of tyres; the only saving grace was that the trials were able to be started straightaway while a fresh set of tyres was ferried out. Some weeks later when the aircraft was released to go home I took the opportunity to let Fitz Fulton, then in the United States Air Force, fly in the Vulcan and we managed to get some unique pictures of the aircraft formating on a B52. In return Fitz let me fly the B52 with him and he also organised a flight in a B47 for me with Jack Allevie who had done the No 14 ETPS Course; both flights were great experiences for me. I also joined the relatively new Society of Experimental Test Pilots based in Lancaster, California.

Ossie Hawkins, also a member of 14 ETPS Course, came back with me on the return flight which was uneventful except that the weather at Woodford was dreadful and at that time Woodford had no ILS. It was dawn, as we had not night-stopped on the way home, so Boscombe Down was not available. Manchester were very accommodating and let us land there, though I suspect we should have landed at a Bomber Command airfield. Dickie collected the aircraft the next day and unfortunately blew a lot of tarmac away as he taxied out, which did not make us too popular.

Unusually, I had yet another trip overseas in a Vulcan. This time it was the first production Vulcan Mk 2 XI1539 to be ferried to Edinburgh Field in Australia for Blue Steel trials. Johnny Baker was my co-pilot and by then he was nominated to be in charge of the Vulcan flying in Australia. To my surprise, no provision had been made to carry any spares and I had to plead for a parachute and one pair of wheels to be put in the bomb bay; what the spares problem was I never found out but I suspect it must have been an accounting one. The ferry started on 7th December 1961 and we went to El Adem and then Aden, where we were parked far away from the usual apron because of a royal visit. The next stop was Gan where there were showers passing through. As the weather cleared I touched down using aerodynamic braking, no parachute as usual and then lowered the nosewheel at about 60 knots. To my horror, when I applied some braking we started skidding, it felt like hydroplaning though we were well below the advertised hydroplaning speed. Luckily the brakes finally started to work and we managed to stop without going into the Indian Ocean, but it didn't do my blood pressure any good.

After landing the ground crew discovered we had a puncture in one tyre which turned out to be due to a Yemeni nail. There were no jacks but the ever resourceful RAF station ground crew constructed a wooden ramp for the good pair of wheels and towed the aircraft backwards up the ramp so that the punctured

Puncture at Gan.

View from officers mess, Gan.

tyre was in the air. Luckily the ramp had a stop at the end because as the wheels went up and got to the back of the ramp they carried the whole contraption along the tarmac for several yards, the undercarriage and aircraft skipping along in spasmodic jerks; without the stop the aircraft would have fallen off the end of the ramp and could have been severely damaged. Once stopped, the punctured wheel and its pair next to it, were in the air and the RAF soon had them changed. We lost a day but I didn't mind as I had my schnorkel and flippers with me and the officers mess was on the beach, with the most fantastic tropical fish swimming in the reef five yards off the shore.

The last leg of the ferry to Australia was from Changi in Singapore and at the time the airfield was still in RAF hands. It was only 2,000 yards long and the temperature would be about twenty degrees centigrade hotter than the standard atmosphere, during the day, ISA+20°C, which meant that the engines would not be producing their full 21,000lbs thrust. The Bomber Command crews refuelled at Darwin if they didn't have a bomb bay tank but I reckoned we could make Edinburgh Field non-stop. I elected to take off at dawn when the temperature had dropped maybe 5° to ISA+15. I had calculated the take-off distance required many times sitting at home in the pilots' office at Woodford and convinced myself that we could take off with full fuel, but when the morning came the airfield looked very short and I wasn't entirely convinced. I applied full power before releasing the brakes but it still seemed as if we used every yard of tarmac as we lifted clear with a big sigh of relief, from me anyway. The flight was six hours five minutes, five minutes shorter than the Goose Bay-Edwards leg but the difference was that we had no close diversion and could see absolutely nothing of Australia except a red cloud underneath us. We must have been making a contrail because I remember the delighted greeting we got from the controller at Broome as we coasted in with over three hours still to go. I suppose we could have landed and refuelled at Darwin but I hated stopping and starting and at least the flight showed what the aircraft could do.

As already mentioned, the Skybolt programme included fitting the Vulcan Mk 2 with Olympus 301 engines of 21,000lbs thrust. I collected the test aircraft XH784 on 9th August 1961 from Moreton Vallance, at that time the home of the Gloster Aircraft Company which made the Javelin and which was yet another Hawker Siddeley company. It was an incredibly powerful aircraft and was extremely sporting, bearing in mind the light weights at which we were flying. Furthermore, each aircraft had an engine rapid start capability from compressed air bottles which were pressurised from ground supplies so that all four engines could be started at once and thus enable the squadron Vulcans to scramble in the event of a missile attack.

The Bristol Engine Company had been taken over by Armstrong Siddeley in 1958 and at this time they had just got their flight test facility going at Filton. Vulcan XI1557 was allocated to Bristol Siddeley to develop the engines and arrived there after a false start, described in Chapter 7. They put first one 301 engine in the port inner position and then later fitted another 301. The installation was difficult as the aircraft was built for 201 engines and consequently I did a lot of the Olympus 301 engine testing to get initial CA release, but Bristol Siddeley also did a lot of work later improving the engine and the installation. In fact I did quite a bit of flying in the next couple of years developing the engine to get it to be surge free at extreme altitudes, which was a very time consuming business.

It was my ambition to fly the aircraft at the SBAC show to demonstrate its rapid start capability by getting it towed to the runway, getting the control tower to fire a red flare and then scrambling the aircraft in less than two minutes, but our new managing director, the aforesaid Sir Harry Broadhurst, would not agree since he said that one of his jobs was to get the development programme for the engine back on track; in fact I don't believe the programme had slipped from the target dates but Sir Harry had only just left the RAF and joined Avros and clearly wanted to show everybody what an effective manager he was going to be. This decision was a great disappointment to me but obviously I could do nothing about it. We could have taken off at less than 110,000lbs with 84,000lbs of thrust, a fantastic power weight ratio for a strategic bomber, but alas it wasn't to be. After we had cleared the engines, however, the RAF were able to demonstrate a four-aircraft scramble.

Looking back now at my log book I was amazed to discover that I did the first flight of the Olympus 301, the first autoland and the first flight with Skybolt missiles all within two months in August/September 1961. I must have been pretty busy at the time but it is only now as I write this, that I notice how close all these events were.

Extract from author's log book – first autoland.

Extract from author's log book – first Skybolt flights.

Extract from author's log book – first flight with Olympus 301.

The last piece of significant test work I did on the Vulcan was the maximum weight trials at 204,000lbs around October 1967. We did accelerate-stops, double engine-cuts on take-off and some performance measurements as well, all at Bedford. Interestingly, the aircraft was XH539, the one I had delivered to Australia for Blue Steel trials and had returned, its work successfully over.

Looking at my log book over the years we developed the Vulcan, it is interesting to see the amount of flying required. Overall I did a total of 850 flights in the Vulcans, 1,327 hours on 105 different Vulcans out of a total of 136 that were built including the two prototypes. The average length of a flight was thus one hour, thirty-four minutes which in my view is surprisingly long for test work. The flying was carried out on a number of aircraft and I made an analysis of my log book showing what the various aircraft were used for and the number of flights on each.

Vulcan Mk 2

Tail Number	Aircraft test programme	ALB flights
VX777	Initial Mk 2 handling	13
XA893	AC electrical development	26
XA891	Olympus 201 engine development	67
XA899	Automatic throttle	31
	MFS	
XH533	Confirmatory Mk 2 aircraft handling	111
	Boscombe acceptance aircraft	
	Flutter	
	Static position error	
	Negative g tests	
	Autopilot trials	
	Automatic landing trials	
XH534	Boscombe Down autopilot aircraft	36
	Blue Steel performance and carriage	
	Bomb bay tanks	
XH535	Skybolt radio systems	22
XH536	MFS1B development	14
	RAT tests	
XH537	Skybolt	19
XH538	Flight refuelling	9
	Skybolt	
XH539	Blue Steel	45
	High weight take-offs	
XH557	Handling squadron then Bristol Siddeley for Olympus 301 development	22
XJ784	Olympus 301 engine development	29

A Comparison with Concorde

The Vulcan had only two things in common with the Concorde, the shape and the name of the engine. There the similarity ended, apart of course from the ear splitting noise on take-off. The Concorde delta was very slender and the wing was comparatively thin and the Olympus had had many developments including reheat added at the back end.

I was fortunate enough to have a long trip in the second UK prototype Concorde and do a couple of landings. Unlike the Vulcan, the Concorde was speed unstable on the approach so that as the aircraft slowed down and the attitude of the aircraft got steeper, more power was required to maintain the slower speed. Consequently, automatic throttles were used on normal approaches and landings to make landing the aircraft a conventional operation rather than a very demanding test of skill. Whether there was something in the delta shape after all I don't know but my first landing scared me because the speed was incredibly low and I had not realised we were on the ground, due to the smooth runway at Fairford. Unfortunately, I made a second landing without the automatic throttles and this time we arrived with a very definite thump. It needed an experienced Concorde pilot to be able to make a steady approach and a good landing without the help of the automatic throttle.

The take-off seemed very routine though the rotation speed seemed ridiculously high at 180 knots and the speed at which it actually left the ground, unstick as we say, even more so at about 200 knots. John Cochrane, the deputy chief test pilot of the British Aircraft Corporation, was in the left hand seat and he asked me to take off following the commands from the flight director, which ensured that I kept to the correct acceleration profile as the aircraft built up speed.

In fact the RAE at Bedford had been developing a take-off director for the Concorde using Vulcan Mk 1 XA899 for flight testing. The right hand instrument panel had had the horizon and compass replaced with the Trident attitude indicator and situation display and the RAE control law was fed into the director bar on the attitude indicator. The real purpose of the RAE trials was to have a climb out law which would enable the pilot to fly at the optimum climb speeds even if there were some engine failures during the take-off. It took about 100 flying hours to optimise the director climb out settings and then RAE had the bright idea of trying the system out with 'dyed in the wool' airline pilots sitting in the tiny cramped flight deck of the Vulcan on an ejector seat without any coffee being served by the cabin attendants! The test pilot they chose to do this initiation was John Farley, later to be the great exponent of vertical take-off in the Harrier.

John managed to get sixteen worthies to try their luck and the trials were clearly an outstanding success despite the unusual environment for the airline pilots. The take-off director added an enormous safety benefit since engine failure on take-off in a Concorde required quite a large reduction of attitude to ensure optimum acceleration. One of the visitors was an examiner from the Civil Aviation Flying Unit who apparently expected, by reason of his position, to be accorded reverential treatment throughout the sortie. Somewhat peeved by this, at the end of the sortie John decided to show him what the big Vulcan wing could do. I can't do better than to quote from John's account of the proceedings:

Vulcan Mk 1 with take-off 'Concorde' flight director. (*John Farley*)

Vulcan buffs will know that the minimum threshold speed in RAF service was 125 knots, a speed determined not by lift requirements but by the need for good lateral control in turbulence. The day was lovely, with not a turb anywhere, so by half a mile out I was nicely settled on finals for runway 24 at 125 knots gear down and airbrakes out. At 100ft, as the security fence slipped beneath our nose, I used my right hand to stream the braking parachute, open the bomb doors and stop-cock the two inner engines while my left kept steadily raising the nose. The lovely monster reared right up and seemed to just hang in the sky before greasing on at a very low speed.

I lowered the nose, put on the brakes and stopped. Then I remarked that if he looked out of his side he would see that we were still a little short of the centre line of the main runway 27.

Getting no response, I looked across to find him rigid in his seat and just staring out of the front. I suspect he was in shock as we had only used the stub of 24 [the very short length at the beginning of the runway] or about 2000ft. Perhaps he thought he had died and was waiting to see some pearly gates appear. Showing him what could be done with a decent wing made me feel quite a lot better though.

Perhaps it was just as well that as a military pilot John did not need a civil instrument rating. Unfortunately, in spite of all the work that the RAE team did and the plaudits from the guinea pig pilots, the Concorde did not use the take-off director, which reminds me of the thirsty horse refusing to drink from the water in front of it.

CHAPTER 6

DEMONSTRATION FLYING

There are two, quite different, types of demonstration flying that a test pilot is required to do. Showing a new aircraft to a potential customer on the one hand and exhibiting the company's product to best advantage to the public at large on the other. Each task requires a different approach. For the Vulcan, of course, the only customer was the RAF and so Roly Falk's early flying demonstrations were crucial. As I have mentioned elsewhere, when I had occasion to fly the 707 later, I was appalled by the handling and appreciated even more the skill needed to successfully sell it to the RAF.

There is a temptation to think of demonstration flying as just a splendid thing to watch and it is not generally realised how vital such flying can be to the aircraft manufacturers who are trying to sell their aircraft, be it to the military or to the airlines. An occasion like the Society of British Aerospace Constructors show at Farnborough, now every other year but in the '50s every year, needs an airshow in parallel with the exhibition to draw the customers to the venue. But for the individual manufacturer, the flying display of its aircraft is vital, to prove that the aircraft is on schedule and of course to show how well it flies.

For a commercial aircraft, the vital thing is to get the people from the potential airline customers into the firm's chalet since, unlike most military programmes where there is probably one key customer, there will be many contracts with many airlines. With a military programme, the customer is almost certainly funding part if not all of the development work so it is vital to display the plane as early as possible, which is usually and inevitably at the most difficult part of the programme when all the problems are appearing and need to be cured. This was particularly true of the Vulcan with its revolutionary shape and the demanding specification to meet. The flying at Farnborough in the early 1950s, spearheaded by Roly Falk, put the aircraft 'on the map' and ensured that the programme would go ahead.

Demonstrating an aircraft to spectators on the ground is one of the more demanding tasks a test piloting organisation has to do, since one is pushing the aircraft to its limit whilst at the same time having to keep to the display organisation rules, as well as conforming to the crucial timing of the whole airshow. Not all test pilots are equally good at this task but certainly at Avros the job mainly fell to the chief test pilot or his deputy since, generally speaking, we were always demonstrating the newest aircraft and probably only they would have flown it. In the case of the Vulcans that we flew, all our major demonstrations were at Farnborough. In fact, in the eight years that Avros demonstrated the Vulcan, 1953 to 1960, only Roly Falk, Jack Wales in the 1953 formation year, Jimmy Harrison and I did the demonstrations. The precursors of the Vulcan, the 707s, were flown by Ric Esler, Roly and Jimmy Nelson, but other Avro test pilots and even some RAF pilots joined in when all the 707s and both prototypes were being flown in 1953.

Of course, there were a number of private Vulcan demonstrations at Woodford airfield and the first of these was the first flight of the full scale Vulcan on 30th August 1952, when Roly Falk flew the first prototype VX770 and showed it off to all the people who had designed and built the aircraft. At that time it was not called the Vulcan but was known by the manufacturer's design number of 698; Avros gave every new design a number, whether it flew or not so the Tudor 1 was the Avro 688 and the Tudor 2 the Avro 689. The Vulcan basic design was 698 and the models were called Avro 707s. The rocket fighter was the Avro 720, the supersonic bomber the Avro 730, the model 730s were designated Avro 740s and the civil airliner the Avro 748.

During the first flight of VX770, both main undercarriage fairing doors fell off when Roly put the landing gear down but, fortunately, no-one was hurt and in no way did this spoil this historic flight. After the flight Roly announced to the outside world that everything worked perfectly, but then I have never heard a test pilot, after a first flight, ever say how terrible it all was, however difficult it may have been.

In fact I did one Vulcan demonstration myself at Woodford on the first carriage flight of the Skybolts, but on that occasion I was an unwilling display pilot as I have described in an earlier chapter. Unplanned demonstrations are potentially very hazardous.

Tragically, the de Havilland 110 flown by John Derry crashed at Farnborough only a day or two after Roly's first flight in the Vulcan. This was on 6th September 1952 when the aircraft hit a lot of spectators and a total of thirty-one people were killed, including the two crew. Immediately following this accident new rules were introduced for display flying which, in summary, prevented aircraft from coming below 100ft and from turning towards the crowd. These restrictions made it very hard for a pilot to fly fast and still keep the aircraft in front of the spectators, since the required turns had to be done away from the airfield. The rules were relaxed in later years, but all the time we were flying the Vulcan we were subject to the 'no turns towards the crowd' rule which made demonstrations difficult for us, since we needed to keep the gap between consecutive runs as short as possible to avoid boring the crowd. This meant pulling maximum g out of sight of the crowd in order to turn the aircraft round while keeping the aircraft close to the ground, not a particularly desirable manoeuvre to say the least.

The new rules were enforced by a flying control committee composed of a knowledgeable collection of senior test pilots, an SBAC representative and the SATCO, senior air traffic control officer; the committee was chaired by the group captain flying at Farnborough who in reality had the last word. The supervision by this committee became stricter and stricter through the years as the wartime bravura of the pilots faded into the distance and the issue of safety became ever more important. Everything was recorded using the latest technology as it came along and there were more and more cameras filming every second of the display. The critical parameters were the height below which the pilot must not descend and the display line which the pilot was not allowed to cross and, therefore, get too close to the crowd. In fact these two rules were very sensible, since if an aircraft got too low or too close to the crowd it could only be seen by a relatively few people. It was the prohibition of turning towards the crowd that was the 'spoiler' as far as giving an 'exciting' demonstration was concerned.

John Cunningham was the de Havilland chief test pilot and had been a nightfighter ace during the Second World War, known affectionately as 'Cat's Eyes Cunningham' as a tribute to his apparent skill at seeing in the dark, though it later transpired that apparently he was using and testing the very latest top secret radar. He used to demonstrate the Comet and later the Trident by doing two decelerating flypasts, spaced minutes apart, so that the aircraft whistled by with the throttles closed. Everybody said how splendid his demonstration was, while Jimmy and I thought it was rather dull. But then it was the reaction of the marketing department that mattered, not what we as pilots thought.

The first public demonstration of the delta shape at Farnborough was the 707 VX784 in 1949 when the aircraft flew in for the static display on the Tuesday. It did not fly at the show because a lot of work including adjusting the controls was required before it would be safe to fly in a demonstration. In 1950 the 707B VX790 made its first flight at Boscombe on the Wednesday of show week, in the hands of Roly Falk. The moment the flight was over Roly took off for Farnborough and made a low pass in the blue-painted aircraft. It remained on static display for the rest of the week, again because there had not been time to adjust the controls and some of the systems.

In 1951 Avros managed to get their demonstration aircraft ready a month before the SBAC show which was unusual. The delta this time was the 707A WD280 and Roly flew it for the whole week doing an inverted run and demonstrating very rapid rolls as part of his display. He displayed very clearly the outstanding agility of the aircraft.

Meanwhile Jimmy Nelson flew the slow speed 707 VX790.

In 1952 Roly was being stretched because not only did he do the first flight of the first prototype Vulcan VX770 on 30th August, he also flew one of the 707s at Farnborough. In fact he had hoped to fly VX770 at the show on the Monday after positioning the aircraft at Boscombe but after he took off for Farnborough he had undercarriage problems again, a left over from the first flight when the fairings came off, and so he had to return to Boscombe. However, Tuesday was the big day when everything worked. The white Vulcan led a formation of the red 707B flown by Jack Wales and the blue 707A flown by the one-legged Jimmy Nelson. The formation then broke up and Roly demonstrated the Vulcan doing steep turns as if he was in one of the 707s, a spectacular performance. Unfortunately his routine had to change due to the crash of the de Havilland 110 later in the week.

Avros seemed to have had a tradition at that time of producing the aircraft they wanted to fly at the SBAC show only a day or so before the show itself. In fact the event was invariably the spur to getting the aircraft ready in time. In the case of VX770 the story goes that Sir Roy Dobson himself was at the flight sheds every evening with his wife, producing fish and chips for the servicing crew and telling everybody how vital it was for the aircraft to be at the show. He explained that the future of the Vulcan programme, and indeed of Avros itself, could depend on getting the airplane to Farnborough. At the time, with there being three V Bombers under contract and the competition with the Victor intense, Dobbie could have been absolutely right when he said that if the programme slipped and the Vulcan did not appear, the politicians in London might try to stop the project, saying that the delta shape was not possible. He realised only too well that once it had appeared and the spectators had been dazzled, it would be much harder to stop the Vulcan programme.

By 1953 the three deltas at Farnborough had grown to six. True to tradition, Avros managed to get the second prototype flying just before the show, so that five days later a perfect formation appeared of VX777 flown by Roly, VX770 flown by Jack Wales with, on one side two 707As, the original one flown by Squadron Leader Murley and a new one, WZ736, flown by Flight Lieutenant Hough. On the other side was the 707B flown by Flight Lieutenant Burton and a new twin-seater variant called a 707C flown by Squadron Leader Potocki. These 707s at the time were being evaluated by the RAF in Aeroflight and, consequently, it was agreed they could take part in the show. 'Spud' Potocki later became chief test pilot of Avro Canada. The entire formation was flown successfully for the first five days which was a triumph of servicing and organisation.

In 1954 there was just one Vulcan VX770 and it was flown by Roly again accompanied by Jimmy Harrison, who had just joined Avros from Aeroflight, as his second pilot.

In June 1955 Roly demonstrated XA889, the first production aircraft still with a straight leading edge, at the Paris airshow. However, Roly had decided that with Handley Page displaying the Victor in September at the SBAC show something special had to be done. On 31st August he took off from Woodford and he practised a few barrel rolls to the east of the Pennines; he used the barrel roll because in this type of roll there is some small positive g on the aircraft and crew throughout the roll, unlike a slow roll in a fighter-type aircraft when the altitude is kept constant and the pilot is hanging on the straps when the aircraft is upside down. Having perfected his technique he returned and then, at 1830, after the main body of people had left, he did an SBAC display, rolling the aircraft perfectly as he flew by. Incidentally, he never warned Ted Hartley and the rest of the crew in the back before doing these manoeuvres and of course they could only tell what was going on by looking up through the minute window in the roof or by the sunlight and shadows moving rapidly round the cabin. I gather from Ted that I was always more considerate when I decided to do aerobatics.

Roly knew that his first obstacle at Farnborough was going to be his firm, which had forbidden him to roll 770 the previous year at the show. His second difficulty was going to be the SBAC organisation who, egged on by Handley Page, would also try to stop him rolling the aircraft. His solution was not to tell anyone what he was going to do, except for Charles Gardner the commentator. On his second flypast he appeared climbing slightly and executed his barrel role in front of the SBAC president's tent. This roll caught the imagination not only of the aviation community but the world's press. The Vulcan was on the map as a UK icon and even now, over fifty years later, the thought of a Vulcan flying again has excited the public's imagination.

After two days flying XA890, Falk, forever afterwards called Roly by all who met him, was called in front of the service and civil aviation heavy breathers and told that he must not continue rolling the Vulcan as it was dangerous in so large an aircraft. Roly of course had anticipated such a reaction and produced his flight records showing that there was positive g on the aircraft all the time and the aircraft was climbing throughout the manoeuvre. However the die was cast, the 'top brass', politically and not technically driven, had made their minds up and that was the end of the rolls, for that year anyway. Roly felt it was no business of these people to interfere with the flying control committee who well understood the inherent safety of the climbing barrel roll and had made no objection. Unfortunately, though I went to the show from Boscombe that year it was later in the week when the rolling prohibition had been applied so I never saw Roly with his show stopper, though the commentator told us all about it.

However, the SBAC and the MOD could not spoil Roly's week of triumph, despite the attempted curbs by the bosses. Dobbie had,

Top: Vulcan VX777 with Mk 2 wing.

Bottom: Vulcan 770's leading edge breaking up during a flying display at Syerston.

Top: Early pressure clothing.

Middle: TSR2 engine disintegration, Vulcan XA 894, 3rd December 1962 at Filton. *(Rolls-Royce)*

Bottom: Vulcan Mk 2 XL390 on the tarmac at Glenview before the display accident, 12th August 1978.

unbelievably, managed to persuade Prime Minister Sir Anthony Eden to fly in the aircraft. When the show was over on the 6th, Eden was given some flying overalls and got into 890 followed by Dobbie who stood on the ladder between Roly and the prime minister, presumably to watch and possibly to prevent Roly rolling the aircraft! The flight, without aerobatics, went perfectly and the prime minster even flew the aircraft for a bit. Interestingly, one of the things that impressed Sir Anthony the most was the low noise level which he said was much less than the airliners he usually flew in.

Thanks to Roly's showmanship in 1955 the Vulcan has a secure place in British aviation history and if Vulcan XH558 does manage to fly again in 2007 there can be no doubt that once again it will attract the world's attention.

In 1956 Roly flew Vulcan XA892 at Farnborough and in 1957 Jimmy Harrison flew VX777 with the Mk 2 wing and Roly flew XA889 which was the first time the production Mk 1 had been seen in public. Also at the show was Rolls-Royce, flying VX770, now fitted with the Conway engine being developed for the Victor Mk 2.

As I have emphasised, the Vulcan was always a show stopper whenever it appeared, due to its dramatic shape, its nose high attitude on the approach and lastly, the enormous noise generated from its Olympus engines. While many tens of thousands of people have watched this magnificent machine flying at air shows, very few have been fortunate enough actually to fly the aircraft and even fewer have had the chance to do aerobatics in it during a show and for this reason I feel privileged to able to describe doing so.

*   *   *

Author flying Vulcan XA891 at Farnborough. (*A V Roe*)

I had the good fortune to fly the Vulcan for three years at the show, but the first time will always remain the greatest occasion in my memory. Vulcan XA891 had been fitted with the prototype Olympus Mk 201 engines and, at the time, the engines gave 16,000lbs of thrust each. As described elsewhere, we had discovered that we could do rolls off the top in the Vulcan, the so-called 'toss bomb' manoeuvre, and so I was very keen to exhibit this manoeuvre at Farnborough. Jimmy was taking the first production Vulcan Mk 2 down and we had been allotted just six minutes for our combined demonstration. We sat down and discussed what we both wanted to do and what was possible in the time scale.

Ideally, I would have liked to have taken off at the far end of the Farnborough runway so that I could start my pull up for the roll off the top in front of the crowd. I had already discovered that it was possible to do a roll off the top if I started from 270 knots, since there was just enough speed at the top of the manoeuvre, 145 knots, to be able to roll safely back to level flight. I knew from tests at Woodford that I would have 270 knots at the end of the Farnborough runway. However, taking off from the far end of the runway would have caused some problems for Farnborough Air Traffic and, if it was a windy day blowing from the west, I might not have enough speed to start my pull up at the end of the runway. I decided therefore not to press with Jimmy the idea of taking off from the wrong end.

Jimmy of course was constricted by the demonstration rule of not turning towards the crowd and, in the end, our plan was for Jimmy to take off first, being immediately followed by me. I would then do two rolls off the top and turn downwind for landing. Jimmy would do another two runs including a roll and then land in turn. Unfortunately, in true Avro tradition it was a cliff hanger deciding whether the first production Mk 2 XH533 was going to be ready to go to Farnborough; to be on the safe side we positioned VX777 at Farnborough which was aerodynamically the same as the Mk 2. Luckily, XH533 did just make it and Jimmy did not have to fly VX777 since its structure was damaged as explained in the next chapter. On Wednesday, after the show, I flew it back to Woodford and only then was the damage discovered.

The great day finally arrived, it was a Saturday, and we set off for Farnborough. There were three of us in my aircraft, Dicky Proudlove, one of my regular flight test observers in the right hand seat, and Eric Burgess was my AEO. One of the interesting facets of flying military aircraft at Farnborough was that the aircraft was leased back to the company and was no longer flown under Procurement Executive operating rules and procedures. The AID inspector duly cleared the aircraft for flight and then we had to sign the paperwork with all the small print. Avros had then to insure the aircraft for third party damage themselves and, I imagine, the premium must have been enormous.

The first thing we had to do on the way down was to have our photos taken from an elderly four-piston-engined Handley Page Hastings transport aircraft, with the rear freight door removed so that what seemed like an enormous number of photographers could lean out into the slipstream in turn to take pictures of the aircraft they fancied. Avro's photographer, Paul Cullerne, was clearly visible and as I formated behind and to the right of the Hastings I could see him gesticulating for me to go in, out, up, down until he was satisfied. When the photography session was over I landed behind Jim who had already had his picture taken.

Saturday was practice day to have our display watched and authorised by the flying control committee. However, in 1958 things were a bit more relaxed than in later years and the committee was chaired by Group Captain Pat Hanafin who was a splendid pilot and very understanding officer. He appreciated that all the pilots flying their aircraft wanted to put on the best display they could, not only to please themselves but also to please the marketing guys in the firms' chalets. I remember I heard one of the bosses at Hawker Siddeley remarking 'our pilots are never put under pressure', but the facts were that inevitably we were all under pressure and, as described elsewhere, pressure is a great generator of accidents.

Jimmy and I taxied round to the take-off point of runway 25 and I looked across and saw what looked like thousands of flags streaming in the breeze with serried ranks of chalets climbing up the hill to the south of the runway. Air Traffic called Jimmy on to the runway for take-off and, as he commenced his take-off run, I followed and lined up XA891 behind him on the runway. I opened all four throttles in anticipation of clearance from Air Traffic and stood hard on the toe brakes. I heard 'Vulcan Two you are clear to go' and opened the throttles up to full power. The aircraft shuddered and slithered on the runway as I waited until there was full power on all engines; the noise was enormous inside the aircraft and it must have been deafening outside, getting everybody's attention. Of course one of the features of flying at Farnborough was that nobody carried much fuel because the lighter the aircraft the livelier the display. I had therefore elected to have only 5,000lbs of fuel per engine which made the total weight 105,000lbs with 64,000lbs of thrust from the engines. Consequently, when I released the pressure off the toe brakes I was not disappointed; the aircraft leapt forward like a startled deer.

I hauled the aircraft into the air at about 130 knots and then had to push the stick forward as hard as I could to prevent it from climbing since I needed XA891 to accelerate quickly so that I was as close as possible to the spectators when I started the pull up. It was necessary to push the electric trim control switch at the top of the stick continuously to try to keep the push force from getting out of control as the aircraft hurtled down just above the runway at an unbelievably fast rate. The end of the runway rushed towards us and as soon as I had my target pull up speed of 270 knots I had to stop pushing the stick like a lunatic and immediately start pulling back and rotating the aircraft in order to start the climb straight up and over without overstressing the aircraft.

We had fitted a very large accelerometer to the instrument panel and Dicky started calling out the accelerations. Normally, the aircraft would be limited to 2.4g but as it was very light we had a special dispensation to apply up to 3g. Dicky's job was to call out the g all the time and my job was to try to keep to 3g without ever exceeding this limit and possibly causing the aircraft to break up. Of course we had been practising this manoeuvre at Woodford and I think we all knew, as we were pressed into our seats by the application of g, exactly what 3g felt like. Dicky, I suspect, called 3g more rapidly and more often if he thought I was pulling too hard and likely to go over the limit.

I also had to try to keep the wings level, but the view out of the Vulcan's windscreens was so poor it was very difficult to do this with any certainty. As we were pressed down in our seats it seemed to take for ever for the ground to appear, albeit upside down, in the windscreen letter box slits in front of us. Eventually it showed up, but by this time the speed had dropped to below 150 knots, which was by no means the optimum speed to half roll a Vulcan! Applying full aileron generated a lot of adverse sideslip and so it was necessary to apply full rudder at the same time. The aircraft reluctantly rolled the right way up but there was no time to celebrate.

I slammed the throttles shut and dived down just in front of the crowd and then pulled up for another roll off the top. At the top, after rolling out, I turned left downwind for landing and with the power almost completely off I managed to touch down just in time before Jimmy came towards me on his first run. The whole trip took three minutes and nineteen seconds. Obviously, I was feeling pretty pleased with myself but some of the gilt was taken off the gingerbread when we heard in the Empire Test Pilots School bar that night that the Handley Page Victor had also done a roll off the top. Whether they had heard on the grapevine what we were doing I don't know, but it was a bit disappointing; I consoled myself that Johny Allam had only done one Immelmann and he was already airborne and therefore had lots of airspeed when he started, whilst we had done two in succession from a standing start. Incidentally, the ETPS bar was always the meeting place for the test piloting fraternity during the Farnborough show and as we were staying in the Queen's Hotel just across the road we could walk over. Farnborough never seemed quite the same after the Empire Test Pilots School was moved to Boscombe Down some years later.

The following day, Sunday, we had to go to the morning briefing in the pilots' tent to hear about the weather, receive the very important first briefings from Pat Hanafin and get the flying programme for the day. Sunday, the first day of the show, was a long briefing as every detail was discussed so we all knew exactly what has going to happen. In fact the programme varied from day to day because firms were often bringing in new aircraft at the last moment, aircraft were going unserviceable or it was a public day and the three services were joining the display programme – whatever the reason there were always some changes and the SATCO always brought a pile of sheets with the day's programme listings. The display was controlled to the nearest minute so it was vital to know what was going on and note carefully the aircraft immediately ahead since, even if the show timing went wrong, the day's order was seldom changed. We had lunch in the pilots' tent which was situated by the control tower near the start of the main runway and on the opposite side to the exhibition and chalets. It was a wonderful social occasion for us, meeting all our friends, most of whom we hadn't seen since the previous Farnborough. Of course, watching the show from the pilots' tent gave a false impression of the individual displays in some ways, since they were naturally aimed at the chalets and the customers, quite a long way down the runway from our tent.

As our flight time approached we got changed in a room at the bottom of the control tower, got into our cars parked in our special car park and drove out to where the Vulcans were parked, situated a long way from the runway. Cars were vital at Farnborough and especially the 'sticker' on the windscreen. Unless one had the right sticker it was impossible to get from the chalets to the pilots' tent and from there to the aircraft. Once there we slowly got settled in and waited first for our clearance to start, then to taxi, and finally for take-off. This time there were photographers standing very close to the runway and we could see lots of people watching from the steps between the exhibition hall and the chalets. We saw the aircraft ahead of us in the programme land and then we were cleared for our display. Our exhibition was uneventful if it is possible to use that description about any SBAC display and, in particular, a Vulcan aerobatic one. Once again, three minutes nineteen seconds later we were on the ground. I taxied slowly back to the parking area wondering if there was any way I could have improved the flying.

The next day I was still feeling extremely pleased with myself and decided to have lunch in the Avro chalet rather than in the pilots' tent. Philip Kidson, the very experienced public relations officer, nowadays probably called public relations executive, sat me down somewhere, I've forgotten who I was with. To my delight I saw our managing director, Jimmy Kay, rushing over towards me and I was pretty confident what he was going to say. However I'd got it wrong. 'Hurry up with your lunch, we need your table' was his only comment.

Looking back, I realise that Jimmy Kay's remark was extremely good for me. It cut me down to size at the right time. I don't think for one moment he meant to deflate me but it certainly did; he was just ensuring that the official guests were going to be able to sit down when they arrived. As I got up to leave, Philip Kidson told me that a lot of the secretaries wanted to fly in the aircraft. I couldn't believe it. We had two spare seats since Eric Burgess was as usual also the navigator, but it was terribly claustrophobic in the back with only two tiny windows situated in the roof. It would be like the worst fairground ride in the world. Nevertheless, Philip told me that the secretaries were really keen and so I agreed to allow one at a time; Eric briefed them each morning on how to escape in the event of an emergency so that they were ready in the afternoon. In fact, if anything had happened it would have been most unlikely that they could have got out of the aircraft using the escape chute since we would have been too close to the ground. Furthermore, if by chance the landing gear was down it would have been impossible, since the escape chute was in front of the nose gear. However, we were fully booked all week with people wanting a ride during the show. As far as I remember Jimmy didn't have any passengers, but whether that was because he didn't want any or because he had not made any arrangements I don't know.

At the weekend, my wife Margaret arrived and wanted to know what was going on. She immediately said that if the secretaries were going to fly then she wanted to fly as well and on the final Sunday she had her turn. She asked me afterwards whether having her on board made any difference to my flying, and I just managed to hide my astonishment. Those three minutes were frantically action packed and there was certainly no time for extraneous thoughts. However, I managed to murmur some non-committal reply. It has always been my view that pilots do the best they possibly can, regardless of the passengers in the back. Certainly, whenever I was in an aircraft I would always try to get it down smoothly and of course safely, whatever the weather, who I had on board or indeed anything else.

It was the tradition then that at the end of the week all the pilots and their partners, they were usually wives in those days, were invited to the SBAC president's tent for a champagne reception. It was a great occasion which was very enjoyable, except that I made the mistake of thinking the champagne was going to run out, for the first and only time in my life.

In the morning it was time to go home and back to the real world. Margaret said she didn't fancy going back by train on her own, and so I offered her the right hand seat of my Vulcan which was spare because Dicky had gone home and Ted Hartley had driven down so wanted to drive back. As I mentioned before, I could have flown the aircraft by myself since I had discovered that I could push the pressurisation switches on after take-off with the end of the cg slide rule. Anyway I rather fancied showing off the Vulcan to an appreciative audience.

We made an early start with Eric Burgess, my AEO who had been with me all week. On the return to Woodford I did one or two rolls to show Margaret how it was done and we landed uneventfully. I knew that Leysa Falk had flown in a Vulcan with Roly so I checked if she had flown in the pilot's seat. She told me that she had only flown in the back, so Margaret was the first lady to fly in the right hand seat of the Vulcan and I suspect that there may have been only one other, Maureen Harrison, Jimmy's wife. In fact when Maureen discovered that Margaret was coming back with me on the Monday morning, she virtually insisted that Jimmy should take her back in the front. Jimmy was a superb test pilot but not an early riser and, unfortunately for him, the weather was deteriorating at Woodford by the time he took off, at about lunch time. The problem was compounded by the fact that XH533, which Jimmy was flying, had the Smiths Military Flight System installed which he detested and normally he flew with an RAF liaison officer, Max Savage, who would lean over and set Jimmy's compass. On the return flight to Woodford, Jimmy was faced with having to fiddle with the compass card himself as well as trying to land in the poor weather. Woodford at the time had no ILS and only had a radar which gave positioning relative to the runway centre line. How Jimmy managed to land I shall never know; the visibility was extremely poor and it took him three goes, but then he was a magnificent pilot. We all had nightmare visions of the aircraft landing at Manchester airport and Maureen having to get out onto the tarmac. We never took wives up again.

My final memory of my first SBAC show was the comment from my friend and expert Polish aerodynamicist in flight test, Zbigniev Olenski, who had visited Farnborough during the week. He said rather dismissively, 'I watched your rolls off the top but they were not quite straight.'

Regrettably, I have only managed to find one poor video of the aircraft doing a roll off the top and I have been unable to find any still pictures, though I do remember seeing a splendid shot of the Farnborough runway with a vertical Vulcan at the far end and a spectator next to the runway with his hands over his ears.

Sept	1	Vulcan	XA891	Self	S. Robinson	S.B.A.C Show
Sept	2	Vulcan	XA891	Self	R. Proudlove	S.B.A.C Show
Sept	4	Vulcan	XA891	Self	R. Proudlove	S.B.A.C Show
Sept	4	Vulcan 2	VX777	Self	—	Farnborough - Base
Sept	4	Anson	GAGPG	Self	R. Pogson	Base - Farnborough
Sept	5	Vulcan	XA891	Self	E. Hartley	S.B.A.C Show
Sept	6	Vulcan	XA891	Self	E. Hartley	S.B.A.C Show
Sept	7	Vulcan	XA891	Self	E. Hartley	S.B.A.C Show
Sept	8	Vulcan	XA891	Self	M. Blackman	Farnborough - Base

Extract from author's log book.

I flew for many years at Farnborough, but only twice more in a Vulcan. We were never allowed to do aerobatics again because a few weeks later the first Vulcan prototype, doing a demonstration at RAF Syerston on their open day, had a structural failure of the wing and crashed killing all the crew; what happened is discussed in detail in the next chapter and gives my personal opinion that the aircraft's structure was almost certainly damaged before it took off.

Looking back at my Vulcan demonstrations at Farnborough, I realise now that I did not make the most of my opportunities, though as I have mentioned, we were hampered by the rules following the John Derry accident. First of all, when landing the Vulcan Jimmy told me that he used to like landing in the 'bottleneck', the narrow bit of tarmac at the start of the runway. Unwisely I followed his example and always tried to touch down as slowly as possible right at the beginning of the runway, opposite the pilots' tent.

This was extremely satisfying for the ego but quite useless as a demonstration of the landing ability of the Vulcan because no one in the chalet area could see it landing, incredibly slowly in a fantastic nose-up attitude like a praying mantis; the pilots in the pilots' tent loved it but for the chalets to have seen the approach and touchdown it would have been necessary for me to touch down not earlier than the correct 'displaced' touchdown point, clearly marked on the runway, to be visible from the Avro chalet. When I was having my first lunch in the Avro chalet at the beginning of the week, I should have realised this but it was not until some years later when I was flying the Nimrod that I started to optimize my display for the guests in the company's chalet.

The other point about landing was that we always chose to do a left hand circuit, which meant that the aircraft was invisible to the onlookers until after touchdown. We clearly should have done a right hand circuit, but I was nervous of relying on the person in the right hand seat for accurate positioning. The difficulty, once again, was down to the poor visibility out of the Vulcan and, from the left hand seat, there was absolutely no view of the runway out of the right hand side. Perhaps I should have flown the aircraft from the right hand seat but it would have taken a lot of practice. In the Nimrod in later years I did do right hand circuits with an experienced pilot in the right hand seat, but even then I remember very nearly having to be diverted because we had overshot the runway centre line and the first thing I saw as I rolled level was the runway in a seemingly impossible position on our right. Somehow I rescued the situation and there was a splendid shot in *Flight* magazine of the aircraft very steeply banked about to touch down, rectifying the situation.

In the other two years when I flew the Vulcan at Farnborough we had only time for two runs and our difficulty was always that turning the aircraft out of sight of the crowd took a long time, though we were working like crazy applying large angles of bank and g. In retrospect we should have kept the speed right down so that we would have spent less time turning the aircraft. After all, the best view of the Vulcan was always flying very slowly with a very steep attitude. However, hindsight makes things very easy.

The wind was always very important during display flying, particularly when turning. An 'on crowd' wind was the most challenging since it meant that if care was not taken it was difficult to stop the aircraft crossing the display line. Because of the Derry restrictions the Vulcan display was not too affected by the wind, but if the wind was away from the crowd then doing a tight left hand circuit could mean that the turn onto finals was tighter than planned. I well remember looking down on the Farnborough houses whilst turning finals with what seemed like well over 60° of bank.

I only blotted my copybook once at Farnborough. In my eagerness to land as early as possible on the runway, or even the bottleneck, in my competition with Jimmy, I misjudged things in the rain. In the ETPS bar that night I was ribbed for landing on the grass. In the morning I drove out to the bottleneck and to my chagrin I saw some very light tyre tracks about six feet to the left of the bottleneck and ten feet short of the start of the main runway. By chance I met Pat Hanafin in the exhibition hall a bit later and I immediately apologised to him. He told me not to worry. Nowadays it would be a 'cause celébre' and I suspect that we would be sent home.

In summary, in the many years I spent flying at Farnborough, I detected that the stature of the display pilots decreased steadily through the years. In the '50s, pilots like Roly Falk, Neville Duke and Peter Twiss were almost worshipped, but later on the demonstration pilot was regarded as just doing a routine job. The pilot was viewed as just one member of the team developing an aircraft and it was considered that it would be wrong to over emphasise his or her importance. In fact that view was probably the correct one, except perhaps for John Farley bowing to the crowd in his Harrier, since in later years aircraft became easier to fly and there were automatic control systems between the pilots' stick and the controls themselves, which were vitally important in protecting it and making it safer to fly. Nevertheless, flying at an air display will always make the adrenalin flow for the pilot, even if the chief designer is unimpressed.

* * *

Before leaving the subject of demonstrations it should be mentioned that towards the end of its life, the RAF had a Vulcan display team initially using XL426 as a great publicity and advertising tool. However, the airplane was switched to XH558 since it had more flying hours left before needing a major overhaul. The type of display was very different from the type we were able to do at Farnborough because, generally speaking, they were allotted more time and because by then there were no restrictions on turning towards the crowd.

The RAF very sensibly issued a document in 1979 on Vulcan display flying in which I learnt for the first time in the introduction that apparently, despite the request from the MOD for us not to do aerobatics, there was an RAF Vulcan flown at a Paris show in the early '60s doing rolls off the top. The introduction goes on:

> However our imagination may be fired by these displays, reality controls the event, and aircraft fatigue and other considerations dictate that the limits set out in Group Air Staff Orders 1-1-8 are to apply. The aircraft is impressive anyway, and the best use of its qualities must be made within the limitations laid down whilst observing the most rigorous Flight Safety Parameters.

The limitations imposed by the Group Air Staff Orders, GASO, were 45° of bank in a steep turn, 90° bank in a teardrop turn, and not below 500ft. The teardrop turn is an ideal demonstration manoeuvre for the Vulcan as by doing a climbing wingover at low speed, rolling and then letting the nose drop, the g is kept low and the aircraft is kept in front of the crowd. I shall always regret not being allowed to do this manoeuvre myself at Farnborough because of the Derry rules in force at the time.

I am grateful to Guy Bartlett for the diagrams shown below, taken from his web site[4]. The pictures in fact are taken from the GASO order referred to above. As can be seen, there were seven flypasts specified and, by the look of the diagrams, the aircraft very sensibly flew at a slow speed.

The GASO finishes with a section on pitfalls and understandably the first pitfall mentioned is the wind to which I referred earlier and would be very critical for the type of display shown above. There is another very valid caution in the document called 'Extemporization'; the [4]

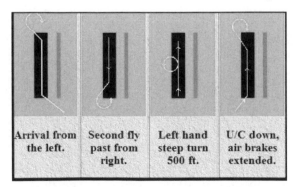

| Arrival from the left. | Second fly past from right. | Left hand steep turn 500 ft. | U/C down, air brakes extended. |

http://www.users.zetnet.co.uk/mongsoft/vulcan display flight page all.htm

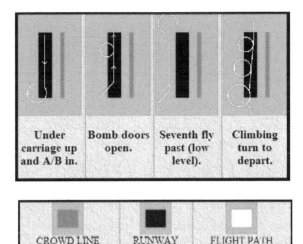

Under carriage up and A/B in.	Bomb doors open.	Seventh fly past (low level).	Climbing turn to depart.

CROWD LINE	RUNWAY	FLIGHT PATH

display pilot is warned never to agree to an extension of a programme in the middle of a display, or even a curtailment, since this could lead to getting into dangerous situations and, certainly in my experience of demonstrating aircraft, the warning is a very sensible one, particularly extending a demonstration off the cuff. Furthermore, anything which upsets the timing for other aircraft could be potentially dangerous and certainly annoying.

As has been said, the RAF did a magnificent job demonstrating the Vulcan in the UK and all over the world and, hopefully, XII558 will be able to 'take up the torch' and continue the tradition.

CHAPTER 7

INCIDENTS
AND ACCIDENTS

As has been previously mentioned, flight testing an aircraft has two key objectives, first to try to make certain that the aircraft will be safe to be flown by the 'worst' pilot likely to be authorized to fly it within the conditions specified by the aircraft limitations. The second objective is to try to ensure that the performance of the aircraft fulfills the requirements laid down when it was ordered by the customer. Very often, meeting the performance requirements makes satisfying the handling requirements much harder to meet; for example, in military terms a particular armament requirement might demand a very aft centre of gravity.

Judgement on the acceptability of aircraft handling is often very difficult and pilots may disagree on what is acceptable. This very often occurs between the aircraft manufacturer's pilots and the acceptance pilots, though in the case of the Vulcan I cannot recall any significant disagreements, possibly because both the firm's pilots and the acceptance pilots had been trained at the RAF Empire Test Pilots School and knew the standard required. However, one method of judging whether the handling qualities of an aircraft is or was indeed acceptable is by looking at the incidents and accidents that eventually occurred.

Unfortunately, it is very difficult to find and explore unusual occurrences that have happened to a military aircraft, as distinct from civil ones, because the proceedings of the Boards of Inquiry are seldom made available to the general public, though some stories are passed on by word of mouth. It is of course a pity that even after the thirty-year cooling off period permitted by the Freedom of Information Act the proceedings are not put in the public domain, though the reluctance of the services to make available some of the accident documentation is understandable since, even after thirty years, the circumstances of some accidents may still be very upsetting to the relatives, particularly if fatalities have happened. However, another consideration which might be relevant is that there is reluctance within the services, encouraged by the government, not to let the reports of any Board of Inquiry be made available since they might disclose mistakes that were made which could be subjects for criticism.

Incident and accident investigations are particularly important on aircraft that are currently in service, whether military or commercial or private flying for that matter, in order to understand immediately why something happened and try to take action to prevent a similar event occurring. The Vulcan is of course no longer in squadron service, but in fact there were about nineteen major accidents, as distinct from incidents, listed for the Vulcan and all were investigated; about nine of the listed occurrences might be attributed to crew error but these issues are never clear cut. As explained, not all the documents investigating the accidents are available and, consequently, some of the description and analysis below will inevitably be subjective. Nevertheless, it is felt useful to consider and comment on each incident or accident as appropriate. Of course, the problem with the government not allowing disclosure is that incorrect conclusions may be drawn when the accidents are discussed, as inevitably they will be. The object of this chapter is not to go into any details of the people concerned but merely to discuss the cause of each occurrence and consider what lessons can be drawn.

One final but very important point about investigations into a happening is that there may be different opinions for the cause of the event. As a general rule, it is always easy to blame the crew, particularly if they are not available to debate the investigating board's conclusions, but the reasons why a crew member makes a mistake may be due to the design of the aircraft requiring the crew to do more than they can reasonably be expected to do; this point sometimes gets overlooked.

This dilemma in accident investigation is best illustrated by the terrible accident to the Chinook helicopter on 2nd June 1994, taking some extremely important intelligence people from Northern Ireland to Scotland. The aircraft hit the mountainside in the Mull of Kintyre and the Board of Inquiry found that the pilots had been guilty of gross negligence. The decision of the board has been, and still is, a subject of debate because there was no substantive evidence and no flight data recorder. It is difficult to believe that the crew would have flown in cloud below the safety height which would have been a major consideration in their planning. Furthermore, there were problems with the digital engine control which had been reported by A&AEE, Boscombe Down. The authorities were very sensitive to the report of this accident since there was some criticism of the decision to send the whole of such an important team in one aircraft. The reason for the accident will never be fully understood but it is a very good example of how careful a board should be in coming to definite conclusions on the cause of an accident.

Aircraft design teams and their test pilots are always asking themselves whether something could have been improved, whether something could have been done differently or if more warnings of certain flight conditions should have been given? This is always a major concern. The test pilot is always having to make decisions on whether something is safe *enough*, since nothing is intrinsically and totally safe. It is all a matter of judgement. If one tries to make an aircraft too safe it becomes too expensive; as I have mentioned elsewhere, I was always teaching my pilots that safety costs money. For this reason I have looked at the incident and accident record of the Vulcan to try to see if we got it right. I have tried to classify the incidents into types of occurrences – landing accidents, asymmetric approaches, display flying, low flying pilot error, engine malfunction, electrical failures and miscellaneous occurrences. The listing and discussion will take place in this order though the classification of each accident into a particular grouping may be debatable.

LANDING ACCIDENTS

Vulcan Mk 1 XA897   1st October 1956   London Heathrow
This accident was the first major one concerning the Vulcan and has been analysed *ad nauseam*. It took place when almost the whole UK aviation world was waiting for it to land at London's Heathrow airport after completing a brilliant world tour. On approach, the aircraft hit the ground short of the runway, went briefly up into the air again and then crashed. The two pilots ejected and survived but the four rear crew members were killed; with the nose undercarriage leg down they had no chance of escape.

Vulcan XA897 was the first aircraft to be accepted by the Royal Air Force and it had been decided that it should go immediately on a world tour after delivery to 'show off' the RAF's new bomber. The captain was Squadron Leader Howard who had been with Avros for many months at their Woodford aerodrome, flying with the firm's test pilots while they were testing all the early Vulcans prior to CA release. Air Marshal Sir Harry Broadhurst, C-in-C Bomber Command was in the co-pilot's seat. In the back there were three RAF crew from Waddington, the AEO, the navigator and a Vulcan co-pilot, part of Howard's official crew; in addition there was an Avro support engineer.

The plan was that the final leg of this world tour should land at London Heathrow to massive publicity but, as bad luck would have it, the weather was not good. At the time of the accident it was given as calm, heavy rain, visibility 1,100 yards, scattered low cloud at 300ft and 7/8ths cloud at 700ft.

The accident raised all sorts of questions in the newspapers and discussions were played out in the full spotlight of publicity. One question was how was it that the pilots had ejection seats and not the rear crew? Another question was whether the landing radar being used at the time, called Ground Controlled Approach, GCA, was being operated correctly. However, if more cogent questions were being asked such as querying why this military aircraft was landing at a civil airport or why, if it was planned to land there, it wasn't fitted with the standard civil approach equipment, the Instrument Landing System, ILS, it was not at all obvious.

Besides the standard RAF Board of Inquiry, there was a special limited investigation of the accident by a Dr Touch to check the correct functioning of the GCA, because the GCA was being severely criticised as being a likely cause of the accident. In fact Dr Touch in his report remarks:

> At the time of the accident there was mist and slight drizzle in the region of the runway threshold. Horizontal visibility looking outwards along the centre line was about 800 yards. The aircraft was seen over the airfield at ranges in excess of 1,000 yards.

The report mentions heavy rain but goes on in the next paragraph:

> Further back along the approach path, at approximately 1¼ nautical miles from touch-down, horizontal visibility at ground level was around 200 yards, but the aircraft was seen at a distance of about 400 yards. In this area it does not appear to have been raining heavily, observers speaking of mist and slight drizzle.

The pilot was passed the weather and elected to make an approach. The aircraft was not equipped with an ILS indicator and the supporting radio receivers which was the standard civil approach aid, but Heathrow had a GCA and so the approach was made using this equipment. At about 2,000 feet short of the runway and 250 feet north of the 10 Left runway the aircraft touched the ground just as engine power was being applied according to eyewitnesses. It then rose back in the air followed by the two pilots using their ejector seats and baling out. It hit the ground and broke up. The fact that the aircraft was not able to continue flying after it had hit the ground was almost certainly due to the geometry of the Vulcan structure and controls. In the design of the aircraft, the two Vulcan main undercarriage legs were prevented from swinging backwards and forwards by two very strong folding links, one for each undercarriage leg, called drag links attached to the wing structure forward of the legs. When the aircraft hit the ground it is highly probable that the drag links were broken so that the legs would have swung backwards and hit the underside of the trailing edge of the wing. Unfortunately, the Vulcan control operating rods ran along this part of the wing and would have been critically damaged by the undercarriage legs so that it would have been impossible to carry on flying. The pilots therefore would have had no alternative but to eject and inevitably the four rear crew members were killed.

The Touch report analysed in great detail the correct functioning of the GCA, and the second conclusion of the report was that, 'the controller failed to warn the pilot of the closeness to the ground', the first being that the GCA equipment was functioning correctly. The report also analysed the performance of the tracker, whose job it was to look at the aircraft with the vertical radar, and the performance of the controller who had to look at the aircraft on the horizontal radar and pass both lateral and vertical information to the pilot. On balance, Dr Touch felt that the tracker performed correctly but felt that the main controller in passing information to the pilot had concentrated too much on trying to get the aircraft to regain the runway centre line from which it had strayed and had not passed the fact that it was below the correct glide slope sufficiently strongly. It was of course possible that the tracker lost the aircraft in the heavy rain but Dr Touch did not feel that this had happened. I read somewhere in an account of this accident that the trackers at Heathrow were not allowed to track below 500ft but this clearly was not the case; the tracker tried as hard as she could to follow the aircraft but the rain clearly did not make matters easier.

Whatever happened during the approach however, the most obvious and key question is why the pilot came so low. The aircraft approach limitation for the Vulcan was set at 300ft 'height true' and 350ft 'height altimeter' so it is quite clear that, regardless of any instructions from the GCA controller, the pilot for some reason did not take missed approach action when the aircraft reached the approved minimum approach altitude.

The RAF accident report found that the indicated altimeter height would have been probably reading an extra 50ft higher than the correct indicated height due to the fact that the altimeters fitted at the time of the accident had an indication lag due to friction. This friction error would have been a contributory factor but would not have caused the accident. In time, all the Vulcan altimeters were changed to include vibrators to remove this error.

Another aspect that clearly made life difficult for the pilot was the very poor view out of the front of the Vulcan through the windscreens. Furthermore, the Vulcan windscreen wipers were extremely poor so that if indeed it had been raining heavily at the final part of the approach, a possibility suggested in the Touch report, then it would have been very difficult indeed for either pilot to have seen the ground.

The final ingredient for the cause of this terrible accident was almost certainly the pressure the pilot must have been under to land in front of a very high powered reception committee. Perhaps the most obvious point is the fact that Howard's official co-pilot was in the back of the aircraft unable to help; in the normal course of events he would have been calling out the heights from the altimeter and Howard presumably would have taken overshoot action at the approved minima. It is not known whether the actual co-pilot was calling out the heights. Pressure on a pilot has always been a contributory cause of accidents and this one must be another glaring example of the effect of pressure.

In summary the factors causing this accident could be listed, not in any order as follows:

1.   The decision to send a relatively inexperienced crew with a brand new RAF aircraft on such a long trip round the world.
2.   The decision for the aircraft to land at Heathrow instead of at a military airfield.
3.   The poor weather at Heathrow.
4.   The poor visibility from the Vulcan, particularly in rain.
5.   The significant static error on the Vulcan and the friction lag on the altimeter.
6.   The lack of ILS on the Vulcan.
7.   The controller not warning the pilot he was too low.
8.   The pressure on the pilot to land when his diversion airfield was clear.
9.   The usual co-pilot being in the back of the aircraft, with a very senior pilot who was almost certainly out of practice flying in very poor weather conditions, in the co-pilot's seat.
10.   The pilot coming below his decision height, perhaps inadvertently, due to the pressure of the situation and possibly not being advised of the aircraft altitudes at the critical part of the approach.

Clearly this accident was caused by a combination of circumstances as is so often the case but, in my opinion, the key cause was the pilot coming below his decision height under the great pressure put on him to land and without his accustomed co-pilot to help him by warning him of the aircraft altitude.

Vulcan XA894　　　　　**10th June 1957**　　　　　**Avros, Woodford**
This was an accident that didn't happen but might easily have done. The aircraft was being flown by a Boscombe Down test pilot who was not used to large aircraft, especially the Vulcan. This was his first landing at Woodford, which seemed very short compared with Boscombe and he came in steeply ready to touch down early. Apparently, he failed to start his landing flare early enough and his co-pilot, my friend Milt Cottee of 'supersonic' Vulcan fame, grabbed the stick, perhaps a bit late, and the aircraft touched down early, short of

Tyre Marks

XA894 wheel marks at Woodford.
(*A V Roe*)

the runway but luckily just above the lip of the bank of a stream which ran in front of the runway.

It was clearly a very heavy landing as evidenced by the fact that the starboard pitot tube was bent due to the impact. Milt went to look at the touchdown marks and it was a miracle that the undercarriage drag struts had not been broken, as at London Heathrow.

The explanation of this event is almost certainly that in principle pilots get used to the width of the runway they are landing at and it is one of the cues for starting the flare. I knew from my own experience how difficult I found it at first to judge the flare at Woodford with its narrow runway, having got used to landing at Boscombe; it took me a little time when I started flying from Woodford to learn to use some of the other cues for starting the flare. On other aircraft types, the view was so much better that there were plenty of ways of judging when the aircraft was near the ground; the real secret, for me anyway, on the Vulcan was to check through the circular side window.

Once again I am indebted to Milt for the description of this incident. I was at Woodford at the time but unlike Milt I don't remember inspecting the wheel marks:

> The flight test observer and I set out to drive back to Boscombe Down. Access to the south across the airfield at Woodford was by way of a road which crossed the runway on which we had just landed. The tower-controlled crossing traffic lights flashed amber during non-active times. So as we approached the runway crossing now with amber flashing light showing, I remarked to my passenger that it would be interesting to see the under-run of the runway where we had first hit on landing.
>
> I turned and drove down to the end of the runway. The double wheel tracks of both bogies were deeply rutted in the cinder hardened under-run which extended back from the runway about 200ft to end at the edge of a small stream which crossed between the runway and the railway viaduct. I followed the left wheel tracks back to the splurged earth where we had made first contact. This was about 20 feet from the edge of the stream. I walked over to

the right wheel tracks and followed them with horror to the edge of the stream. Erosion by the stream had cut vertically down and those wheel tracks went over the edge.

In the air, the rear bogey of the double bogey undercarriage of the Vulcan hangs down some two feet below the front bogey. The beam between the bogeys has hydraulic shock absorbers cushioning the action as all wheels lower on to the runway. On this occasion, the trailing bogey on the right side had hit the top edge of the bank of the stream. Just six inches lower and the right gear would have been sheared off. I expect that had this occurred, we would have cart wheeled inverted. Both of us were staggered at how close we had been to disaster.

Vulcan XA902   February 1958
Damaged during landing. Repaired. Details not known.

Vulcan Mk 1 XH498   25th October 1959   Rongotai, New Zealand
This was a landing accident when the airport was being officially

Vulcan XH498 touchdown. (*Bob Mitchell*)

Vulcan XH498 climb out.
(*Bob Mitchell*)

opened. The aircraft landed short and, unfortunately, there was a bank just before the runway. The port landing gear hit the bank and the drag link broke so that it swung back, hit the underside of the wing skin and ruptured a fuel tank. Luckily the gear did not hit the control run, as in the London accident, so the aircraft was still controllable. The decision was taken to land at the RNZAF base at Ohakea where the aircraft could be repaired more easily. It made a very good landing indeed with minimum damage and an Avro repair team completed repairs by 3rd January 1960. There were no injuries.

Apparently wind shear caused the wing to drop and for the undercarriage to hit the bank but one has to wonder whether pressure on the pilot was a contributory cause, bearing in mind he must have been aiming well short of the correct touchdown point. I have landed

a Vulcan short myself under pressure but luckily there was no bank to catch the landing gear.

Vulcan XH498 after landing. (*Bob Mitchell*)

Vulcan Mk 2 XH557   16th September 1960   Filton Airport
This aircraft was being flown to Bristol Siddeley at Bristol to be fitted with Mk 301 engines. The weather was poor with low cloud and rain. The following is a report on the accident from an expert test pilot eye witness:

> Delivery flight to Filton from Boscombe Down for engine handling trials with the new larger Olympus engine. The aircraft had been allotted to Handling Sqn to enable flight trials to be undertaken to update the advanced issue Pilot's Notes. The captain ...... had 15 hours on type and the co-pilot ..... none. After touching down fast, from a radar approach, 550 yards beyond the threshold on a flooded runway in moderate rain at Filton, the pilot applied the wheel brakes with no apparent effect. The drag parachute was then deployed but again no retardation occurred.

Another eyewitness told me the parachute came off:

> Engine power was applied 600 yards from the end of Runway 10 and an overshoot executed, the aircraft was pulled off the ground 50 yards from the end of the runway. During the overshoot the aircraft struck a sodium light bursting four of the eight starboard bogie tyres and struck a commercial garage situated at the end of the runway, blowing all four petrol pumps away, and damaging two cars. As the aircraft climbed, the streamed brake parachute fell away.

One of the eye witnesses clearly got it wrong! The aircraft then diverted to St Mawgan and landed safely. The weather at Filton was marginal for the Vulcan especially using the ACR 7 radar, which the captain had never before flown in a Vulcan. This had been compounded by the failure of the brake parachute to fully deploy. No substantial damage was done to the aircraft which was ferried back to Filton to have the larger engines installed. Clearly the accident was due to a combination of bad weather, landing too fast, streaming the parachute too late and general lack of experience on the type. It was extremely fortunate that no serious accident resulted either to the crew or to people on the ground.

Vulcan Mk 1 XA904 1961 Waddington
Damaged during landing. Aircraft later scrapped. Details not known. Board of Inquiry report not available.

Vulcan Mk 2 XL384 1971
Heavy landing. Not repaired. Details not known. Used for crash crew training.

Vulcan Mk 2 XM645 14th October 1975 Zabbar, Malta
The aircraft was coming in to land at 1310 hours and made a touchdown just short of the runway. It managed to overshoot but the aircraft had been severely damaged. The pilots managed to eject but the rear crew members were killed in the aircraft which turned into a fireball. The aircraft should not have landed so early but the problem was exacerbated by the fact that the runway at Luqa had a lip so that any aircraft that touched down short was likely to be severely damaged.

It is not known whether the undercarriage drag links broke or whether some other malfunction occurred following the touchdown but clearly something very serious happened as a result of the heavy landing.

Discussion on Landing Accidents
A successful landing always depends on the skill of the pilot. The Vulcan perhaps was more demanding than a lot of aircraft, particularly if it was touching down slowly since the attitude was very high and the pilot needed to be a long way off the ground to keep the wheels from touching prematurely. Bomber Command pilots did not like streaming the parachutes on landing, any more than we did at Woodford and so they would often choose to touch down slowly, very understandably, but the danger was that the aircraft might touchdown earlier than planned, as I did at Farnborough in the rain. The landings at Luqa and Rongotai are clearly in that category and they were classic 'accidents' as they would never have happened if there had been no lip at the beginning of the runway. The landing at Woodford was very similar but luckily the ditch had a soft bank and the aircraft was not badly damaged.

The London crash was a classic bad weather landing accident and I find it interesting that as far as I know this was the only case of a Vulcan landing accident due to coming too low in bad weather.

ASYMMETRIC APPROACHES

Vulcan Mk 2 XM601   7th October 1964   Coningsby

The aircraft, fitted with Olympus Mk 301 engines, was returning from a normal sortie at night with the captain using the RT, and the assumption was that the co-pilot was flying the aircraft with Nos 3 and 4 engines at idling power. At the start of the approach the captain said that they would do a practice ILS asymmetric approach using the two port engines followed by a touchdown and then taking off again, a roller landing. The last call was 'three greens for roller'. Power was applied over the runway and the aircraft was seen to bank to starboard and then turn sharply away from the runway. When the aircraft was 300 yards along the runway but 175 yards to the right of the centre line the starboard wing tip hit the ground. The aircraft caught fire on the first impact and the fire continued severely as the parts came to rest. The fuselage ended up 350 yards away from the runway, outside the airfield.

Both pilots ejected but were too close to the ground for their parachutes to work. All the crew members were killed. The probable cause of the accident was that all four engines were opened together by the co-pilot and the live engines would have responded almost immediately whilst the two engines at idling power would have taken a relatively long time to accelerate and produce significant thrust. The speed would have been below the speed required to be able to control with the rudder the differential thrust being produced by the 'live' engines and so the pilot would have lost directional control. The captain clearly failed to take over in time.

Vulcan Mk 2 XH576   25th May 1965   Scampton

The co-pilot was to carry out an asymmetric approach and roller landing using Nos 3 and 4 engines with Nos 1 and 2 engines throttled. The aircraft was just to the right of centre line before reaching the runway but regained the centre line, but then it started to go to the left. It flew along the left side of the runway and the captain decided that the aircraft would touchdown off the runway. He took over control and opened up all four engines. The port wheel rolled along the runway 25ft in from the edge 2,375ft down the runway. The aircraft then drifted on to the grass with 15° of bank. It lifted off the ground after another 150ft, and flew for 320ft turning left.

The port wing ran along the ground causing the aircraft to swing round, the port undercarriage hit the ground and then the nosewheel broke off. The port undercarriage then collapsed, the starboard undercarriage hit the ground, the nose dug into the ground and the aircraft slid into the car park and struck the control tower. A small fire was rapidly extinguished. All the crew survived.

The cause of this accident was the opening of all four throttles without sufficient speed for the rudder to be able to control the differential asymmetric thrust which resulted from the live engines opening up before the idling ones.

Discussion on Asymmetric Approaches

These two accident are very similar and I find it strange that after the first one, new regulations were not issued to prevent pilots doing asymmetric approaches and roller landings without first opening up the idling engines before opening the live engines. Unfortunately, the pilots notes did not warn of the danger of trying to do roller landings from asymmetric approaches.

DISPLAY FLYING

Vulcan XA903   4th September 1958

This aircraft was being flown at Farnborough showing Blue Steel for the first time to the general public. It was based at Woodford and flew to Farnborough each day. After the third day the half weight dummy Blue Steel was removed for servicing and the ground crew noticed that the structure had been damaged and 'grounded' the aircraft so that it was not able to go to Farnborough for the rest of the week. The archaic g recorder showed 4.5g, way outside any permitted Vulcan structural limit. Apparently the aircraft had been 'demonstrated' at Moreton Vallance on the way back from Farnborough without any authorization and it was assumed that the damage was done at this time. Surprisingly no disciplinary action was taken against the pilot though apparently he was called to see Dobbie, Sir Roy Dobson, perhaps because it could not be proved exactly when the damage was done to the aircraft. Interestingly, as a result of the inspection of XA903 the decision was taken to inspect VX777 mentioned in the description of the VX770 accident below and serious damage was discovered.

Vulcan VX770   20th September 1958   RAF Syerston

The Vulcan first prototype VX770 was taking part in a flying display at Syerston and the aircraft broke up in front of the crowd during a fast run. All the crew were killed.

Vulcan VX770 was the first prototype Vulcan and fitted initially with Rolls-Royce Avon engines. The aircraft was then handed over to Rolls-Royce to be fitted with the development engines for the Victor Mk 2, Conway engines with 17,500lbs thrust each. Whilst taking part in a flying display at RAF Syerston it broke up during a fast run. One picture of the accident shows the starboard leading edge peeling off before the aircraft crashed. In addition on the amateur cine film the leading edge can be seen breaking off first.

This aircraft was not as strong as a production Mk 1 and its maximum speed was 380 knots. There was also a g limitation on the aircraft compared with a Vulcan Mk 1. Some amateur film was obtained of the aircraft and detailed analysis took place. It was said that the aircraft was flying at over 400 knots and some g was being applied as well, making it a rolling pull-out which would mean that lower g margins would apply. The accident was therefore said to have been caused by the pilot flying too fast.

By chance I knew the pilot well as he was on my flight on No 5 Venom Squadron, at Wunstorf in Germany and I felt uncomfortable with the explanation of the accident, since I didn't feel that the pilot in question would have been reckless and flown well above the briefed flypast speed of 300 knots.

This accident occurred just after we at Woodford had been practising doing rolls off the top in our Vulcans prior to the SBAC show and, of course, I had carried out rolls off the top at Farnborough throughout the week. Unbeknown to us, the Rolls-Royce pilots had been doing rolls, rolls off the top and, I have it on unimpeachable authority, even one loop in VX770; the knowledge that a Vulcan had done a loop really amazed me since Jimmy Harrison and I with our knowledge of the structure, always felt it would be a very unwise thing to do. Whether other aircraft have been looped on the RAF squadrons is an interesting question; clearly it was not an event to be talked about in the pilots' office or the officers' mess or anywhere else for that matter.

Unfortunately, what was not generally known was the fact that after each aerobatic flight at Woodford we had a special small man in the ground crew who could and would climb up and inspect inside the leading edges for damage, because sometimes the nose ribs buckled and had to be repaired. As far as I know Rolls-Royce knew nothing of these inspections and they may not have been looking at the leading edges internally between every flight; we did not advertise our problems, especially since if the ministry AID inspector thought we had damaged the aircraft unnecessarily, the firm might have been liable for some expensive repairs. For example, the decision to inspect VX777 after the damage to XA903 had been found, was not taken by the maintenance organization but was suggested by Laurie Trier, a specialist in structures in our flight test organization since he had been on a flight with Jimmy Harrison when Jimmy inadvertently pulled 3.5g practising for Farnborough.

Knowing the history of nose rib damage to our aircraft, the chance of structural damage to VX770 would almost certainly have been accentuated by the fact that it had been doing aerobatics, since it was the first prototype and, as mentioned, it was not built to the production standard. I found it very significant that the break-up occurred starting with the leading edge. Consequently, in my view the aircraft may well have been severely structurally damaged before it took off and that was probably the reason why it crashed. My view is reinforced by the fact that when I returned VX777 to Woodford halfway through the SBAC show after Jimmy had collected the production Mk 2 a day or two earlier, it was discovered that the leading edges and the bomb arches at the top of the bomb bay were in poor shape and needed repair. It was not certain when the damage was done but Laurie Trier blamed the Farnborough practice mentioned above though some damage may have been there for some time since the aircraft had certainly being doing rolls off the top besides lots of barrel rolls.

For the record, it was not the pilot who was flying the aircraft at Syerston who carried out the loop. Furthermore, the Rolls-Royce chief test pilot at the time did not do any aerobatics as far as I can ascertain, though it is difficult to believe that he did not know what was going on since I have heard from two crew members flying from Hucknall at the time that rolls were routinely carried out over the airfield at the end of a flight.

Unfortunately, we shall never know the whole story and the official report will always blame the pilot for flying too fast but I remain unconvinced. On so many fatal accident investigations the pilots get blamed because they are not there to defend themselves, whereas perhaps more investigation was required into the design of the aircraft and the regulations governing its maintenance and operation.

Vulcan Mk 2 XL390   12th August 1978   Glenview, USA

This aircraft was briefed to do a practice display at Chicago Lakeside airport but the captain decided to carry out an unauthorized air display at Glenview before departing for Lakeside. The aircraft made a run over the airfield starting at low level, probably below 100ft, it was then pulled up for a teardrop turn which was not executed correctly and the aircraft crashed killing all on board.

Interviews with the eyewitnesses, naval aviators, suggest that the manoeuvre was not properly executed and that the aircraft sideslipped downwards so that the pilot then found it impossible to pull out. Display rules stated that Vulcans doing displays should not come below 500ft so that the captain had less height than usual to attempt to rectify the poor execution of the wing over. In addition it is believed that the aircraft was heavier than usual since it was carrying extra fuel to transit to Lakeside for the display there.

Discussion on Display Flying

Flying displays and the practices beforehand always put extra pressure on pilots and the aircraft. It is necessary to be especially careful to ensure that accidents do not take place because the display pilots are trying too hard to do their best; they may get too close or even beyond the corner of the aircraft's flight envelope or perhaps try to do manoeuvres which are beyond their capabilities. The RAF were very good at dealing with this problem, but in spite of their regulations the accident to XL390 took place. The VX770 accident could have been due to a pilot trying too hard, we shall never know, but the aircraft was almost certainly damaged before the flight. The overstressing of XA903, assuming it did take place at Moreton Vallance, was presumably an example of a pilot trying too hard; it was amazing that the aircraft did not break up.

LOW FLYING

Vulcan XH477　　　　12th December 1963　　　　Scotland
The aircraft was briefed for a low level exercise in Scotland, not less than 1,000ft, above ground level. Seventeen minutes later a normal position report was given but after that nothing was heard. Sometime afterwards it was discovered that it had hit a saddle of ground between two hills while climbing slightly.

As far as is known the aircraft wasn't fitted with terrain following radar. It was assumed that it crashed while low flying in bad weather.

Vulcan Mk 2 XH536　　11th February 1966　　　　Wales
This aircraft was briefed to do a low level exercise. It is believed that it coasted in at Porthcawl. One position report was given at a turning point and nothing further was heard. The aircraft hit the ground at 1,910ft near the summit of Fan Bwlch Chwyth, 2,635ft, twenty miles NE Swansea. All the crew members were killed. At the time of the accident the weather was misty with cloud covering the hills above 1,400ft.

The accident was assumed to be due to the pilot not complying with the Air Staff Instructions, in that he probably encountered instrument meteorological conditions and did not climb up immediately. The hills at the time were covered with snow so it is likely that the mist would have merged with the ground.

There has been some debate whether the aircraft was fitted with terrain following radar but it seems fairly clear that in fact it was testing the TFR. However the following is a partial excerpt from a web site which specialises in discussing the Vulcan:

> They did not have TFR at that time. TFR was only introduced in 1967... No... his crew were doing map based terrain following. It should only have been done in daylight and VMC. The technique called for the radar to get accurate fixes and for the plotter to 'track' the aircraft using a chinagraph pencil and a half-million chart. He would call the terrain height and height to fly while the radar would call 'cut-off' ie the black hole that marked the next ridge. As the black hole got smaller and returns appeared behind it the assumption was made that the aircraft was above the ridge. The fallacy was the 'hill behind a hill' when the second hill was much higher than

the first. In this case there was 'no hill behind a hill' on their track. Unfortunately they were not on track but about 2 miles off.

In the absolute certainty that the nav team were in control, the pilots followed the height calls in VMC. The height demanded meant that the aircraft just kissed the tops of the clouds. Unfortunately it was not cloud but ground mist.... A similar incident had happened at Scampton a year or so earlier called the 'Hills of St Clone' where the aircraft hit a saddle in ground mist.

Discussion on Low Flying
Low flying accidents will always occur but particularly in the case of military aircraft practising operation sorties. The RAF group orders clearly tried to cover all eventualities and prevent their aircraft flying too low but the accidents occurred in spite of the regulations.

PILOT ERROR
Vulcan Mk 2 XH535   11th May 1964   near Andover
This aircraft was being flown from A&AEE by an Avro test pilot and a test pilot from B Squadron at Boscombe Down. It crashed nine miles west of Boscombe and the rear crew members were killed; the two pilots ejected and the sequence of events seems to have been as follows.

The aircraft had been doing routine tests and the Avro test pilot was trying to demonstrate to the Boscombe pilot very low speed flying, apparently as low as 85 knots at 20,000ft. It was said that the particular manoeuvre which the Avro pilot was trying to demonstrate was a very high rate descent at very low speed culminating in a normal landing. However, on this occasion the aircraft went into a spin and the tail parachute was streamed to try to recover normal flight. Though the spin was stopped momentarily, the aircraft entered into another spin and the captain ordered the crew to abandon it at 2,500ft and the pilots ejected shortly afterwards. The rear crew did not bale out, presumably because of the g forces associated with the aircraft spinning.

I find it difficult to comment on this accident as the manoeuvre being demonstrated was way outside anything I had done or would have thought of doing. The Vulcan could be flown at very low speeds with full up elevator when a very high rate of descent would occur; however, it was necessary to be extremely careful not to let sideslip build up. As the manoeuvre has since been described to me, it sounded unwise to say the least and certainly outside anything that was officially permitted. A friend of mine had the manoeuvre demonstrated to him by the pilot of this aircraft followed by a landing and he felt very nervous throughout the whole operation.

Vulcan Mk 2 XJ823   5th February 1970   Akrotiri

The description of the incident below was written after conversation with the pilot concerned. There were no formal documents available. However, there is no doubt that the aircraft was structurally damaged after the flight.

The captain was authorized to do an air test and carried out a high speed run starting at 50,000ft. However the aircraft was 'reluctant to slow down'. The air brakes didn't seem to help and the aircraft entered a steep dive. The captain pulled the stick back as hard as he could during the dive but at first was unable to pull out of the dive. Understandably, he ordered the crew to abandon the aircraft which they were unable to do because of the g forces but luckily the mach number finally started to reduce as the altitude decreased below 30,000ft; the captain was then able to pull the aircraft out of the dive and start to climb. The pilot thinks that the highest mach number that he saw was 1.0 IMN. However, there was a discontinuity in the elevator feel during the manoeuvre and, after the recovery had been made and the aircraft landed, it was discovered that there was some 'rippling in the top surface of the wing'.

This is the only case that I have come across of a Vulcan Mk 2 getting out of control by diving too fast due to the aircraft's inherent instability at high mach number. The indicated speed of 1.0 would probably have been about .975 true mach number. What may not have been known at the time, because it was not described in the pilots notes, was that there was a spring strut fitted to the Mk 2 elevator circuit set at 150lbs to enable pilots to recover at very high mach number. However, in the circumstances described by the pilot where the airspeed was very high as well as the mach number, the probability is that too much g was almost certainly pulled; the aircraft was damaged because the elevator forces would have been less than the normal airspeed forces programmed at this high speed due to the operation of the spring strut. Unfortunately, the Vulcan was flying before the days of flight data or crash recorders. The general view at the time in Cyprus was that the pilot had operated the elevator feel relief, which would have made the forces very light indeed. He was pretty sure he didn't and had he done so he would almost certainly have broken the aircraft, bearing in mind he was pulling as hard as he could. In my view this was a case of the emergency spring strut 'relieving' the artificial feel in a flight regime which was almost certainly outside the flight envelope.

Surprisingly, the aircraft was flown back to the UK to be repaired; perhaps they didn't know as much as we did about looking after the nose ribs! In fact the aircraft was repaired at Bitteswell and I went down to fly it on 14th August to check that it was fully serviceable after repair, though at the time I knew nothing about how the damage was caused.

Discussion on Pilot Error

The accident to XH535 resulted in my opinion from a combination of insufficient pilot supervision and unwise flying, but perhaps I am showing 20/20 hindsight. The high speed dive by XJ823 is of course due to pilot error and as far as I know there has never been another similar event, though it was only by chance I heard of this one. However this type of accident could only happen on an aircraft like the Vulcan, where the penalty for going too fast is complete lack of control.

ENGINE MALFUNCTION

Vulcan Mk 1 XA894   3rd December 1962   Filton, Bristol

The aircraft was sent to Bristol Siddeley to test the TSR2 engine and after the engine had been installed under the bomb bay it was being run at full power on the ground with reheat. The whole rotating turbine disc came off, hit the ground, bounced up and hit the fuselage, hit the ground again, bounced up again and went though the wing, setting fire to all the fuel tanks and then flew for half a mile to the turning circle at the start of the runway where the brand new Bristol 188 stainless steel prototype was sitting having final tests. By a miracle the turbine disc did a circuit around the 188 and finally came to rest.

There were five engineers on the aircraft as well as the chief test pilot of Bristol Siddeley and they managed to scramble out onto the ground and run before the whole aircraft was completely burnt out. The running bay was on a 2% gradient and the burning fuel from the tanks ran across the perimeter track straight for a brand new fire engine which was trying to put the fire out but instead was set on fire itself and destroyed.

Vulcan Mk 1 XA909   16th July 1964   Anglesey

This aircraft was on a navigation exercise when an explosion occurred and both No 3 and No 4 engines were closed down. At the same time the captain experienced difficulty with the lateral control. The plane was ten miles north of Aberystwyth and the co-pilot sent out a mayday call. It then headed for Valley in Anglesey but the captain realised that even with asymmetric power he had insufficient aileron power. A Gnat formated on the aircraft and saw extensive damage to the starboard wing. In addition both airspeed readings were grossly inaccurate.

The captain then decided to abandon the aircraft and the three rear crew members were clear by 3,000ft. The co-pilot and the captain then ejected. All crew members were found in a few minutes and rescued by helicopter.

The cause of the accident was a failure of an engine bearing in No 4 engine.

Vulcan Mk 2 XL385   6th April 1967   Scampton
The aircraft was cleared for take-off and as the captain opened the throttles there was a loud bang and Nos 1 and 2 engines wound down in unison. XL385 was brought to rest after travelling no more than 20ft. The captain noticed a fire on the port side and ordered the crew to abandon the aircraft. He operated the fire extinguishers and shut down all engines. He then rapidly left the aircraft which was destroyed by fire despite all the efforts of the fire crews.

Inspection of the wreckage showed that No 1 engine turbine rotating disc, had disintegrated at high rpm. Part of this disc was found 250 yards away. No 2 engine was also damaged and both the low pressure and high pressure turbine discs were missing. The HP disc was found 500 yards away on the port side. There was evidence of fatigue cracking at all bolt holes of No1 HP disc and this was considered to be the primary cause of the accident. Pieces of the disc and also pieces of No 2 disc had penetrated the fuel tanks and started the fire. It is possible that No 3 combustion chamber might have caused a resonance condition at the HP disc which resulted in the subsequent failure at the bolt holes.

The large distances travelled by the rotating parts is a reminder of the enormous energy contained in them and shows why an aircraft is nearly always destroyed if the rotating parts cannot be contained.

Vulcan Mk 2 XM604   30th January 1968   near Cottesmore
The aircraft took off from Cottesmore on a routine flight. During the climb the bomb bay was observed to be overheating. The air bleeds were turned off and the temperatures returned to normal but the sortie was abandoned. When the aircraft returned it was above maximum landing weight, 140,000lbs, and a period of continuation training was started to try to get the fuel down before landing. After the second circuit, as the aircraft was climbing away at 800ft, a double bang was heard, the control column became free and there was complete loss of control. The captain ordered the aircraft to be abandoned but due to the low altitude and the aircraft being out of control all the rear crew members were killed. The co-pilot ejected safely but the captain ejected when the aircraft was nearly inverted. Incredibly, he survived because his undeveloped parachute got caught in electrical high tension cables and he was able to release his harness and drop to the ground.

Examination of the wreckage indicated that there had been a failure of the No 2 engine low pressure compressor shaft in the region of No 4 bearing. (There was no protection device in the event of a shaft failure.) Various eyewitnesses reported seeing fire in the region of the bomb bay and the No 2 engine location. It is clear with hindsight that an immediate overweight landing would have saved the aircraft and the rear crew but in this case there can be no criticism of the captain for acting as he did. One can only do what seems best at the time.

Vulcan Mk 2 XM610   8th January 1971   Wingate[5]

The aircraft was climbing with 85% power on all four engines when there was an explosion on the port side. No 1 engine ran down, the associate jet pipe temperature gauge reading went to its limit and the fire warning light came on. The standard drills were then carried out and the fire warning light went out. The aircraft continued to climb on three engines but then the jet pipe temperature on No 2 engine started to climb and No 2 fire warning light came on. The fire drill was carried out and again the fire warning light went out. At first the AEO could not see any problems underneath the aircraft but then he noticed a glow in his periscope and saw a fire in the region of No 1 engine. The No 2 fire warning light re-illuminated for about two minutes and went out again but the fire was now firmly alight.

The captain made a Mayday call and the rear crew were ordered to prepare to abandon the aircraft. When the aircraft was clear of cloud the captain ordered the crew to bale out which they did successfully. The captain tried to save the aircraft but when he started to lose control he ordered the co-pilot to eject. The captain followed safely and the aircraft entered a spiral dive before hitting the ground.

The engines were Olympus Mk 301s. The cause of the No 1 engine failure was a blade root fatigue failure on the high pressure rotating turbine. Apparently the blade then rotated with the turbine disc, causing an imbalance in the engine which finally resulted in an explosive rupture of an engine combustion chamber. The debris from the explosion caused damage to the No 2 engine and to the aircraft fuel system which resulted in an uncontrollable fire.

Vulcan Mk 2 XH558   6th November 1975   Scampton

Apparently Vulcan XH558 which hopefully is going to fly again soon had an Olympus Mk 201 engine problem and I can't do better than include the following report from a relevant Vulcan web site:

> On 6 Nov 75 I was part of the crew on the day the damage came about. As I recall, both the captain ...... and myself were undergoing a check. Being 27 Sqn we were off to do a very long northbound maritime sortie so we also had both drum tanks full in the bomb bay. There we were rolling down Scampton's runway when the inevitable happened for a training check and (the training captain) announced simulated double engine failure one and two. Sometime very close to this there was a massive bang, lots of expletives and four throttles being firewalled as number three and four wound down. We staggered off the runway, thank the Lord for the Lincoln Edge, climbed to height for

---

[5] Vividly described in Roland White's *Vulcan 607*.

the GCA pattern, carried out the drills for a double engine failure and some semblance of order returned. However, as we flew downwind the navigator was in the door well ready to open the door and the AEO looking through the periscope was announcing we were on fire. There was no indication of fire from where the pilots sat so rather than open the door and throw our pink bodies at the nosewheel the rear crew stuck with the aircraft. My log book shows 15 mins for this flight but the instrument pattern that day seemed to take a very long time.

Suffice to say the pilots did a great job, we landed overweight, stopped on the runway and six Vulcan crew members ran away bravely leaving it to the fire crews. However, when we looked back there was no fire. A few minutes later we were able to approach the aircraft and see what had occurred. The biggest shock was the huge hole blown in the starboard wing. It is very strange to stand underneath an aircraft and look through where the wing upper and lower surfaces should have been. The other sobering thing was looking at HP fuel pipe to the number three engine. As I recall, the number three engine had moved damaging the pipe but all along the exposed area were cuts and nicks where parts of the compressor had damaged it.

So what had happened? The number three engine had managed to find a seagull during the take-off run which caused it to disintegrate taking the number four engine with it. In so doing it modified the wing. Oh and the fire we experienced downwind. There was lots of twisted metal around the hole in the wing and the anti-collision light was reflecting on it. All of this did make me think though when we landed at Macrihanish one JMC just ahead of an Atlantique that suffered a multiple seagull strike. I seem to recall in excess of thirty were found in and on the aircraft. As much as I enjoyed my time flying the Vulcan I was quite pleased to then fly with two Spey engines and a bang seat.

Discussion on Engine Malfunction

The Olympus engine was a pretty dangerous beast when it failed. I was very fortunate since in all the hours I did testing the engine handling I never had any serious problems. The crews faced with these catastrophic failures of the engines handled the aircraft very well indeed though some failures could not be controlled. The Mk 301 engines seemed to be less reliable than the Mk 201 though the statistical sample is very small. The Vulcan Mk 1 engines seemed to be very reliable and there was only one malfunction resulting in aircraft loss.

Top: Author piloting the first flight of Vulcan Mk 1A showing production leading edge modification at Boscombe Down.

Middle: Blue Steel missile fitted to a Vulcan Mk 2. *(Fred Martin RZF Digital)*

Bottom: Vulcan XH537 with Skybolts fitted.

Top: Author piloting Vulcan XH535 as it formates with B52 Stratofortress 20008 over Edwards Air Force Base, 7th July 1961.

Middle: Author after flying B47 20221 at Edwards Air Force Base.

Bottom: And after piloting B52 20008 at the same base.

Top: Vulcan scramble during a rapid response exercise.
(Fred Martin RZF Digital)

Bottom: Vulcan refuelling showing the tanker role capability.

Top: Vulcan XH558 with hose drum unit. This aircraft is due to fly again summer 2007. *(Fred Martin RZF Digital)*

Bottom: Author with the 707A WD280 at RAAF Museum, Pt Cook, April 2007.

ELECTRICAL FAILURE

Vulcan Mk 1 XA908   24th October 1958   Detroit, Michigan, USA

The aircraft was flying on an exercise from Goose Bay, Canada to Lincoln AFB, Nebraska. When it was sixty miles NE of Detroit a mayday call was received announcing complete electrical and control failure and that it was descending through 40,000ft. Another call was received a minute later asking for a heading to the nearest airfield, the aircraft then being at 34,000ft. It was next seen over Detroit where it crashed in a residential area. All the crew were killed and several residents were injured. The cockpit canopy had been jettisoned and the second pilot's ejector seat was found in Lake St Clair, 10 miles from the crash site. The second pilot's body was never recovered.

Examination of Nos 1 and 4 generators indicated that they probably failed from internal faults. In addition, one of the voltage regulators inspected showed the system had been varying in voltage, possibly for several hours. By chance when investigating another malfunction on the ground, shortly after this accident, it was found that XH476, with exactly the same electrical standard, had a wiring fault as a result of a new modification which had only recently been done on XA908. This modification was being carried out on the rest of the Vulcan fleet. It was thought that this fault might have caused the accident to XA908. Eleven other aircraft which were having the modification installed were examined but no fault was found. The exact reason for the accident will never be known.

However, the 112V battery system should have been able to supply emergency power to the power controls for at least twenty minutes, but it was clear from the pilot's radio transmissions that control was being lost after three.

Two things happened after this accident, firstly a pre-flight load check was introduced into the servicing before flight; a realistic group of loads was put on the busbar, the ground power was switched off and the performance of the batteries confirmed before the ground power was restored. The time was then taken for the voltage to return to full value thus fully checking the batteries. The second action was to raise a modification to introduce two latched contactors between the busbars to try to prevent a fault on one side of the aircraft affecting the other side and thus obviate a similar occurrence.

Vulcan Mk 1 XA891   24th July 1959   near Hull

The aircraft took off and almost immediately afterwards warning lights for Nos 2 and 3 generators came on (there was no No 1 generator fitted, see below) and No 4 generator light flickered and went out. The busbar voltage dropped rapidly to 70V from 112V and the controls were not responding properly. The captain, the chief test pilot of Avros, put out the airbrakes and the controls started to malfunction. He immediately retracted the airbrakes and climbed to 14,000ft. The

AEO was unable to reset any of the generators and the captain realised that it would be necessary to abandon the aircraft. He gave the necessary instruction and the crew, including a test engineer from Bristol Engines, exited cleanly followed by the ejection of the co-pilot and then himself. No-one was hurt and the aircraft crashed in open space without doing any damage.

Before discussing the fault it should be remarked that the captain saved the day by realising that it would not be possible to land, though obviously that was his first instinctive reaction. Had he tried to land the aircraft, it would almost certainly have crashed on landing killing the crew. His decision to turn away from the airfield and climb to the east was first class.

This aircraft was developing the engines for the Vulcan Mk 2 and Sundstrand constant speed drives, CSDUs, and alternators had just been fitted to the Nos 1 and 2 engines instead of the normal 112V DC generators. However No 2 CSDU was not being used and No 1 CSDU was connected to an alternator which drove a 112V DC motor generator connected to the port busbar. The RAE experts examined the wreckage and tried to reconstruct what happened. The motor generator was in good condition but the fuses connecting the battery busbar and two starboard busbars were blown. The view was expressed that the most likely cause was an earth fault on No 4 generator which damaged No 3 generator and also put the motor generator off line, blowing the fuses connecting the busbars. The moment that happened the batteries took over the load on the battery busbar and the AEO found it impossible to reset the motor generator. From that point onwards the aircraft was doomed as more and more services came off line.

The RAE report remarked that it was unfortunate that there was only one generator supplying the port busbar and that Mod 697, which introduced latched contactors, had not been carried out on the aircraft. This modification disconnected the busbars on a peak load and prevented reconnection unless the AEO manually selected them.

Vulcan Mk 2 XM600   17th January 1977   near Spilsby
The aircraft was flying a normal training flight and was briefed to carry out a practice emergency electrical descent by dropping the RAT which would immediately shed some loads and power the controls. At 30,000ft the airborne auxiliary power unit, AAPU, would then take over the electrical supplies. The captain dropped the RAT at 40,000ft but the voltage was fluctuating up to 185 volts, way above its proper value of 115 volts. The voltage finally stabilized after about three minutes and the RAT was brought on line to take over from No 2 alternator. The RAT voltage rose to 155 volts and after about a minute when the aircraft was below 30,000ft the AEO brought the AAPU on line.

At this point the bomb bay fire warning light flashed on followed by the No 2 engine warning light. The captain shut down the engine but the AEO reported flames were coming from the area of No 2 engine about four feet behind the RAT. The engine fire warning light went out but came on again with the bomb bay fire warning light. The AEO confirmed that the fire was getting worse and the captain transmitted a mayday call and immediately ordered the crew to bale out. There was a problem with the way the entrance door was operated manually but using the electrical switch solved it, unfortunately catching the nav radar operator who was half in the chute by surprise causing him to slide out when he wasn't quite expecting it. Eventually all three rear crew members dropped clear by 6,000ft. As control was lost the captain ordered the co-pilot to eject and he followed at about 3,000ft The aircraft crashed in open country near Spilsby.

The primary cause of the accident was arcing at a terminal block on one of the three phase outlets of the RAT due to a bad connection and this arcing burnt a hole in an adjacent fuel pipe and set fire to the fuel. The heat from this fire then damaged other fuel pipes in the vicinity and the aircraft was doomed.

Discussion on Electrical Failure

The Vulcan Mk 1 electrics were not as reliable as the Mk 2 and depended heavily on the ability of the four 28V batteries being able to supply power for a reasonable length of time. After the loss of the aircraft in the States a modification was done which almost certainly prevented similar occurrences and would have prevented the accident to XA891 had it been embodied. The only Mk 2 accident resulted from an installation fault on the RAT wiring; I find that explanation a bit surprising, but at least it wasn't an electrical design fault.

MISCELLANEOUS OCCURRENCES

Vulcan VX777   27th July 1954   Farnborough

The second prototype Vulcan landed at high speed at Farnborough and was unable to stop on the runway; the aircraft went onto the grass and the undercarriage got caught in a ditch and collapsed. No one was hurt.

The aircraft had been carrying out stalls and slow speed manoeuvres involving large applications of aileron and rudder. After one such manoeuvre the rudder jammed at full deflection and the aircraft was sideslipping in a disturbing manner. The crew were unable to diagnose the exact cause of the problem since there was no way of looking at the rear of the aircraft in VX777, unlike production aircraft which had a periscope, and pushing the rudder pedals in the opposite direction did not seem to work. The pilot was worried that there might have been damage to the fin or rudder and flew past the control tower for an examination. He was reassured that the fin seemed to be undamaged and so he decided to land using bank and asymmetric power to enable the aircraft to be lined up and landed on the runway. The parachute failed, presumably because the speed was too high and the accident resulted.

The reason for the accident was that one of the spring struts in the rudder circuit jammed and the rudder was held at full deflection by the control circuit. Analysis after the accident suggested that if the pilot had kicked the rudder pedals the spring strut might have freed and normal flight would have been regained. However, the pilot was clearly very worried that there might have been some structural damage and was unwilling, understandably, possibly to exacerbate the situation. As explained in Chapter 2, the managing director had no inhibitions in blaming Roly Falk who was the pilot, but being wise after the event may not be a fair way to judge how the pilot should have behaved.

Vulcan XH497   **3rd July 1958**   **RAF Scampton**
This accident was an emergency landing caused by the steerable nose gear falling off during take-off, complete with landing wheels. The rear crew members baled out and sadly the navigator was killed due to a failure of his parachute. The captain managed a successful emergency landing on foam with minimum damage to the aircraft, stopping all four engines during the landing run. The death of the navigator was particularly sad as the captain had done everything perfectly and the decision to bale the crew out was agreed by the duty officer in the control tower.

The accident was caused by over steering the aircraft on the ground with a tractor which broke the pivot bracket on the nose gear.

Vulcan Mk 2 XH556   **April 1966**   **Finningley**
Undercarriage collapsed. Details not known.

Vulcan Mk 2 XJ781   **23rd May 1973**   **Shiraz, Iran**
The aircraft had an undercarriage malfunction and suffered Cat 5 damage on landing (ie, written off). There were no fatalities.

XJ781 was completing a training sortie at Shiraz and the captain selected undercarriage down about eleven miles from the airfield. The main hydraulic pressure fell to zero and no undercarriage lights appeared. The AEO confirmed that no undercarriage doors had opened. The aircraft cleared the circuit and after consultation with the duty command flying decided to operate the emergency air system. Only the starboard undercarriage leg and the nosewheel came down and initially only the starboard gear showed a green light. After some delay the nosewheel eventually locked down.

The captain tried a firm touchdown in an effort to dislodge the port undercarriage leg but to no avail and so preparations were made for a landing. The captain could not order the rear crew to bale out as the nosewheel leg was down and therefore would have prevented the rear crew escaping down the emergency chute, since the leg was situated immediately behind the chute.

At 400ft the pilot jettisoned the escape hatch which left cleanly with no significant increase in cabin noise. The touchdown was smooth and at 80 knots the captain lowered the nosewheel on to the runway. As he felt lateral control reducing the captain allowed the port wing tip to touch the ground and managed to keep straight with full rudder and brake. Unfortunately, as the aircraft came to the end of the foam strip it veered off to the left at approximately 60 knots and pitched down into a gulley. The nose leg was torn off followed shortly by the main undercarriage leg. The nose of the aircraft then hit the far side of the gulley and came to rest.

The crew cabin floor was forced upwards by the crash and the ejection seat brackets were broken. However, the ejection seats did not fire because the safety pins had been inserted as part of the emergency landing drills. The bomb aimer's window was broken and the rear cabin filled with dirt and smoke reducing visibility to two feet. All the crew escaped up the pilots' entrance ladder to the flight deck but the AEO and the nav radar were partially trapped by the bench and had to be freed.

The accident was attributed as so often happens to a double failure. There was a crack in the body of the nose undercarriage port door jack which resulted in loss of hydraulic fluid in the main system. In addition there had been a fatigue failure of the emergency air supply pipe to the main undercarriage.

An eye witness account taken from a web site that specialises in Vulcan stories follows:

> I am not a pilot or aircrew but was present when XJ781 did the crash landing at Shiraz Airfield in 1973. I was in fact a telegraphist on support of the exercise from 12 SU Episkopi in Cyprus. I was a member of the communications support of the exercise. We were accommodated in the Shiraz Inn (nice place with a pool and beers). XJ781 flew over the Inn to show there was a problem with a main undercarriage leg. Not being engineers we thought he was just showing off and never noticed the undercarriage problem.
>
> We were soon alerted to the fact he had crashed on one of the parallel runways at Shiraz and the aircraft had sustained cat 5 (write off) with components. The components (ie all the secret stuff) was stored securely overnight until it could be recovered safely. It was a textbook crash landing by all accounts but the pilot (who I engaged in conversation on the way back to Akrotiri on

a C130) told me a few problems he encountered.

1. He was not aware of a massive ditch between the two parallel runways at Shiraz (otherwise he would have landed on the other one).

2. It was a textbook undercarriage hang up landing.

3. Sadly as the aircraft slewed to the port it was on a hiding to nothing. Big ditch, still a lot of speed, remainder of undercarriage ready for impact and Iranian observer ready for a surprise.

4. The ditch actually broke the back of the aircraft hence cat 5.

5. On the recovery back to Cyprus I was sitting next to the captain who told me he had tried to evacuate the aircraft after jettisoning the canopy but when he stood on his ejector seat it rocked forward a few degrees so he sat down again. He mentioned also the ingress of sand and dust, which stung just a little.

He also told me on the complete evacuation of the aircraft most of the crew approached him and shook his hand. The Iranian observer asked what the congratulations were for and someone in the crew said, ''ell it's a better landing then we usually get'.

Discussion on Miscellaneous Occurrences

These accidents were all random and it is this type of accident which can never be prepared for, even in a modern simulator. The rudder jamming at full travel was unfortunate and possibly a large kick on the rudder pedals might have freed the control but who can tell. Certainly the pilot did a great job landing with full rudder and doing relatively little damage even though the pictures suggest otherwise. The aircraft was soon back in the flight test programme.

The two undercarriage problems were dealt with well by the crew. It is interesting that there was only one case of hydraulic failure which resulted in a major accident which speaks well for the aircraft design.

Summary

The Vulcan was a magnificent aircraft to fly with its fighter type stick and very powerful engines. However like any aircraft it could be mishandled, sometimes with horrendous results. Furthermore, the engines and design of the systems were very new at the time since it was constructed to the very limit of what was possible and therefore was not as reliable as a commercial airliner. The incidents and accidents discussed above have been classified as follows:

Electrics	Engines	Miscellaneous	Pilot Error
908 total failure	909 Mk 104	497 nose gear	897 IMC too low
891 total failure	385 Mk 301	781 hydraulics	894 misjudged landing
600 RAT	604 Mk 301	777 rudder jam	557 misjudged landing
	610 Mk 301		**645 misjudged landing**
	558 Mk 201		**498 misjudged landing**
			770 display
			390 display
			903 display
			535 inadvertent spin
			477 low flying
			536 low flying
			823 excd. max speed
			601 asymmetric
			576 asymmetric

(aircraft in bold type were accidents rather than incidents)

Looking at all the occurrences I believe Avros did a very good job dealing with the aerodynamic problems on both marks of Vulcan as there were no fatal accidents due to the aircraft diving out of control, notwithstanding that the aircraft was incredibly unstable at high subsonic mach numbers. The only unusual handling accidents were in fact as a result of practising double-engine failures and, as already mentioned, there seems to have been a lack of understanding of the dangers in doing double-engined overshoots or rollers. The pilots notes gave a limitation of descent altitude with two engines throttled, but no explanation of the danger of losing directional control at low speed due to differential engine acceleration and no prohibition of roller landings. With hindsight perhaps we might have discussed this with Handling Squadron, but we were not aware of the training that the operational conversion unit and squadrons were doing.

Dealing with system design, the hydraulics were clearly well done but the Mk 1 electrics needed, and got, improvement in the Mk 2. There was never any problem with the pressurisation system.

Engine reliability on the Mk 2 was not as good as it might have been and because the engines were not 'contained' if there was a failure, as in civil aircraft, the results of an engine failure could be catastrophic on the Vulcan.

The only other type of accident where there was a pattern was the landing. The aircraft was unusual in that heavy braking was seldom required either due to using the drag chute or landing in a very high attitude. However it required more skill to land on a runway without using the 'chute as can be seen from the three landings described above.

In summary I do think we at Avros did a good, professional job developing the Vulcan, getting the right compromise between performance and safety.

Not an accident, just the end of an era. (*Fred Martin RZF Digital*)

CHAPTER 8

WEAPONS AND OPERATIONAL ROLES

The Vulcan had been commissioned by the UK Government to be a part of the nuclear deterrent, a bomber carrying nuclear weapons. This was the whole raison d'être of the V Force, an essential part of the UK defence system, so I will briefly mention the main types that were carried by the Vulcan fleet between 1953 and 1992, concentrating on Blue Steel and the Skybolt programme because they were the ones that affected the Vulcan systems, the Vulcan structure and, to a lesser extent, the handling.

WEAPONS

Blue Danube

The original weapon was a free fall fission bomb, Blue Danube, carried internally in the bomb bay with retractable fins to allow for easier loading. This was the UK's first operational nuclear weapon. It had a yield of between 10 and 15 kilotons of TNT and all the V Force was designed to carry it. Only about twenty of these weapons were actually produced and they stayed in service until 1961. One of the problems with these nuclear free-fall bombs was trying to ensure that the V Bombers would not be caught by the explosion of the weapon itself, and it was for this reason that the concept of the 'toss bomb' delivery manoeuvre was considered, known in the States as an Immelmann, and which I demonstrated at Farnborough in 1958.

Blue Steel

This was a stand-off weapon carried under the bomb bay. Avros, as the firm providing the Vulcan, did not get particularly involved with the handling of the free fall weapons, but were very much involved with Blue Steel since the missile was manufactured there also. We had to have the carriage trials for handling and weapon development and then carry out drop trials. The missile was an air-to-surface weapon carrying a nuclear warhead, initially with a nominal range of 100 miles, giving the Vulcan the ability to attack a target from outside the range of the enemy defences and it remained in service until 1970.

The Blue Steel programme started in November 1954 and the contract was awarded in March 1956. The missile climbed to 70,000ft after release reaching a speed of over 2,000 miles an hour. This performance was outside the safety capability of the Aberporth range and so live firings at full range were carried out in Australia on the Woomera range with the aircraft based at the RAAF Edinburgh Field, but we did a lot of the development and initial firing using Aberporth and in fact I did a lot of these flights myself.

The basic design of the missile was a fuselage length of 35ft and a wing span of 13ft. The weapon was made of steel because it flew up to Mach 3.0. The aerodynamic configuration was a canard, that is the pitch controls were ahead of the wing instead of behind as in a conventional aircraft. The guidance system used inertial gyros, quite independent of any external navigation system, but with the parent aircraft's navigation system giving the correct start position to the weapon's navigation system at the moment of launch. The flight control and trajectory came from the internal guidance system only after launch. The propulsion system was driven by a hydrogen peroxide/kerosene fuel mixture while the power supply came from a hydrogen peroxide hydraulic pump.

The first phase of the project was mainly design but some free flight model testing was carried out. The second phase was the carriage of test vehicles, initially made in aluminium and then later in stainless steel. These flights were to check out all the systems in the missile and the inter-relationship between the aircraft systems and missile. This was the first UK production steel aerospace project and there were a lot of teething problems whilst learning how to make the structure of the weapon. Structural test rigs were required to verify the design. At the same time, not only did the missiles have to be built but also the supporting test equipment to make certain all the systems were serviceable during assembly and loading.

The initial 2/5ths scale model Blue Steels were in fact made of steel and were carried by Valiants inside the bomb bay. The motor was a solid propellant rocket and a 24 channel telemetry set was carried to allow monitoring of the key parameters. The models were dropped like a normal bomb, the autopilot took over and the rocket was fired a few seconds after launch. The missiles accelerated to about 1.5 mach and flew for several minutes before the destruct system was operated by the range control. All this work was carried out from Woodford and the range at Aberporth was used. These tests enabled the design team to check their assumptions on the missile handling in the transonic region and at the same time the instrumentation system and the missile destruct system were developed and verified. Looking at my log book, I did some of the Valiant carriage flying in this phase using Valiant WZ375, though I was not concerned in any detail with the object of each test.

Towards the end of 1958 full scale test missiles started to appear but, rather like the Vulcan development programme, the initial engine was not the final one but the de Havilland Double Spectre engine, since the production Armstrong Siddeley/Rolls-Royce Stentor for the operational weapon was not ready. These early test vehicles were required to get more experience of the high supersonic speed environment, to assess the level of vibration in order to know what specifications were required for production components, to check that there were no undesirable aerodynamic transients at missile release and finally to be sure that the system transfers worked correctly at missile release; this last test objective was essential because the aircraft provided hydraulic supplies and temperature control for the missile during the carriage phase and the transition from aircraft to missile supplies at launch had to work satisfactorily.

Because there were still manufacturing difficulties in stainless steel at this time, some of the test missiles were manufactured in aluminium; in addition the hydrogen peroxide turbine was not available and so hydraulic reservoirs and batteries had to be used. The first two test vehicles were launched in 1958 without motors and then in 1959 and 1960 powered missiles in this series were employed. Unfortunately, it was not possible to do valid transition tests with these vehicles because they were not representative of production missiles but they were then followed by suitable missiles and the trials began.

The guidance system consisted of three computers, the navigation computer supplied by Elliotts, and the flight rules computer, FRC, plus the autopilot both provided by Avros. The navigation computer also had a homing computer into which the co-ordinates of the target were fed. The procedure was for the missile navigator and the aircraft navigation system to be operated together until launch, to try to ensure that the launch position was as accurate as possible. The FRC was loaded with the desired trajectory and continually compared the present position with the target position to compute the necessary climb, cruise and glide signals to be sent to the autopilot. The trajectory chosen had a cruise element rather than full boost as it was necessary to choose a flight path that was simple to control. Initially, the designers thought that the propulsion motor would have to have variable thrust since the missile was going to be flown at constant altitude and mach number after the climb. However, after a few full scale flight trials they were able make the motor have fixed cruise thrust and allow the mach to increase as the weight of the missile reduced due to fuel usage.

A significant amount of work had to be carried out to ensure that the missile did not hit the aircraft on release and allowance was made for control runaways, but happily none ever occurred. It had been hoped that the autopilot would be able to have fixed gearings for the whole of the flight but it was found as a result of the trials that, because of the great range of airspeeds, a pitot system had to be introduced which varied the gain of the autopilot controls to match the missile speed during the flight.

I made a considerable number of carriage trials with the missiles to prove the whole guidance system. At the theoretical release point, the connection between the aircraft and missile navigation systems would be broken and the aircraft would fly to the target while the missile navigator calculated the missile position by itself. These positions and other information were telemetred back to the range to assess performance; the full scale test missiles were able to transmit 200 parameters to the ground. As mentioned in Chapter 5, Vulcan Mk 1 XA903 was assigned to the task of carrying and dropping the initial rounds. The aircraft did over one hundred hours flying from Woodford and then carried a Blue Steel out to Australia in November 1960. As described in Chapter 5, I ferried Vulcan Mk 2 XH539 out to Australia for the final trials in December 1961.

The RAF had to decide how the trials had to be supervised to obtain CA release from Boscombe and also how the squadron servicing crews were to be trained. It clearly was essential to avoid a duplication of work and so No 4 Joint Service Trials Unit was formed, initially at Woodford but then it travelled out to Edinburgh Field in Australia for the full range trials. These started in Australia in 1962 and about fifty missiles were launched altogether. The first CA release trials took place on 25th February 1962 using a Valiant. Another missile was released in June but the whole programme was complicated by the sudden decision to change from high level release to low level release because of the new Russian high level interceptor missile system. This capability had been anticipated but came rather sooner than expected and it made the task of Avros developing the missile that much harder, not to mention the JSTU and the squadrons. Consequently, the missile trajectories had to be re-evaluated and the CA releases did not start again until 22nd October 1963. Furthermore, the whole pattern of Vulcan operational crew training had to be revised to introduce long, low level flights.

The formal approval for the change took place in October 1963 when a government meeting took place in Whitehall, where it was agreed that the Vulcan/Blue Steel low level role should be sanctioned at a cost of £2.25m for research and development and £0.8m for production, numbers that seem insignificant these days.

A total of thirteen more missiles were then released, ten from 1,000ft and the final three from 50,000ft. Interestingly, two of the releases were actually abortive due to electrical failure, one at high altitude and one at low altitude and the missiles had to be destroyed by the range safety officer. The first squadron aircraft were fitted in September 1962 and Blue Steel remained in service until 1970.

Though Blue Steel was an effective weapon that could not be

jammed after release, rather like the V1s in the Second World War, it was a difficult weapon to be kept immediately available because the on-board electronics had to be protected from extremes of temperature. The other problem was the highly dangerous nature of the fuel so that the weapons always had to be kept near a water reservoir so that the fuel could be dumped if there were any leaks.

Skybolt

It was becoming very clear by the late 1950s that in order to extend the life of the V Bombers a replacement weapon for Blue Steel would be required, since its range was no longer nearly great enough. The Americans were also of that opinion though they thought at first that a stand-off range of about 400 statute miles would be enough. However, they changed their minds and agreed with the UK Air Staff Requirement that a stand-off range of 1,200 statute miles would be needed in order to reach strategic targets within Russia. A ballistic missile would be desirable since it would be very difficult to intercept because of its high speed and it would be impossible to 'jam'. Consequently, the Douglas Aircraft Corporation received a study contract in May 1959 to design a rocket-fired aircraft-launched missile with a range of over 1,000 miles. In February 1960 Douglas was awarded a contract to build research and development missiles which were designated GAM-87A but was dubbed Skybolt almost from the onset of the programme. Aerojet General was to provide the two-stage solid-propulsion system and General Electric was to provide the re-entry vehicle which carried the warhead whilst Nortronics were to provide an astro-inertial system with a star tracker and a ballistic missile computer. In March 1960 the UK were offered Skybolt and in May the British Government decided that they would buy one hundred Skybolts.

Notwithstanding the launch of this programme, the concept of a V Force continuing to carry nuclear weapons was always suspect because of the US Navy's Polaris missile which was very attractive, since the enemy could never know the launch position because the submarines were very difficult to locate. The Royal Navy were advocating the use of Polaris at the same time as the Skybolt programme was authorized. When Kennedy became President in 1961 he called for a review of the Defense Program by McNamara, Secretary for Defense, but Skybolt proceeded in spite of these difficulties. Clearly, what was needed if Skybolt was going to go ahead was a fast, fault-free development programme but unfortunately this did not happen. There were a variety of problems which resulted in the missile not going anywhere near the distance or target and, ironically, the only completely successful launch occurred just as the decision to cancel was taken.

I was personally involved in the Skybolt programme and my first task was to ferry XH535 to Edwards Air Force base in June 1961 for radio compatibility trials to be carried out on the dry lake, as far away as possible from radio interference. At the same time Vulcan XH537 was being structurally modified to be able to carry the missiles which weighed 15,000lbs and were 38ft long. By 28th September 1961 XH537 was ready and after a quick flight to check handling with the pylons on, I took it up with two dummy missiles the following day. I have described the handling of the Vulcan with Skybolts in Chapter 5. From then on through 1962 we carried and dropped Skybolts with increasing sophistication, but at the same time the launches that were taking place in the States were very disappointing. It became clear that the programme was under threat of termination and the United States Government was beginning to think that the Polaris submarine-launched missile would be a better way to maintain a nuclear deterrent.

In December 1962 Macmillan met Kennedy in Nassau and the programme was virtually stopped. Kennedy offered the UK the programme but it was deemed too expensive. Kennedy then generously offered to fund half the programme but Macmillan still refused. The programme was finally cancelled in February 1963 but not before I had had the opportunity to attend a training course in Santa Monica in January 1963 which I found absolutely fascinating as a keen navigator, both on the water and in the air.

The Vulcan was an ideal carrier for Skybolt, unlike the Victor where a lot of time and money was wasted trying to adapt the aircraft for Skybolts for which it was basically unsuitable with its shorter undercarriage and large wing span. There is still a school of thought that the Skybolt programme should have been continued, but in my view, both the United States and the United Kingdom probably did the right thing in not persevering with the missile because it was much harder to know where the submarines were than the aircraft, in spite of their rapid dispersal capability. However, the modifications to the Vulcan wing to carry Skybolts strengthened it enormously and gave the Vulcan a greatly extended fatigue life, very useful in the new low level role. Furthermore, the pickup points fitted for the Skybolts under each wing proved a godsend for carrying jamming radar during the Falklands campaign.

As mentioned, it was somewhat ironic that the last firing of Skybolt, the second guided round, was a complete success. The missile travelled the full distance and the error from target was 1,230ft. As a matter of interest, at the end of 1962 the total cost of Skybolt to the USAF was $356m with a budget of $492.6m, though it was expected that the final spend would have been $550m. Production procurement was expected to be $1.8 billion for 1,000 missiles. Thanks to the generosity of the Americans, the UK was not asked to contribute to the basic R&D costs but only to the additional R&D costs to make the weapon applicable to the Vulcan. At end of 1962 we had spent $21m on US contracts and expected to spend a total of $30m. The manpower investment in the project was significant; there were eighty-seven full time staff based in the US, service and civilians, 250 including dependants. These numbers do not include representatives from Avros, AEI, and Elliotts, also based in the States and over 250 short duration visits made by government and contractors.

My personal view is that Skybolt would have been a very elegant programme to have completed, but its cancellation in favour of Polaris is well understood.

Yellow Sun

In parallel with Blue Steel development and the consequent equipping of some of the Vulcan squadrons, a new nuclear weapon became available, Yellow Sun, to be carried by the non-Blue Steel squadrons. Yellow Sun underwent successful trials off Christmas Island, and was operationally deployed in 1962, at the time of the Cuban missile crisis. It had a yield of up to 1 Megaton of TNT.

WE177

This weapon replaced Yellow Sun and again was used by non-Blue Steel squadrons. Originally conceived for the TSR2, it was given to the V Force when the aircraft was cancelled in 1965. There were several variants and the yield was in the region of 400 kilotons. The weight of the bomb was 950lbs. When WE177 went out of service in 1992, the RAF became a non-nuclear force.

OPERATIONAL ROLES

High Level Strategic Bomber

When the idea for the Vulcan was first conceived it was accepted that the safest way to attack an enemy was to fly as high as possible. At that time flying high had a number of advantages including:

- The aircraft was out of range of enemy surface-to-air missiles
- It was out of range of enemy radar
- It was too high to be intercepted by enemy fighters
- The higher an aircraft flies in the atmosphere, the less is the density of the air, so the operating range will increase.

At this time the fleet of Vulcans were painted white. This colour scheme was known as anti-flash white. White was chosen as it was thought to be the most effective high-level camouflage colour. When the aircraft was flying at 40,000ft or above, anti-flash white made it very hard to detect from the ground. As the name suggests, anti-flash white also had another purpose. It was believed that white would help to reflect any thermal energy which could damage the Vulcan or her crew resulting from a nuclear blast. Whether this is valid thinking is open to debate, as any Vulcan delivering a nuclear device correctly would have been many miles away at the time of detonation.

The Vulcan/Blue Steel method of attacking a designated target would be to fly towards it at around 48,000ft. It would then climb to a launching altitude of 50,000ft. When within range (anywhere between 100 and 120 miles) the missile would be released. At this point the Vulcan captain would fashion an escape as fast as possible away from the target area. The missile, travelling at mach 2.5, would climb to 70,000ft. Four minutes after release it would have completed its 100-mile journey and been over the target when it would descend at around 1.5 mach and destroy it. During the operational life of the Blue Steel system the Soviets did not have any suitable defence against its high speed and small size.

Dropping a free-fall nuclear weapon from the bomb bay would clearly be a more hazardous task because the aircraft was much more likely to be attacked and it would be much nearer the nuclear explosion when it went off. The aircraft would need to turn as quickly as possible to minimise the effect of the detonation, hence consideration of the aforementioned 'toss bomb' manoeuvre.

Low Level Strategic Bomber

On 1st May 1960 a USAF U-2 spy aircraft was shot down by a Soviet surface-to-air missile. The U-2 was struck at an altitude of around 68,000ft. This effectively meant that the days of the Vulcan as a high level strategic bomber were over. With the advancement of enemy radar and missile technology, it was necessary for the role of the Vulcan to change from high level bomber to low level tactical strike aircraft. The risks of low level flight were great, but not as great as being illuminated by enemy radar and attacked with ground-to-air rockets or missiles.

The navigational and bombing equipment being used at the time was not designed to work at low level; however, tests quickly proved that the Vulcan's systems were able to cope remarkably well with the change in role. Thus, by early 1963 Vulcan Mk 1A crews were being trained for low level sorties. A year later Mk 2 crews were being offered the same training. It was around this time that the anti-flash white paintwork of the Vulcan was changed to the green and grey camouflage subsequently used to help prevent Soviet interceptor pilots distinguishing the approaching bombers.

Blue Steel was test fired at low level, below 1,000ft, at Woomera in Australia and as described previously, the trials were successful. However the range of the missile was now drastically reduced from up to 200 miles to just 25-50 miles. The Vulcan captain also had to climb sufficiently high before releasing the missile so that its boosters were able to fire before crashing into the ground. Once released, Blue Steel would quickly climb to 70,000ft before descending towards its target. The accuracy of the weapon was stated to be within 300 yards.

The Vulcan airframe was designed for an average life of 3,900 flying hours in a high level role. At lower altitudes the stresses that the airframe was subject to were much greater due to turbulence. This of course was why the Valiant's life was so short and why the Victor too had problems. The use of reinforcing iron plates and strengthening modifications implemented when the Skybolt missile system was destined to be carried by the Vulcan, allowed the fleet of aircraft to continue in their new role until the implementation of the Tornado in the mid 1980s. In theory, should it have been necessary, Avros could have modified the Vulcan fleet to continue until the turn of the century.

The aircraft was fitted with terrain following radar in the mid '60s so that it could carry out its low level role more safely, though the equipment had to be used with care.

Considering that the Victor B2 was unusable in the low level role due to fatigue fractures, before its major conversion to tankers after 1969, as was the Valiant in 1964, there is no argument that the original Vulcan delta design was robust.

Maritime Radar Reconnaissance

Further advances in missile technology during the mid to late 1960s eventually led to the demise of Blue Steel. Long-range intercontinental ballistic missiles were developed which could be launched from huge distances. These were seen as preferable to risking the lives of air crew. On 30th June 1969 the responsibility for the NATO strategic deterrent forces was passed to the Royal Navy and their Polaris-equipped submarines. From December 1970 all remaining Vulcan squadrons were equipped with free-fall nuclear bombs.

Sampler on Skybolt attachment. (*Fred Martin RZF Digital*)

Samplers with locator. (*Fred Martin RZF Digital*)

Once Polaris had taken over Britain's nuclear defence, the Vulcan was to have a new role. Clearly it could be used as a conventional bomber, capable of carrying up to twenty-one, 1,000lb bombs. Some were also converted to a maritime radar reconnaissance role. For this duty the Vulcan was fitted with two under-wing air sampling pods, together with a smaller, locator pod under the port wing. Eight aircraft were converted to this MRR role, five having fixed fittings, the others having removable ones.

As this role took place mainly over sea water, the selected Vulcans had a tough gloss polyurethane coating applied to them to prevent unnecessary damage to their airframes from the corrosive salty air. Tasks assigned to this handful of converted aircraft included working in collaboration with Nimrod aircraft to fly over the North Sea oil rigs on anti-terrorist patrol, and the much more hazardous collection of dust samples from the upper atmosphere down wind of nuclear test explosions. The gloss paint finish had an additional advantage here, in that it was easier to clean off any radioactive particles which might have attached themselves to the fuselage.

Refuelling Tanker
Towards the twilight of her years in the RAF, some of the remaining Vulcans were converted into tanker aircraft, as the large bomb bay made an ideal location to store extra fuel tanks. The rear ECM housing was emptied and the refuelling rig stored in the new-found space.

Mk 17 hose drum under ECM fairing. (*Fred Martin RZF Digital*)

The Mk 16 hose drum unit example, HDU, was fitted to the Valiant bombers during their conversion to tankers. The HDU had a 105ft (32m) hose wrapped round a rotatable drum. One end was connected to the fuel system, the other to a drogue which helped stabilise the hose and was used as a target for the receiver aircraft. Radio contact between the two aircraft was unnecessary as a system of lights on the tanker could be used to inform the receiving aircraft of how the process was progressing. The rate that fuel could be pumped from the tanker aircraft was around 500 gallons a minute. The Vulcan tankers were not fitted with the Mk 16 HDU. Instead, they had the newer Mk 17 units installed.

50 Squadron operated these aircraft between 21st June 1982 and 31st March 1984, thus becoming the last RAF squadron to operate the Vulcan.

Black Buck
For the Falkland campaign, so excellently described by Rowland White in his book *Vulcan 607*, the aircraft had to have extra equipment. Luckily, the aircraft chosen were fitted with Olympus 301 engines and incorporated the Skybolt modification so it was possible to hang jamming equipment onto the Skybolt hard points. The Westinghouse AN/ALQ-101D equipment was chosen and hung on the starboard Skybolt attachment and a Shrike anti-radar AGM-45 was hung on the port Skybolt attachment.

Shrike anti-radar AGM-45 on port, AN/ALQ-101D jammer on starboard.
(*Fred Martin RZF Digital*)

Summary

The Vulcan was, and still is, a most remarkable aircraft. The fact that it was designed and built in the 1950s makes the technical accomplishment of the design team even more astonishing. The Avro Vulcan has often been compared with the USAF Boeing B52 Stratofortress strategic bomber, since both aircraft were in service simultaneously. However the Vulcan was smaller and lighter, much more agile and marginally faster than the B52 with a much higher service ceiling. The two aircraft were designed to have very different roles. As mentioned previously, the Vulcan was aimed at operating in the relatively short-range European theatre and needed to be operated from medium-length airfields. The life expectancy of the Vulcan was probably only in the region of twenty years as a nuclear deterrent whereas the B52, with regular updating and modification, is still operating today carrying large payloads of conventional weapons.

Fortunately, the Vulcan was never required to drop a live nuclear device in anger. Clearly, throughout the cold war the concept of the nuclear deterrent worked since it would have been impossible for the Soviets to make a pre-emptive strike to attack all the dispersed Vulcan squadrons with their four-minute scramble capability, and a 'tit for tat' nuclear war was unthinkable. Hence the Vulcan squadrons patrolling the skies helped not only to protect Europe from attack but acted as a front line defence force for the USA.

Finally, the appearance of the Vulcan over Port Stanley acted not only as a real threat to the Argentinian armed forces on the ground but also as a key warning to the Argentinians that even Buenos Aires might be attacked. This consideration was a decisive factor in the Argentine strategic planning and ensured that the life of the Vulcan ended on a high note.

CHAPTER 9

VULCAN MK 2 558 G-VLCN

Author delivering XH558 to RAF Waddington (*Vulcan to the Sky Trust*)

So far this book has been about what we did to make the Vulcan work, how we sorted out all the problems and managed to make it not only a safe but also a delightful aircraft to fly. However, the exciting thing about chronicling this history is that the Vulcan project is not dead. One aircraft Vulcan XH558, like the Phoenix, has arisen from the ashes. I must declare a personal interest here as I was the first person to fly this aircraft in June 1960 on its production schedule; I flew it twice, totalling three hours and fifteen minutes. As far as I can remember there was nothing unusual about the flights, just the routine of checking the engines, auto stabilisers, power controls, electrics, and all the systems in the normal way. In fact as this aircraft was the RAF's first Mk 2, I finished up by delivering it to Waddington on 1st July 1960, with Wing Commander Calder, Officer Commanding of the Operational Conversion Unit who had been flying with us to get up to date and ready for the Mk 2. I flew the aircraft twice again in June

1965 for another two hours twenty minutes after it had had the Skybolt modifications fitted at Woodford. Eventually of course, there was no Skybolt programme but 558 had a lot of the structural Skybolt modifications installed to strengthen it and to extend the life of the airframe. After the modifications XH558 went back into squadron service, later became a tanker with a hose drum unit fitted and finally went to the display flight. It is an interesting point that though XH558 was the first Mk 2 aircraft, it finished up by being the last one to fly in 1993. Luckily, thanks to David Walton, who bought the aircraft from the RAF, and Robert Pleming, who believed that he could climb every mountain and did not understand the word 'no', this fantastic aircraft took to the air again on Thursday 18th October 2007 to thrill us all once again and inspire the youth of this generation as it did thirty to forty years ago. Since that day in 2007 it has flown at 14 air displays during 2008 totalling 35 hours 55 minutes and 31 flights.

Designing the Vulcan and making it work from its inception in 1947 to its first flight in 1952 and then further developing it into the Vulcan Mk 2 was a monumental task for Avros, for Bristol Siddeley, for the RAF and for the politicians who had to justify the project. The costs were enormous and the whole programme was always under the threat of cancellation. The design was at the technical edge of what was possible at the time; nobody knew how the delta shape would handle. Over 50 years later the dedicated team at Bruntingthorpe and the generous firms who helped them in getting the aircraft to fly again faced as great, if not a greater task than we did in developing the Vulcan in the first place.

The safety rules that applied to getting the aircraft to fly again were very different from the procedures in the past. Not only did the aircraft have to be cleared to fly by a civil organisation, the rules were no longer just to UK standards but were to a European standard, the Joint Air-worthiness Requirements. The Safety Regulation Group of the Civil Aviation Authority had to ensure that all the safety criteria for the aircraft flying, whilst not meeting the criteria for the latest airliners, were acceptable for the type of flying that it was to undertake. Not only were the rules different but also the way the aircraft had to be repaired and inspected had to satisfy today's civil standards and not the military practices of the past. Indeed, if the original Vulcan had had to meet present-day specifications and procedures it probably would never have flown at all or at least it would have been far too heavy and certainly far too expensive. These maintenance challenges, together with many more, made the cost of this project very great indeed and there can be little doubt that, though the money spent on XH558 has been small compared with the original sums of money that were spent developing the Vulcan, to the team operating the aircraft the challenges have seemed just as great. Furthermore in order now to keep the aircraft flying beyond 2008, the team have a very great financial challenge to meet.

Reviewing the history of the project, the Royal Air Force had come reluctantly to the conclusion in the early 1990s that it could no longer justify keeping XH558 serviceable just to do air displays. The aircraft was put on the market and tender documents were circulated. I cannot do better than to quote an article which I saw on the web in 1993 by David Walton whose firm submitted the winning tender:

> Several weeks after the arrival of the last Lightning, Tony Hulls, the Bruntingthorpe leading member of the Lightning Preservation Group, suggested that we should tender for the Vulcan XH558. After many months of indecision the Ministry of Defence had finally decided that this most famous of all post-war aircraft should be put up for disposal. Without any prompting, tender papers duly arrived in the post. An appointment was made with RAF Waddington for us to view the aircraft and when we arrived we were shown around by a somewhat discon-solate ground crew member. XH558 looked immaculate, standing proudly in her hangar being worked upon by the service crew. The bomb bay doors displaying the word 'FAREWELL' said it all. We were told that a petition 'Save the Vulcan' with over 200,000 signatures had been submitted to Parliament, but all to no avail. The service crew told us of the prospective purchaser who had been to view her and of some of their plans for her, including an anonymous group who proposed to disembowel her and turn her into a restaurant – presumably the chef's special would have been 'Bomb Bay Duck'...!
>
> Such atrocities could not be permitted so the answer was to put in a bid – but where to pitch the bid? We had heard all sorts of rumours of large bids coming from overseas parties, but the grapevine informed us that there were already several Vulcans in various parts of the world outside the UK and that there would be a public outcry if 558 was to depart her native land. Even the politicians would have to accept the public will that if she was to be grounded at least it should be where her devoted followers would be able to see her from time to time.
>
> So with a finger in the wind a figure was arrived at and entered on the Tender Bid form, despatched by first class post on Friday 5th March 1993 to MOD disposals, to arrive ready for opening on Tuesday 9th March 1993. All we could do then was wait. Tuesday 9th came and passed then Wednesday, then Thursday, by Friday we were beginning to think that we had not been successful or that our bid had not been received. We phoned MOD and were

assured that they had received our offer but her fate was in the hands of the Minister and no decision as to her future had yet been made.

On Wednesday we were called by MOD and asked to be present at a Press Conference at RAF Waddington scheduled for 1300 hours on Thursday 18th March. An announcement would then be made about what was to happen to the RAF's last Vulcan aircraft... but congratulations were in order! We duly arrived at the officers' mess at Waddington at about 1300 hours on Thursday to be met by the Vulcan Display Team, who led us into the officers' mess where we were introduced to the Waddington Commanding Officer, Group Captain Uprichard, and several of his staff and senior staff from the Ministry of Defence. After some time we were led into a room where a large press gathering was assembled.

Air Commodore David Hurrel made the official announcement and introduced us as the lucky purchasers. It was then open to the press to ask questions about our intentions for the aircraft – what was her future to be? Would she fly again after being delivered by the RAF? Would the public be able to see her? How much did we pay? Were we pleased with ourselves?

Having faced and answered the barrage of questions it was only just beginning to dawn on us as a family the responsibility we had taken on. We were now the proud owners of the famous Delta Lady and woe betide us if we did not look after her...! Since that day, letters from well-wishers and Vulcan devotees have dominated our postbag creating a major task in replying individually to each one.

What does the future hold for 558? Well, for our part the first major hurdle to get over is to get the aircraft inside a hangar before the onset of winter. Ambitious plans are currently on the drawing board for a prestigious museum building to house our growing collection of working British 1st and 2nd generation military jet aircraft. Hopefully, planning permission will be granted and the construction works got underway. We are hopeful that a successful Airshow on July 18th will help fund the initial phase of the building works.

The successful purchase of XH558 was just the start. Walton also had the foresight to buy not only the aircraft but a whole raft of vital spares including eight brand new Olympus 202 engines from the RAF as well as all the servicing documentation. Dr Robert Pleming appeared on the scene in 1996 and discussed with David Walton what it would take to get the aircraft into the air again; he produced a document showing exactly what needed to be done and who needed to be convinced that it really would be possible for XH558 to fly again. Together they decided how to set about getting the permissions that would be needed to proceed with the project. They needed to get the support not only of British Aerospace but also of the many, many firms who had had their original equipment on the aircraft. In fact, when I first heard about the proposal I was the Technical Member on the Board of the Civil Aviation Authority and we were getting frequent requests to give a Permit To Fly to a rebuilt Lightning fighter. Our Safety Regulation Group refused to grant a permit since the last thing that they wanted was a retired fighter aircraft with a rather dubious safety record flying around the United Kingdom giving air displays. I therefore rather assumed that a similar request for the Vulcan would in due course also be turned down. My stay on the board came to an end and I thought no more about it.

The next thing I heard (in 2004) was that the Vulcan programme was go, that the Lottery had granted some money for the project and that the CAA was prepared to grant a Permit To Fly to XH558 providing the necessary maintenance steps were carried out. I was amazed but delighted and realised straightaway what an enormous amount of work must have already been done to get the aircraft to the 'starting gate'. Robert Pleming and David Walton had been having long conversations with the CAA to get their view on the feasibility of the project and the procedures that would be needed. CAA had not ruled out granting a permit to XH558 but discussed the large number of things that needed to be done first before a permit could be granted.

British Aerospace, who now owned Avro, had also been approached since without their support as the designer of the aircraft with their library of drawings it would have been impossible to proceed; predictably they could not give an immediate decision. Finally, by 1999 the B.Ae Board agreed to support the project and nominated their organisation in Manchester as the design authority; getting XH558 back into the air now seemed a possibility. With this hurdle surmounted, Pleming and Walton reckoned that technically it would be possible to proceed.

Technical feasibility had been determined during the project definition workshop of September 1999 and the technical survey in November 1999-February 2000. Of course being technically feasible was a great step forward but the other side of the coin was who was going to pay for the work? Pleming and Walton naturally realised that the project was going to be incredibly expensive and in fact Walton's company had already spent over £500,000, counting spares and lost revenue though the aircraft itself was purchased for only £25,000. In 2002 Felicity Irwin DL and Robert Fleming decided that private donations, necessary though they were, could not produce enough money and that an approach had to be made to the Heritage Lottery Fund, notwithstanding that it was apparently against the fund's policy to provide money to enable old aircraft to be prepared to fly again.

In fact, surprisingly, the fund were very helpful in suggesting ways the project could be supported, but it took several iterations of draft proposals and discussions before the final and successful submission to the Heritage Lottery Fund in 2003 was achieved. The basis of the submission was the emphasis placed on the educational aspect of the project, stressing the role the aircraft played in the Cold War; XH558 taking to the air would be a reminder to the budding engineers and scientists of today of the excellence of the aircraft, then at the forefront of technology, the importance of manufacturing in the contemporary environment and showing what this country could achieve given the right incentives. The Fund decided initially at the end of 2003 to provide £2.5m for the project and this was increased to £2.73m in June 2004 when the programme was then firmly in place, though of course there was a fund matching requirement of £900,000 which was an ongoing challenge.

The management of the project was changed from TVOC, The Vulcan Operating Company with Pleming as executive director and Walton as a director, to VTS, the Vulcan to the Sky Trust a registered charity, with Pleming as chief executive. Trustees were appointed, the first chairman being Air Chief Marshal Sir Michael Knight. In addition, a Vulcan to the Sky club was formed with Geoffrey Pool as the original chairman; this club has been vitally important in getting a steady flow of funds to the project and enabling XH558 back into the air and it is still very much needed if the aircraft is to be kept flying.

Even though the CAA had agreed in principle to grant a Permit to Fly, the path they laid down to obtaining this permit was extremely onerous. The Vulcan was quite unlike the normal run of aircraft that have permits to fly and the SRG at Gatwick decided that an approved engineering organisation was needed to go through the many required stages before the aircraft could be declared ready for flight. Pleming and Walton decided that Marshalls of Cambridge should be approached and the firm agreed to be the approved engineering/ inspection organisation; the hangar at Bruntingthorpe became an outpost of the main maintenance base at Cambridge, suitably connected with all the modern communication technology. SRG approved the fitness of the maintenance hangar and the procedures to be adopted; in fact these procedures proved and are proving to be very demanding when applied to a fifty-year-old military aircraft which of course had never met them in the first place.

A technical survey of the aircraft was started in 1999 and the Vulcan operating engineers, supervised by Marshalls, stripped it down to find out what actual condition it was in. In 2005 the work started in earnest and the complete aircraft was inspected minutely. Technically, the team had to deal with all the decay and corrosion that had taken place over the years and this was not an easy task because a lot of the deterioration of the structure was not obvious. Visual inspection could only get so far. It was possible to crawl down the air intake tunnels so the jet pipes could be examined. By removing access panels in the wing it was also possible, for example, to get into the claustrophobic fuel tank bays. But there were an enormous number of areas that could not be reached and had to be checked using non-destructive techniques like X-rays, eddy currents and ultrasound. These inspections were a vital first task to assess the work and, happily, the aircraft passed the survey in that nothing that could not be fixed was found. On the other hand, there was a lot of work that had to be done. Some repairs could be done in house but some, like certain of the control surfaces, were corroded and had to be sent out for repair. Of course there was an enormous amount of equipment to be overhauled by outside suppliers, Original Equipment Manufacturers, OEMs, and all their equipment had to be checked. From the results of the survey the work programme was established to get the aircraft back in the air.

Repairing the damage was not straightforward as a lot of the material used at the time was no longer available; for example some of the metal skins, nuts and bolts were no longer manufactured. Of course there were still some old aircraft spread around the UK and one way the team at Bruntingthorpe got this outdated material was to try to get what was available from them. This method of getting spares, by robbing other aircraft, is of course a very standard one called 'Christmas Treeing' and has been around since the maintenance of production aircraft began. However, where the parts or material could not be found then substitutes had to be obtained and approved and, though the new materials were almost certainly better, approval had to be obtained from Marshalls acting on behalf of the CAA and, in some cases, special testing was specified.

Vulcan 558 consisted of a lot more than a metal structure. There was all the wiring and the piping – fuel, pressurisation, hydraulics, oxygen and pneumatics for a start. Testing the electrical circuits, the relays, the switches and the actuators was not a trivial task and this work had to be carried out in accordance with the original designs. For example, the operating and signalling circuits to the power controls was fundamental to the safety of the aircraft and the basic design had to be fully understood; luckily the manuals were all available but they had to be found, read and absorbed by the engineers so that everything could be checked for correct functioning. The rigid piping for the different systems was another challenge since it all had to be physically inspected and checked for damage and leaks. In addition, actually getting some of the piping out of the aircraft was not easy because of the way it was attached to the structure.

Another difficulty which had to be dealt with was the flexible piping and seals. Understandably, a lot of this material was no longer usable and, as mentioned, substitute pipes and seals needed to be chosen, approved and tested where necessary.

A lot of the military weapons systems, equipment and wiring was removed, weighing in the region of 7,000lbs, but then ballast weights had to be installed to ensure that the centre of gravity was in the correct place. So meticulous was the procedure for preparing the aircraft for its first flight that it took into account the weight of the three crew who flew the aircraft, something that I never had to consider when I flew Vulcans, though the flight briefing must have had token weights for the crew on the briefing sheet. I have a strong suspicion that when my wife accompanied me back from Farnborough to Woodford in 1958 in the right hand seat, her actual weight wasn't top of our priority list!

A typical problem which the team encountered was with the pilots' instrument system. Smiths Aerospace, now part of General Electric Aviation, was then very much in business but they were no longer able to support their original Military Flight System and so modern instruments had to be substituted and the design approved. A Bendix Flight System together with a Garmin GPS system was fitted. Satellite navigation systems were definitely not available when I was flying Vulcans though I wish they had been, so that I need not have been quite so dependent on the navigators in the back! Not that they didn't do superbly but, fundamentally, I would have liked a Vulcan which I could have flown by myself. Interestingly, the Garmin repeater on the flight deck is fitted where the machmeter used to be, since 558 has a speed restriction of 300 knots flying with the Red Arrows and 250 knots otherwise, instead of the original 415 knots. There is also a height

XH558 instrument panel mock up (*Vulcan to the Sky Trust*)

restriction of 17,500ft and clearly with these restrictions a machmeter is not required.

The way the aircraft is now flown is a very important consideration because, in order to comply with the certification requirements, it is necessary to measure the fatigue usage not only of the airframe but also of the engines. As mentioned, there are a total of eight spare engines available, which should enable the aircraft to fly for quite a few years using a system of rotating engine changing.

558 is not fitted with a flight data recorder since, in the event of an accident, it would not be rebuilt and the exact cause of the accident would be immaterial, since no other Vulcan aircraft will ever fly. XH558 is limited to flight in clear weather, Visual Flight Rules; it is being proposed that in the future the position of the aircraft will be tracked using a satellite position reporting system, Skytrac, which will be available to the whole world on the internet. Personally, if I had had a choice at the time I was flying XH558, I think I would have preferred the flight data recorder so that there would have been no argument over what was actually done on the flight; however the flight test department would have found Skytrac useful and, as chief test pilot, I would have loved to have known what my pilots were up to.

This brief description of the inspection and work that had to be done to get 558 flying and the current work that still needs to be done to keep it going has been included in this book to give an idea of the enormous magnitude of the task at Bruntingthorpe . To summarise the extent of the problem I am grateful to Guy Bartlett's website for the facts below:-

Each Vulcan contained 430,000 bolts, nuts and rivets.

Each Vulcan was constructed from over 100,000 different components.

Each Vulcan consists of 2.5 miles of rolled sections.

It has 9,500 feet of tubing.

14 miles of electrical cable.

Each Vulcan has up to sixteen fuel tanks.

Contains enough sheet metal to cover 1.5 football pitches.

The Vulcan was a fully electric aircraft. A fore-runner of the modern fly-by-wire jets used by the RAF today.

The Vulcan can weigh up to 100 tonnes fully loaded.

The Vulcan gulped 25 tonnes of air per minute through her intakes.

A Vulcan could carry enough fuel to power a Ford Escort motor car for 35 years at 10,000 miles a year.

The 4 Olympus jets produce as much power as 18 railway engines. They were capable of delivering 80,000lbs of thrust.

Vulcans could outmanoeuvre F-15s in high altitude mock dogfights.

If necessary the Vulcan could be started in 27 seconds, and be airborne within 2 minutes of a squadron scramble.

The record altitude flown by a Vulcan was 64,000ft.

Fortunately, the Bruntingthorpe management is first class and the team work is superb. Whenever I walk round the hangar I am lost in admiration for the dedication of the team. Interestingly, because of the size of the whole task, in August 2006 the programme very nearly came to an untimely end due a financial crisis. The work was going very well indeed but there were insufficient funds to proceed with the project. It was necessary to appeal to the general public for funds and to find a donor to ensure the completion of the maintenance task. Thanks to the generosity of Sir Jack Hayward who agreed to supply £500,000 at the very last moment, and pledges of support and contributions totalling about £700,000 from supporters all round the country the project was saved, the work could be continued and the aircraft flew. In 2008 two benefactors Mike Neal and Eddie Forrester came forward to enable the aircraft to fly throughout the display season.

The situation is of course changing from minute to minute as new critical paths and financial hurdles become apparent, but the enthusiasm of all concerned, from managers, inspectors, engineers and volunteers hopefully will enable the aircraft to fly again in 2009 and onwards and keep thrilling the crowds and inspiring a new generation. The Vulcan was always a show stopper and, in that respect, nothing has changed.

GLOSSARY

A&AEE	Aeroplane and Armament Experimental Establishment.
Aileron	Controls aircraft in roll.
Aileron float	The movement of all the aileron surfaces in the same direction when g is applied thus effectively introducing an extra elevator movement.
Amplitude	Normally the size of an oscillation.
Angle of attack	The angle between the chord of the wing and the airflow.
Artificial feel	Springs connected to the pilot's control so that the forces required to operate the controls resemble the natural aerodynamic forces without power controls.
Asymmetric power	When the engine powers from each side of the aircraft are not equal.
Autostabiliser	A stability aid/device which automatically controls the way an aircraft flies.
AAPU	Auxiliary Airborne Power Unit to provide emergency electrical power for the Mk 2 below 30,000ft.
AEO	Air Electronics Officer, Vulcan rear aircrew member who controls the aircraft electrics and ECM equipment.
Bag tank	A very large flexible container, bag, which contains fuel.
Balance tab	A secondary control fitted to a primary aircraft control surface to adjust the control forces.
BLEU	Blind Landing Experimental Unit.
Boundary layer	The airflow next to the aircraft skin which, because of friction, does not travel at the speed of the aircraft.
Buffet	Vibration felt in an aircraft due to disturbance in the aerodynamic airflow.
Buffet boundary	A 'chart' of where buffet occurs as the

	mach number, altitude, and g is varied.
Busbar	Common electrical point for connecting supplies and loads. Note that the busbar may be one point or a collection of points all connected together.
CA release	A document which gave permission, with limitations, for an aircraft to be used by RAF pilots.
Camber	The shape of a cross-section of a wing in the fore and aft direction, normally curved.
CG	Centre of Gravity.
Chord	The line and distance between front and back of wing.
CSDU	Constant Speed Drive Unit used to produce constant frequency alternating current.
Damping	Positive damping is when an aircraft oscillation gets less without any interference from the pilot or stability aid. Negative damping is when the oscillation gets larger and goes out of control.
Electronic countermeasures ECM	Aircraft electronic equipment fitted to confuse the enemy's detection system and weapons.
Elevator	Controls aircraft in pitch.
Elevator angle per g	The elevator angle needed to apply one g acceleration.
Elevon	Aircraft control combining pitch and roll control.
ETPS	Empire Test Pilots School.
Fatigue life	The number of vibrations of a given amplitude/size a structure can withstand before it breaks, often expressed in hours.
Flare	The act of a pilot rotating the aircraft in order to make a landing.
Flight envelope	The complete set of aircraft limitations in height, speed and g.
Flight system	Integrated flight instrument system in front of the pilot.
Flutter	Rapid oscillation of a control surface and/or structure.

Fly-by-wire	A control that is connected to the crew compartment by electrical wiring instead of metal control rods.
Fulcrum	A balance point round which a lever rotates.
Houchin	Ground electrical power rig for a Vulcan.
GCA	Ground Controlled Approach. A controller passes deviation information from the ideal glide slope and runway centre line to the pilot, as measured by precision radars.
IAS	Indicated airspeed.
ICBM	Intercontinental Ballistic Missile.
ILS	Instrument Landing System. Deviation information from ideal glide slope and runway centre line is shown on pilot's instruments.
IMN	Indicated mach number.
ISA	International Standard Atmosphere. At sea level 15°C and 760 millibars.
Incidence	The angle between wing chord and airflow.
Jet pipe temperature, JPT	The operating temperature of the jet engine turbine blades.
Lateral effects	Aircraft being affected in roll.
Lift coefficient	A measure of the amount of lift being produced by the wing.
Longitudinal effects	Aircraft being affected in pitch.
Mach number	The aircraft's speed measured as a decimal of the local speed of sound.
Mach trimmer	An electrically controlled strut, the length of which is controlled by the speed of the aircraft.
Overbalance	The control surface tries to go to full travel without being operated by the pilot – a very dangerous characteristic.
Pitch damper	An electrically controlled strut, the length of which is controlled by a pitch gyro in order to damp out the oscillation.
Pitot tube	A device for measuring the pressure of the moving airflow, pitot pressure. The difference between the pitot and static pressure is a measure of airspeed.

Phugoid	A long period oscillation, normally in pitch.
Polaris	Submarine-launched ICBM.
Position error	The difference between the true (ambient) pressure and the pressure measured by the aircraft itself.
QFE	Altimeter setting which makes the instrument read zero on the ground.
QNH	Altimeter setting which makes the instrument read the airfield height above mean sea level when aircraft is on the ground.
Rate gyro	A gyroscope which senses directional changes at right angles to its axis of rotation.
Resonance	When a turbine blade or similar structure develops an uncontrollable vibration which, in the case of a turbine blade, would shorten its fatigue life.
Rudder	Controls aircraft directionally.
Short period (oscillation)	A rapid oscillation which is too fast for the pilot to control.
Spring tab	A small control surface at the back of a control which helps to reduce the control forces.
Stability	A stable aircraft is one which, when it diverges from a set condition, tends to return without any action from the pilot.
Stall	When an aircraft flies so slowly that the lift developed by the wing reaches a maximum, the aircraft is said to stall. The stall can be gentle or violent.
Static	A cavity on the side of an aircraft or part of a pitot/static tube which measures the ambient(stationary) pressure. The difference between the pitot and static pressure is a measure of airspeed.
Stators	Engine-fixed aerodynamic blades placed in front of the rotating turbine blades to control the air flow.
Stick force per g	The force needed to apply one g acceleration.
Sweep back	The angle that the leading edge of a

	wing trails behind a straight wing.
Thickness chord ratio	The ratio of the thickness of the wing divided by the chord of the wing. The chord is the physical fore and aft dimension at that point on the wing.
Trailing static	A device for measuring the pressure, which is towed behind an aircraft.
Unstable	The aircraft tends to deviate from the desired flight path without any input from the pilot.
V_R, V_2	Pre-calculated rotation and lift-off speeds used during take-off to ensure optimum and safe take-off performance.
Vortex generators	Small blades fixed to the top surface of the wing to re-energise the stagnant boundary layer as it travels over the wing.
Wing fence	A long vertical piece of metal attached in a fore and aft direction to the wing surface to ensure the airflow does not move sideways.
Wing root	The inboard part of the wing next to the fuselage.
Yaw	Transient angle between aircraft direction and aircraft heading.
Yaw damper	An electrically controlled strut, the length of which is controlled by the gyro in order to damp out an oscillation.

TIME CHART

7 January 1947	Requirement Specification B.35/46 formally issued.
March 1947	Type 698 first sketched out as a pure delta flying wing.
27 November 1947	Avro's design tender to B.35/46 accepted.
June 1948	Specification B.35/46 re-issued with amendments.
June 1948	Two prototypes ordered.
September 1948	Detailed design completed.
4 September 1948	First flight 707 VX784.
6 September 1950	First flight 707B VX790.
February 1951	First flight 707B VX790 modified intake.
June 1951	First flight 707A WD280.
July 1952	First B. Mk 1 production order.
30 August 1952	First prototype maiden flight, Rolls-Royce Avons.
October 1952	Type 698 officially named Vulcan by the Air Council.
3 September 1953	Second prototype maiden flight.
4 February 1955	First production B.1 maiden flight.
5 October 1955	Flight testing of second prototype with Phase 2 kinked wing commences.
20 July 1956	First B.1 delivery to RAF Bomber Command (230 OCU).
11 July 1957	First B.1 delivery to operational squadron (83 Sqn).
31 August 1957	Second prototype flies with Mk 2 wing fitted.
19 August 1958	First production B.2 maiden flight.
30 April 1959	Last B. Mk 1 delivered.
1 July 1960	First B.2 delivery to RAF Bomber Command (230 OCU).
October 1960	First B.2 delivery to operational squadron (83 Sqn).
9 August 1961	First flight Olympus 301.
31 August 1961	First autoland.
21 September 1961	First Skybolt carriage.
Oct 1960-Mar 1963	B.1 to B.1A upgrade programme.
December 1962	Development of Skybolt missile abandoned.
February 1963	First operational Blue Steel equipped squadron

	(617 Sqn).
late 1963	Blue Steel trial launched at Woomera.
1964	Vulcans switched to low-level attack profiles.
14 January 1965	Last B.2 delivered.
1966-Jan 1968	B.1As retired from squadron service.
1969	Blue Steel missile withdrawn from RAF service – Vulcans tasked with conventional bombing.
1 November 1973	First B.2(MRR) conversion delivered to RAF.
9 June 1981	Phased retirement of B.2s starts.
30 April/1 May 1982	Operation 'Black Buck' flown in Falklands War.
1982	Rapid conversion of 6 a/c to K.2 air refuelling tankers.
31 December 1982	Last B.2 squadron disbanded.
31 March 1982	B.2(MRR) withdrawn from service.
31 March 1984	K.2 withdrawn from service.
23 March 1993	Last RAF Vulcan flight. Delivery of XH558 to Bruntingthorpe.
September 1999	Launch of campaign to return a Vulcan to the air.
22 June 2004	Heritage Lottery Fund awards £2.7m for restoration of Vulcan XH558 to flying condition.
2007	Planned first flight of restored Vulcan XH558.

APPENDIX 1

ACCIDENT TO VX784

Accident to Avro 707 VX784   30th September 1949

This was the first 707 to be built by Avros and had been flying for about a month. The circumstances of the flight were that the aircraft took off, did one very wide circuit of the airfield flying slowly and then crashed near Blackbushe, killing the pilot. The airbrakes on the aircraft were fully extended and investigation by the firm came to the conclusion that there had been a malfunction of the airbrakes which up to that time had only been partially extended.

Interestingly, no mention is made of an internal Aeroflight RAE memo sent to the director which came to the conclusion that the primary cause of the accident was due to aileron overbalance. The full document is available from The National Archives, TNA, AVIA 5/43 and follows this brief discussion. Part of the memo stated:

> You will see that we are fairly convinced that the aileron control was appreciably overbalanced on the last flight (about +/– 20lbs at full aileron displacement). We are also of the opinion that the observed behaviour of the aircraft is consistent with aileron overbalance together with a fairly light elevator control, the significant points being:
>
> (a)   The two sharp wing drops which were noted by flying control immediately after take-off, when the pilot would have first noted the overbalance and then firmly gripped the control column.
>
> (b)   The slow speed of the aircraft as observed by all, for the pilot would wish to keep the speed down in order to limit the stick forces caused by the overbalanced controls.
>
> (c)   The irregular lateral control motion of the aircraft as observed during its run over the aerodrome.

The memo goes on to explain that such an overbalance would be extremely tiring for the pilot and that the pilot probably extended the airbrakes in an attempt to get more power from the engines and therefore make it easier to control the aircraft at slow speed. The memo discloses that Avros had made a change to the aileron balancing before the flight which Aeroflight considered should not have been made because the aileron hinge moments had not been properly assessed from previous flights.

The memo concludes:

> In our opinion, therefore, the accident was primarily due to
> an overbalanced aileron control, leading to difficulty of
> lateral control and subsequent exhaustion of the pilot....

The actual cause of this accident will never be known. The author
considers it significant that the pilot did not talk to the control tower,
perhaps because he was in such dire straights trying to control the
aircraft and determine what to do. This accident is a good example of
how careful one has to be in assessing reasons for such since it is only
if the true cause is established that the correct action can be taken to
prevent a repetition of the occurrence. There follows an actual copy of
the report.

Aero F/1227.43R/DJL/126   Aero Flight Section

                                           14th October, 1949

Director   SECRET

                    Avro 707 Accident

        We enclose a copy of two notes prepared by Aero F
and Aero S on the likely control balance position and on a
theoretical analysis of the lateral stability characteristics
of the Avro 707.

        You will see that we are fairly convinced that the
aileron control was appreciably overbalanced on the last
flight (about ± 20 lb. at full aileron displacement). We
are also of the opinion that the observed behaviour of the
aircraft is consistent with aileron overbalance together with
a fairly light elevator control, the significant points being:-

(a)   The two sharp wing drops which were noted by flying
control immediately after take-off, when the pilot would have
first noted the overbalance and then firmly gripped the control
column.

(b)   The slow speed of the aircraft as observed by all, for
the pilot would wish to keep the speed down in order to limit
the stick forces caused by the overbalanced controls.

(c)   The irregular lateral motion of the aircraft as observed
during its run over the aerodrome.

        While we cannot be any means certain, we feel that the
run over the aerodrome may have been an attempt at landing which
was defeated by the bad visibility and the extreme difficulty
the pilot would have had in trying to turn onto the runway after
discovering he was well out of line. We have rigged up a
simulated overbalanced control in the laboratory with the degree
of overbalance as calculated by us, and we think this would
convince anyone of the extraordinary difficulty in correcting
bank errors and performing any turns.

                                                   /We

- 2 -

We again think it possible that the pilot was on a wide circuit to land when the aircraft spun and crashed. While the exact cause of the spin cannot be determined, we think it possible that he either stalled when trying to fly at even lower speeds in order to limit the overbalance forces when he must himself have been in an exhausted state; or alternatively that he extended the dive brakes in order to help him keep the low speed with better engine control and that the large nose-up change of trim due to the underwing dive brakes previously noted caught him out.

We are afraid that we must consider that Messrs. A.V. Roe made too large a change in the aileron control characteristics between the last two flights (we estimate a change in b_2 of the ailerons as +0.3, while their estimate we believe is +0.25). The firm were largely led to do this by the large estimate of b_2 on the aileron of -0.378 (as against ours of -0.12) but a simple check of the aileron forces in flight in the previous condition would have guided them; incidentally a b_2 of -0.378 at 140 knots would give an aileron force of ± 70 lb. which would be inevitably heavy. _incredibly._

With regard to the lateral stability calculations, these are inconclusive in that the results depend entirely on the value of l_p assumed, and evidence on this derivative is inconclusive. But, the pilot had previously been closely questioned on the "dutch" roll characteristics and he had said that there was no sign of trouble in this direction; this statement taken together with the fact that the calculations show little change of the damping of the lateral oscillation with C_L should indicate that it was unlikely that the pilot would experience a violent change in the character of the lateral oscillation at a lower flight speed than he had hitherto flown the aircraft.

In our opinion, therefore, the accident was primarily due to an overbalanced aileron control leading to difficulty of lateral control and consequent exhaustion of the pilot, and that, probably in an attempt to fly at too low a speed, in

/order

- 3 -

order to keep the overbalance forces as low as possible, the aircraft was inadvertently stalled. Operation of the underwing airbrakes at the low airspeeds may have been a contributory cause as they cause a nose up pitching moment.

Aero Flight Section

Copy to: Aero 1
           Aero F
           Structures (Accident Section)

APPENDIX 2

FLIGHT TEST RECORD 1ST FLIGHT MODIFIED LEADING EDGE

FLIGHT TEST RECORD.

Aircraft Type: 707A.　　　　　　　　**Serial No.** WD. 280.

Flight Nos. 426, 427, 428.　　　　　　**Date of Flights:** 2. 2. 55.

Loading Ref. No. 707A/44/W.41　**T.O. Weight:** 10,557 lb.　**T.O. C.G.** 0.2795c̄

Flight Duration: 426 : 40 mins.　**Total Flying Time to Date:** 236 hrs. 45 mins.
　　　　　　　　　　　427 : 35 mins.
　　　　　　　　　　　428 : 30 mins.

Structural alterations to aircraft since last flight:

　　2nd extended and drooped leading edge fitted (19⅞%).

　　Underslung wing tip booms fitted.

Pilot's Comments:

　　The first of these flights was a general handling assessment with particular emphasis on the low speed characteristics and the other two flights were to establish the buffet threshold.

　　The low speed behaviour was as good as it has ever been and there is probably a substantial improvement in the buffet threshold particularly below .98 I.M.N.

　　General:

　　On take-off, nose wheel raising speed with full up elevator was about 80 kts. and unstick speed 110 kts. This is about the same as before.

　　At 20,000 ft., clean with engine idling, speed was reduced to the full up elevator condition at 85 kts. Very slight buffeting started at 122 kts. and persisted without getting appreciably worse down to the lowest speed attained. Behaviour was very steady, there being no lateral or directional trim changes or directional uncertainty which was characteristic of all recent configurations between 105 and 95 kts.

　　Similarly, during 'g' stalls at 140 - 130 kts. no wing drop or roll occurred. Sideslip was induced at 85 kts. and maintained without difficulty whilst holding full up elevator.

　　In the landing configuration with Dive Recovery Flap fully up the behaviour was equally good until, at speeds below 80 kts., the usual high incidence difficulties developed which required large and rapid rudder and aileron movements for control.

　　Before landing, a rough check was made of the aircraft's ability to climb at various speeds in the landing configuration. At 110 kts. and full power there was no significant rate of climb; this was rather surprising to the pilot because a similar check made a few weeks ago showed a rate of climb of about 1000 ft./min. in this condition.

The approach to land was made at 125 - 130 kts. crossing the hedge at 115 kts. and touching down at about 105 kts. In view of the fairly low final approach speed, the flareout and float were remarkably easy.

Buffet Threshold.

At nominal 300 kts. E.A.S. the usual technique was used to record the buffet threshold between .94 and .70 I.M.N. The threshold varied from about 2.5 'g' at the highest speed to 5.5 'g' at the lowest. This compares with about 2.2 'g' and 4.7 'g' respectively for the last configuration.

At the medium and low Mach No. it seemed that the threshold is now not very far removed from the lift boundary, since very slight right wing drop coincided almost exactly with the buffet threshold. Also there was a noticeable increase, in the intensity of buffeting just beyond the threshold, whereas in the past, a substantial increase of 'g' beyond the threshold gave little change in the level of the buffet.

- 2 -

Before landing on the last flight, I.A.S. was increased to 410 kts. at low level and some general manoeuvring including a few aerobatics at lower speed, showed no change in handling behaviour.

J.G. Harrison.
Test Pilot.

Observer's Comments:

NIL.

Appendix Attached:

Circulation:
Sir Roy Dobson.   Mr. J.H. Orrell.
Sir William Farren.   Mr. R.J. Falk.
Mr. S.D. Davies (2)   Mr. J.G. Harrison.
Mr. J.R. Evans.   Mr. C.F. Bethwaite.
Mr. P.L. Sutcliffe.   Mr. Z. Olenski.
Mr. Connor.   Mr. S.I.R. Nicol.
                            Mr. G. Beardshall.
                            Film Reading Section.

JGH/SMH.

Appendix to Flight Test Record Nos. 426, 427, 428.   Aircraft: Type 707A. WD. 280.

Date: 2nd February, 1955.

Film Record of Events.

Flight and Time	Event No. A/O Camera	Camera Speed fr./sec. A/O	– Event –
Flt. 426. 10.20 – 11.00			Low Speed.
	1	4	135 – 85 kts. clean – 140 galls.
	2	4	'g' stall 140 – 115 kts.
	3	4	Repeat of 2.
Flt. 427. 14.30 – 15.05			Buffet Threshold.
	1	4	.92 I.M.N. – $2\frac{1}{2}$ 'g'
	2	4	.88 I.M.N. 4.0 'g'
	3	4	.84 I.M.N. – 4.2 'g' M low.
	4	4	.80 I.M.N. – 4.8 'g' Slight Right Wing Drop.
	5	4	.76 I.M.N. – 5.3 'g'
	6	4	.68 I.M.N. Maybe unreliable – hurried.
Flt. 428 16.05 – 16.35			
	1	4	.94 I.M.N. – $2\frac{1}{2}$ 'g'
	2 & 3	4	.90 3 more reliable than 2.
	4	4	.86 I.M.N.
	5	4	.84 I.M.N. Extra point.
	6	4	.82 I.M.N. – 4.3 'g'
	7	4	.78 I.M.N. – 5.0 'g'
	8	4	.74 I.M.N. – 5.2 'g'
	9	4	.70 I.M.N. 5.5 'g'

VULCAN MK 2
PROGRESS REPORT

A. V. ROE & CO., LIMITED, MANCHESTER.

⑥

MEMORANDUM

11th August 1958

From .... J. G. Harrison .... | To .... Mr. J.A.R. Kay ....

<u>SUMMARY OF FLIGHT TRIALS IN VX.777 AND XA.891</u>

This morning I received your request from Price for a summary of the results of the flight programme on VX.777 and XA.891 to be available by tomorrow morning. You will appreciate that, in the time scale, it has only been possible to do a very hurried broad summary of the work to date.

Attached is a similar paper on engine development in XA.891 written by Blackman.

<u>FLYING CHARACTERISTICS OF VX.777</u>

<u>MK.2 AERODYNAMIC PROTOTYPE</u>

Introduction

The following details are based on a total of 70 hrs. 25 mins. flying time, 26 hrs. 20 mins. having been flown since the grounding. The aircraft has been flying recently within the following limitations.

> <u>E.A.S.</u> 350 kts. An attempt was made to get this raised to 415 kts. but the R.A.E. would not give the additional clearance without a further programme of ground resonance tests.
>
> <u>C.G. Range</u>: .247 - .2988.
>
> <u>Weight</u>: Maximum take-off 138,000 lb.
>
> <u>Mach Number</u>: Approximately .94 T.M.N. This is a handling limitation dictated by high Mach number instability.

Ground Handling

Taxying is generally straightforward but at aft C.G. nosewheel steering is not very effective because of the light load on the nosewheel. We expect this to be better on the Mk.2 because the nose leg is some 14 inches higher than on VX.777 and also because the extreme aft C.G. is associated with higher all up weight than it is possible to use on VX.777.

Take-off

Take-off is straightforward. In fact, at extreme forward and aft C.G's take-offs have been completed with stick free. The shorter nose leg of the Mk.2 will make slight differences to take-off behaviour and elevon settings recommended for take-off cannot be finalised until the Mk.2 has flown.

Pitch Damping

At all C.G. positions and heights for VX.777 divergent oscillations occur over a small range of Mach numbers but we have in all cases demonstrated a recovery to positive damping. Apart from development flying for the pitch damper, basic damping is of only academic interest since we have four independent pitch dampers.

- 2 -

These have worked very well with no sign of malfunction so far. A compromise
setting has been chosen which gives good damping at all flight conditions. Even
with two channels switched off the aircraft is still no worse than a Mk.1 Vulcan
without pitch damper. This is encouraging since Boscombe Down impose no special
limitations on the Mk.1 Vulcan when the pitch damper is inoperative.

The only tests outstanding on the pitch damper are the runaways which will
be started this week. If these are cleared satisfactorily the pitch damping
problem is largely overcome, although it will be necessary to prove the system at
the much greater height and weight ranges of the Mk.2. It is possible that this
may necessitate a height monitor.

High Mach Number Instability

At a Mach number slightly above the best cruising Mach number the aircraft
becomes statically unstable and this is considerably worse than predicted by Wind
Tunnel. However, even without Mach trimmer the aircraft has been regularly flown
to Mach numbers higher than that achieved with the Mk.1 Vulcan, albeit with some
difficulty. Our knowledge of position error above .9 true is rather scanty but
the available evidence suggests that we have reached True Mach Number of about
.94 at all heights appropriate to VX.777's limitations.

Mach Trimmer

The increasingly severe instability at high Mach number greatly increases the
difficulty of designing a satisfactory Mach trimmer. Revised output requirements
have been drawn up and incorporated as far as possible in three new transmitting
Machmeters delivered by Newmarks but not yet flown. Newmarks are not very confident
about their ability to produce Machmeters on a production basis having the very steep
output and close tolerances required to counteract the aircraft's instability. The
problem here is that if the three transmitting Machmeters are not closely matched
within requirements, spurious failure warnings will occur and the effect of runaways
will be greater than we can tolerate. There are several ideas for overcoming this
problem, such as feeding the Machmeters from a separate static source which provides
an increasing over-reading of Mach number (similar to the Mk.1 Vulcan's static
source), thereby decreasing the slope of Mach trimmer output with indicated Mach
number which would ease Newmark's difficulties considerably. None of the ideas,
however, will reach the flight stage in the immediate future, so no further details
will be given here.

Elevon Float with 'g'

When flying VX.777 last year it was found that the elevons up-floated with 'g'.
Circuit modifications were made during the major grounding and these have lessened
the up-float with 'g'. At the same time basic aircraft damping of the short period
pitching oscillations has been worsened. There are two conflicting factors here:
if we revert to the original degree of float, Mk.2 stick force per 'g' may become
unacceptably low and Mach trimmer and possibly auto-pilot runaways too severe.
If we decrease the float even further the pitch damper may not be capable of
providing sufficient artificial damping. The modifications already incorporated
to VX.777 and also XH.533 may prove to provide the right compromise solution but
we shall not know if this is so until XH.533 has flown.

Buffeting

Two recent flights have been devoted to measurements of elevon hinge moments.
These have been made without vortex generators. Detailed analysis will take some
time but from the flying viewpoint no major problems have been encountered. At
Mach numbers up to about .9, beyond the buffet threshold thumping occurs which
provides a natural deterrent to further increase of 'g'. Above .9 severe thumping
has not been encountered but the maximum output of the P.F.C's has been reached
coincidentally with reaching full up elevon at about 2 'g', .93 I.M.N. at a $V/_p$ of
450. The elevons have also been used in the aileron sense as might occur during
the escape manoeuvre without untoward occurrence.

Outstanding work on this subject will be repeat tests with vortex generators and, of course, an extension of the critical flight conditions which can only be made when the Mk.2 flies.

Stalling

There is good natural pre-stall buffeting and at most flight conditions the stall remains perfectly docile. Directional instability may occur during the extreme aft C.G. stall but this is not considered important since there is even better natural stall warning than for the Mk.1 Vulcan, on which stalling is prohibited.

General Flying

The aircraft is generally very pleasant to fly, control circuit friction and break-out forces being better than the Mk.1 and the elevons providing a more lively response in roll. In some flight conditions side slip resulting from coarse use of the ailerons is greater than on the Mk.1 but this can be minimised with rudder, although fin strength is adequate to permit full aileron throughout the speed range without using rudder. This is no more than a minor peculiarity which is only noticeable when the controls are used coarsely.

Landing

The approach to land is appreciably easier than on the Mk.1 Vulcan. At the same weight an approach speed some five to ten knots lower can be used, the forward view is better as is the aileron control, the latter point being of importance in turbulence and cross-winds. The landing itself is easy, although if final approach speeds are too high there is a tendency to float more than on the Mk.1. At mid and aft C.G's a very high degree of aerodynamic braking is available which should assist the Service by saving wear on the wheel brakes. We have shown that it should be impossible to touch the proposed R.C.M. fairing on landing but if pilots are to be encouraged to take advantage of the aerodynamic braking the fairing may occasionally be scraped during the landing run. Some protection against this type of damage has been requested on the R.C.M. fairing.

Conclusion

The whole programme has gone very well indeed so far. It is particularly gratifying that the pitch damper development has progressed so well. You will remember that this subject exercised our minds considerably when it was seen in the initial flying that the aircraft was so much worse than the Mk.1 in this respect.

It can be said that the only problem known to exist is that of providing a satisfactory Mach trimmer.

On the other hand, we should not delude ourselves that everything will be plain sailing on the Mk.2 since the much greater height and weight range may have an unfavourable influence on such things as buffeting, high Mach number instability and pitch damping. Furthermore, much of the engineering aspect remains to be cleared on the Mk.2.

(J. G. Harrison)
Chief Test Pilot

JGH:SAH

OLYMPUS B.OL.6 DEVELOPMENT IN VULCAN XA.891

Vulcan XA.891 first flew with B.01.6 engines on 20th June 1958 and since then only fourteen flights totalling 23 hrs. 50 mins. have been carried out: a short diary is appended.

The first five flights were spent in determining the engine handling characteristics with convergent nozzles. It was found that the fuel systems did not permit maximum or cruise R.P.M. to be maintained above 30,000 ft. which meant that the aircraft was little better than a 102 engined Vulcan. In addition it was not possible to maintain full electrical load on the alternator installation above 50,000 ft. due to excessive Sundstrand drive oil temperatures.

Two convergent-divergent nozzles and the latest production 17,000 lb. fuel systems were then fitted to Nos. 1 and 2 engines so that they become representative of the Vulcan Mk.2 production standard. One flight was made before delivering the aircraft to B.A.E.L. for the period of Woodford holiday shut-down. Maximum R.P.M. could be obtained to maximum altitude tested, 54,000 ft., but the engine handling had deteriorated in that moderate or slam throttle openings caused the engines to go out above 50,000 ft.

While the aircraft was at Filton B.A.E.L. confirmed our opinion that the engine basically was very good but that the fuel system would need modifying. As will be seen from the diary, they managed only six flights due to the need for two engine changes: one due to a No.5 bearing failure and one due to a split pin in the oil filter.

No more engine handling can be carried out at the moment until modified fuel systems arrive from B.A.E.L. The next few flights will be spent determining the maximum load that the alternator can supply above 50,000 ft. without overheating the Sundstrand drive.

Summarising the outstanding problems then:

(a) The engine handling is not satisfactory due to engine extinctions on throttle openings above 30,000 ft. Modified fuel systems awaited from B.A.E.L.

(b) Sundstrand oil cooling inadequate, causing load shedding above 50,000 ft. Investigation of possible loads being carried out.

AIRCRAFT DIARY

Date	Remarks	
20.6.58.	First flight Langar to Woodford	0 hrs. 40 mins.
	Unnecessary ground cooling fan disintegrated in bomb bay on the flight, luckily missing vital control and electrical runs.	
1.7.58.	Four flights on engine handling.	7 hrs. 45 mins.
	Inspection panels in air intakes not adequately fitted. This fault took two weeks to repair, during which time 17,000 lb. fuel systems and con-di nozzles were fitted to Nos. 1 & 2 engines.	
17.7.58.	Engine handling.	2 hrs. 30 mins.
18.7.58.) 5.8.58.)	Aircraft at Filton. Eight flights including delivery flights. Two engine changes.	13 hrs. 00 mins.
	Aircraft on ground due to no spare Sundstrand being available at Woodford and unserviceable Motor Generator.	
11.8.58.	Some engine performance for B.A.E.L	hr. 45 mins.

(A.L.Blackman)
Test Pilot.

PRODUCTION HISTORY

Head of Design Team: Roy Chadwick (Stu Davies from August 1947)
Chief Aerodynamicist: Eric Priestly (later Roy Ewans)
Project Designer: J.G. Willis (later G.A. Whitehead)
Design Office: A.V. Roe & Co Ltd, Chadderton, Manchester

Version	Quantity	Modified	Assembly Location	Time Period
Vulcan prototypes	2		Woodford	Sept 1948-Sept 1953
Vulcan B. Mk 1	45	28 to 1A	Woodford	1954-Mar 1959
Vulcan B. Mk 2	89	about 40 with 301 engines 8 Maritime, 6 tankers	Woodford	1958-Dec 1964

Total Produced: 136 a/c (All variants)

DIFFERENT MARKS OF AIRCRAFT

Vulcan B. Mk 1A	Conversion of B. Mk 1 with ECM equipment in enlarged tailcone.
Vulcan B. Mk 2	Improved production version with larger, thinner, wing and uprated Olympus 201 or 301 engines. Later fitted with Terrain Following Radar in nose pimple and ARI.18228 passive radar warning system on top of fin.
Vulcan B. Mk 2A	B. Mk 2 converted to carry Blue Steel missile. Olympus 301 engines. Reverted back to B. Mk 2 standard when Blue Steel withdrawn.
Vulcan B. Mk 2BS	Alternative designation for B. Mk 2A.
Vulcan B. Mk 2(MRR)	9 conversions of B. Mk 2 for Maritime Radar Reconnaissance role.
Vulcan K. Mk 2	6 conversions of B. Mk 2 for air-refuelling tanker role, with single hose-drum unit under rear fuselage.

CA DEVELOPMENT AIRCRAFT

NOTE: Numbers in brackets are the number of flights flown by author in each aircraft.

	Development History
First prototype VX770	One aircraft with Avon engines. Later fitted with Sapphire, and Conway engines. Crashed at Syerston.
Second prototype VX777(13)	One aircraft, much closer to production standard. Olympus 100 engines initially. Later flight tested new wing for B. Mk 2. Last flight April 1960.
Vulcan Mk 1 XA889(58)	Initial production version. Olympus 101. Flight tested 102/104 engines.
Vulcan Mk 1 XA890(13)	Radio development aircraft BLEU.
Vulcan Mk 1 XA891 (67)	Olympus engine development aircraft for Mk 2. Crashed in 1959 due to complete electrical failure.
Vulcan Mk 1 XA892(15)	Misc. and A&AEE development aircraft.
Vulcan Mk 1 XA893(26)	Mk 2 AC development aircraft. Nose section at Bicester.
Vulcan Mk 1 XA894(59)	Autopilot development aircraft. Then engine development Bristol. Destroyed by fire.
Vulcan Mk 1 XA895(22)	Mk 1A development aircraft then ECM trials.
Vulcan Mk 1 XA896(0)	Engine test bed, Filton.
Vulcan Mk 1 XA899(31)	Auto throttle and MFS development aircraft. Nose section at Cosford.
Vulcan Mk 1 XA903(18)	Blue Steel development aircraft. Then Rolls-Royce test bed.
Vulcan Mk 1 XH478(16)	Flight refuelling.
Vulcan Mk 2 XH533(111)	First production Mk 2 development aircraft. Autolanding development.
Vulcan Mk 2 XH534(36)	Autopilot development aircraft. Blue Steel handling.
Vulcan Mk 2 XH535(22)	Skybolt radio programme development aircraft. Crashed near Amesbury.
Vulcan Mk 2 XH536(14)	MFS1B development aircraft. Crashed 11th February 1966.
Vulcan Mk 2 XH537(19)	Skybolt handling aircraft.

Vulcan Mk 2 XH538(9)	Skybolt development aircraft.
Vulcan Mk 2 XH539(45)	Blue Steel development aircraft. High weight tests.
Vulcan Mk 2 XH557(22)	Olympus handling aircraft.
Vulcan Mk 2 XH560(14)	Olympus handling aircraft.
Vulcan Mk 2 XJ784(29)	Olympus 301 engine development aircraft.

APPENDIX 6

OPERATORS

MILITARY OPERATORS
UK – Royal Air Force   B.1: 6 sqns + OCU; B.2: 11 sqns + OCU

VULCAN MK 1
230 OCU Jul 56 – Jun 60 Waddington
44 Squadron Aug 60 – Dec 82 Waddington
50 Squadron. Aug 61 – Nov 66 Waddington
83 Squadron May 57 – Oct 60 Waddington
101 Squadron Oct 57 – Jan 68 Finningley, Waddington
617 Squadron May 58 – July 61 Scampton

VULCAN MK 2
230 OCU Jul 60 – Aug 81 Waddington, Finningley, Scampton
9 Squadron Mar 62 – Apr 82. Coningsby, Cottesmore, Akrotiri,
   Waddington
12 Squadron July 62 – Dec 67 Coningsby, Cottesmore
27 Squadron Apr 61 – March 72 Scampton
35 Squadron Dec 62 – Feb 82 Coningsby, Cottesmore, Akrotori,
   Scampton
44 Squadron Dec 67 – Dec 82 Waddington
50 Squadron Dec 66 – Dec 81 Waddington
83 Squadron Oct 60 – Aug 69 Scampton
101 Squadron Feb 68 – Aug 82 Waddington
617 Squadron Aug 61 – Jan 82 Scampton

VULCAN MK 2 (MARITIME RECONNAISANCE)
27 Squadron Nov 73 – March 82 Scampton

VULCAN MK 2 (TANKER)
50 Squadron Dec 82 – Mar 84 Waddington

GOVERNMENT AGENCIES
CA Fleet   A few on loan for test duties

CIVILIAN OPERATORS
Bristol Siddeley/Rolls-Royce   At least 2 B. Mk 1s loaned for engine
   test bed use
The Vulcan Operating Company   Vulcan Mk 2 XH558

SPECIFICATIONS

AVRO VULCAN B.MK 1

Role: Long range strategic medium bomber.
Crew: 5.
Dimensions: Length 97ft 1in (29.59m); Height 26ft 6in (7.95m); Wing Span 99ft 0in (30.18m); Wing Area 3554.0sq ft (330.18sq m).
Engine(s): Four Bristol Olympus 101 turbojets of 11,000lbs (4990kg), or Olympus 102 of 12,000lbs (5443kg) or Olympus 104 of 13,000lbs (6078kg).
Weights: Empty (including crew) 83,573lbs (37,144kgs); Maximum Take-off 170,000lbs (77,111kg).
Performance: Maximum level speed 477mph (763kph), .92 True Mach Number (607mph, 971kph) at altitude, Cruising speed Mach 0.86 (567mph, 907kph) at 45,000ft (13,716m); Service ceiling 55,000ft (16,765m); Range 2607mls (4,171km).
Armament: No defensive guns. Conventional or free-fall nuclear bomb load carried internally. Maximum bomb load 21,000lbs (9,526kg).

AVRO VULCAN B. MK 2

Role: Long-range strategic medium bomber.
Crew: 5.
Dimensions: Length 99ft 11in (30.45m) initially, 100ft 1in (30.50m) over nose 'pimple', 105ft 6in (32.15m) with refuelling probe; Height 27ft 2in (8.28m); Wing Span 111ft 0in (33.83m); Wing Area 3964.0sq ft (368.27sq m).
Engine(s): Four Bristol Siddeley Olympus 201 turbojets each rated at 17,000lbs (7711kg), or Olympus 301 turbojets each rated at 20,000lbs (9072kg).
Weights: Normal Take-off 179,898lbs (81,600kg); Maximum Take-off 204,000lbs (92,727kg).
Performance: Maximum level speed 477mph (763kph) sea level, .92 True Mach Number (607mph, 971kph) at altitude, Cruising speed Mach 0.86 (567mph, 907kph) at 50,000ft (15,241m); Service ceiling 60,000ft (18,288m); Range 3,500mls (5,600km).
Armament: No defensive guns. Conventional (21 1,000lbs (454kg) bombs) or nuclear bomb load in internal bomb bay or provision for one Blue Steel 'stand off' bomb in semi-recessed installation. Many aircraft also included under-wing attachment points for the Skybolt missile, which could be later used for the carriage of Martel-Shrike missiles and ECM pods.

INDEX

NOTES

NOTES

NOTES